D1526757

INTERNATIONAL PERSPECTIVES ON AGING

CURRENT ISSUES
IN INTERNATIONAL AND COMPARATIVE LAW

VOLUME 3

EDITORIAL BOARD

The titles published in this series are listed at the end of this volume.

INTERNATIONAL PERSPECTIVES ON AGING

Edited by

GEORGE J. ALEXANDER
Professor of Law, Santa Clara University, U.S.A.

MARTINUS NIJHOFF PUBLISHERS
DORDRECHT / BOSTON / LONDON

Library of Congress Cataloging-in-Publication Data

```
International perpectives on aging / edited by George J. Alexander.
     p.   cm. -- (Current issues in international and comparative
  law ; v. 3)
    Includes index.
    ISBN 0-7923-1691-6 (HB : acid free paper)
    1. Aged--Social conditions. 2. Aged--Legal status, laws, etc.
  3. Aged--Care.   I. Alexander, George J.  II. Series.
  HQ1061.I5355  1992
  305.26--dc20                                         92-7330
```

ISBN 0-7923-1691-6

Published by Martinus Nijhoff Publishers,
P.O. Box 163, 3300 AD Dordrecht, The Netherlands.

Sold and distributed in the U.S.A. and Canada
by Kluwer Academic Publishers,
101 Philip Drive, Norwell, MA 02061, U.S.A.

In all other countries, sold and distributed
by Kluwer Academic Publishers Group,
P.O. Box 322, 3300 AH Dordrecht, The Netherlands.

Printed on acid-free paper

Printed in the Netherlands

CONTENTS

Preface

Elderlaw is becoming a prominent specialty. Problems of elders are, of course, neither new nor limited to any specific country or region. In this book there is a selection of perspectives from scholars in different parts of the world. All of them focus on some branch of elderlaw. The compilation could not and does not attempt to map out the field nor to make country by country comparisons of the issues discussed. Rather, it attempts to show some commonality of concerns and in identification of problems and proposals for solutions.

Although the legal problems of elders are as old as human-kind, they have taken on current prominence for another reason. Lifespan has increased markedly in recent years. Persons who would, given their age, have been the elders of the past and would have been expected to be focused on their imminent death are now as a group robust and well. They have better survived the ravages of time than have the plans fashioned when life expectancy was much lower.

Questions concerning social status, expectations of living standards, general assistance and medical care all have become far more important and considerably more difficult. As life has become longer and death more controllable, the issue of a person's right to choose death over diminished quality of life has also become far more complicated.

Chapters in the book explore both questions of social obligations to elders and elders' rights and duties. Authors address these issues as they arise in the United States, Japan, Greece, New Zealand, the Netherlands, Canada and England. While the articles naturally demonstrate diversity, it is also interesting to notice the similarities in the perspectives of the authors.

There are, naturally, a number of matters on which there is disagreement. Perhaps the most basic disagreement concerns the reason for the proportionate increase in the elder population. Most scholars have explained that fact by the better health of today's older people but Eric Midwinter proposes that "the main reason why the proportion of older people has increased is because the proportion of younger people has decreased."

No one disagrees that the increase in the proportion of elderly is worldwide. Accordingly, it is important to examine global approaches. Luke T. Lee applies international human rights law to elderlaw. He claims that there is a good fit and suggests that reforms based on his observations will improve the lot of seniors.

There is no unanimity in wanting to adopt a human rights approach or even wanting to improve the condition of elders, of course. Some think that other generations deserve priority and that the elderly have already received more than their fair share of resources. Perhaps it is incorrect to think of either elders or young people as though social programs related to their age would apply equally to later generations of the same age. David Thomson examines the question of intergenerational equity by asking whether a lifetime of contributions for similar members of successive generations secures similar results over time. He concludes that it does not and that the disparity is great. Indeed, he concludes, it is not old age but the political power of a generation that accounts for the advantages of present elders.

David Thomson's conclusions depend on the accuracy of the comparisons and Eric Midwinter disagrees that such comparisons can properly be made.

Whatever conclusion one draws from the discussions of public programs for elders, one should also consider private support obligations. In both the United States and Japan family members are ultimately responsible for elders who cannot provide for themselves. Yukata Tajima analyzes the Japanese law both in this regard and with respect to the effects of limited employment opportunities for the elderly. Compulsory retirement by age is still the rule in Japan.

Robert Levy describes the enforcement of family responsibility in the United States. Both point to needed improvements in their respective systems.

Several authors describe the condition of elders. Valerie J. Grant provides insight into the problems of elders living alone in New Zealand. She paints a clear and poignant picture of the common condition in old age. Her data concerns forty elders in Auckland who were, on average, 81 years old.

Ira Emke provides a wealth of demographic information about older Greeks. The author concludes that, in Greece, the needs of the ever increasing elderly population center on health. Specifically, they center on preventive measures, information on health improvement and on enhancing the quality of general health.

Increased longevity has paradoxically created new concern with dealing with death. Margaret Somerville examines the standard of medical care for elders. She compares levels of disclosure for the old as compared to that of younger patients and focuses on how informed consent applies to them. She addresses and distinguishes pain relief and euthanasia.

J. Wöretshofer and J.L.M. Elders describe euthanasia in the Netherlands, the country which has the most open use of this practice in the world.

In my article, I discuss pressures in the United States which are militating toward rationing health care and encouraging life support termination. I suggest that it is critically important to leave such choices to the individual and describe a method of doing so.

George J. Alexander
January 1992
Santa Clara, California, U.S.A.

AGING:
THE HUMAN RIGHTS APPROACH

Luke T. Lee[*]
United States/United Nations

Introduction

In approaching the problem of aging from human rights
perspectives, it is useful first to clarify the status of human rights.
For if it can be established that the status of human rights is legal,
and not merely moral, such rights can command official compliance
therewith, and not be subject to the whim of officials or the
vicissitudes of the times. The increasing expansion of governmental activities into areas formerly reserved for the private sector,
e.g., education, health, food and nutrition, housing, social welfare
and old-age security,[1] lends urgency to the clarification of the
status of human rights.

---

[*] Director of Plans and Programs of the Office of the United States
Coordinator for Refugee Affairs; Co-author of POPULATION AND LAW: A STUDY OF
THE RELATIONS BETWEEN POPULATION PROBLEMS AND LAW (1971); former Director of
the New York Office of the Rule of Law Research Center and its representative
to the United Nations.

1. For fiscal year 1982, for example, the United States devoted $195 billion -
about 27 percent of the entire government's budget - to programs benefiting the
elderly. Statement of Richard S. Schweiker, Secretary of Health and Human
Services and head of the U.S. Delegation to the U.N. World Assembly on Aging
on July 27, 1982. Text in *Aging in All Nations: A Special Report on the United
Nations World Assembly on Aging* 101-102 (Vienna, July 26-August 6, 1982)
(published by the National Council on the Aging, Inc., Washington, D.C., 1982).
    Medicare alone paid $36 billion a year for personal health care of the elderly.
The 1981 White House Conference on Aging, 2 Final Report 13 (1982); Levine,
Introduction: The Frame of Nature, Gerontology, and Law, 56 SOUTHERN
CALIFORNIA LAW REVIEW 261, 279 (1982).

Status of Human Rights

The status of human rights has traditionally been classified according to the instruments in which the rights are incorporated: if the rights are stipulated in treaties, they are "legal" rights insofar as the states' parties are concerned; if the rights are promulgated in General Assembly declarations or resolutions, they are considered as merely "moral" rights, without any binding legal force. Such classification is faulty for the following reasons:

First, it ignores the non-treaty sources of international law. Article 38(1) of the Statute of the International Court of Justice clearly lists "international custom" and "general principles of law" as also sources of international law. Thus, to the extent that a particular human right has assumed the character of customary international law or a general principle of law, it is legally binding on all states, regardless of the existence of a treaty.[2]

It also has been maintained that human rights have their roots in natural law. According to Lauterpacht, whenever there is an appeal to human rights, to the "dignity and worth of human persons," there is an appeal to natural law and *vice versa*.[3] Thus, human rights are regarded as inherent in human beings, whether or not expressed in positive law. In a less noticed passage in the judgment on the *North Sea Continental Shelf Cases*, the International Court of Justice characterizes the "inherent right" as follows:

> In order to exercise it, no special legal process has to be gone through, nor have any special legal acts to be performed. Its existence can be declared . . . but does not need to be constituted. Furthermore, the right does not depend on its being exer-

---

2. Lee, *Law, Human Rights and Population: A Strategy for Action*, 12 Virginia Journal of International Law 309, 311 (1972).

3. H. Lauterpacht, An International Bill of the Rights of Man 26, 31, 35 (New York, 1945); Gross, *Family Planning as a Human Right: Some Jurisprudential Reflections on Natural Rights and Positive Law*, in Human Rights and Population: From the Perspectives of Law, Policy and Organization 25 (Medford, Mass.: Law and Population Programme, Fletcher School of Law and Diplomacy, Law and Population Book Series No. 5 (1973)).

cised.[4]

The functions of natural law, as Professor Leo Gross puts it, are to serve "as a source and censor of positive law."[5] The first function is to provide a "model for legislation, that is, it comprises precepts which should be incorporated into positive law." The second is to serve as the superior legal "order which 'strikes down' positive law when" the two orders are in conflict.[6] These two functions of natural law may be merged into a "principle of action,"[7] whose usefulness to our approach to the problem of the aged will be elaborated upon below.

The second reason why the traditional classification of the status of human rights is faulty is that even under the positivist precept human rights have already assumed legal status through the Charter of the United Nations. This derives from the fact that Article 55 of the Charter obligates the United Nations to "promote . . . universal respect for, and observance of, human rights and fundamental freedoms for all without distinction as to race, sex, language or religion." Furthermore, under Article 56:

> All members pledge themselves to take joint and separate action in co-operation with the Organization for the achievement of the purposes set forth in Article 55.

Although the Charter does not spell out all of the contents of human rights, the gaps have been filled by subsequent instruments,

---

4. 1969 International Court Justice, *Reports of Judgments, Advisory Opinions and Orders* 22.

5. Gross, *supra* note 3, at 26, 29.

6. Gross, *supra* note 3, at 29-31.

7. Gross, *supra* note 3, at 21. *See also* Paul Roubier, THEORIE GENERAL DU DROIT 186-87 (Paris: Sirey, 2nd ed., 1951).

principally the Universal Declaration of Human Rights.[8] The latter's relationship with the Charter is clarified by Section 3 of Article 31 of the 1969 Vienna Convention on the Law of Treaties[9]

---

8.   Adopted and proclaimed by the United Nations, General Assembly Resolution 217A(III) of December 10, 1948.

While the 18th-century revolutionaries focused on the civil and political rights of man, as manifested in the Constitution of Virginia of 1776, the American Declaration of Independence and the French Declaration of the Rights of Man and of the Citizen, their 20th-century counterparts consider such rights illusory unless accompanied by economic, cultural and social rights. As Prime Minister Attlee said in his opening statement at the first General Assembly session in London:

> The Charter of the United Nations does not deal only with Governments and States or with politics and war, but with the simple elemental needs of human beings whatever their race, their color or their creed. In the Charter we reaffirm faith in fundamental human rights. We see the freedom of the individual in the State as an essential complement to the freedom of the State in the World Community of nations. We stress, too, that social justice and the best possible standard of life for all are essential factors in promoting and maintaining the peace of the world.

9.   U.N. Doc. A/CONF.39/27 (1969), reprinted in 63 AMERICAN JOURNAL OF INTERNATIONAL LAW 875 (1969), 8 INTERNATIONAL LEGAL MATERIAL 679 (1969).
Even for states which have not ratified the Vienna Convention on the Law of Treaties, the Convention may be binding on them as customary international law. Thus, despite the fact that the United States has not ratified the Convention, the Department of State, in its Letter of Submittal to the President, stated that "although not yet in force, the Convention is already generally recognized as the authoritative guide to current treaty law and practice." S. Exec. Doc. L., 92d Cong., 1st Sess. 1 (1971). Indeed, the United States has on various occasions regarded particular articles of the Convention as codifying existing international law, for example, by citing the Convention in its brief in the hostages case against Iran. See Memorial of the Government of the United States of America in Case Concerning United States Diplomatic and Consular Staff in Tehran (United States of America v. Iran) 42 n.2 (1980). The Restatement of the Foreign Relations Law of the United States (Revised) s 328(1) (Tent. Draft No. 1 (1980), p. 72) has accepted the Convention "as presumptively codifying the customary international law governing international agreements, and therefore as foreign relations law of the United States even before the United States adheres to the Convention."
Prior to the entry into force of the Vienna Convention on the Law of Treaties on January 27, 1980, the International Court of Justice stated in its Advisory Opinion on Namibia:

(Interpretation of Treaties), which provides:

> 1. A treaty shall be interpreted in good faith in accordance with the ordinary meaning to be given to the terms of the treaty in their context and in the light of its object and purpose.
>
> 2. The context for the purpose of the interpretation of a treaty shall comprise, in addition to the text, including its preamble and annexes:
>   . . . .
>
> > (b) any instrument which was made by one or more parties in connection with the conclusion of the treaty and accepted by the other parties as an instrument related to the treaty . . . .

Two criteria thus exist under the rules of treaty interpretation for determining whether a subsequent instrument indeed serves to fill the gaps of or elaborate upon a prior treaty: namely, (a) the connection of the subsequent instrument with the conclusion of the treaty, and (b) the acceptance of the instrument by the other parties to the treaty as being related to the treaty.

Whether a subsequent instrument was indeed made in connection with the conclusion of a treaty hinges, of course, upon the professed purpose of the instrument itself, as revealed in its working. The following paragraphs in the Preamble of the Universal Declaration of Human Rights, which was adopted unanimously by the members of the United Nations in 1948[10] and reaffirmed through its repeated recitation, are pertinent:

The rules laid down by the Vienna Convention on the Law of Treaties concerning termination of a treaty relationship on account of breach (adopted without a dissenting vote) may in many respects be considered as a codification of existing customary law on the subject. 1971 International Court of Justice, *Reports of Judgments, Advisory Opinions and Order*, 16, 47 (Advisory Opinion of June 21).

10. The votes were 48 for, none against, with eight abstentions. Although the Soviet bloc abstained from voting, they subsequently affirmed it when voting for the Declaration on the Granting of Independence to Colonial Countries and People of 1960, paragraph 7 of which reads: "All states shall observe faithfully and strictly the provisions of the Charter of the United Nations, the Universal Declaration of Human Rights and the present Declaration . . . ."

WHEREAS the peoples of the United Nations have in the Charter reaffirmed their faith in fundamental human rights . . . .

WHEREAS Member States have pledged themselves to achieve, in co-operation with the United Nations, the promotion of universal respect for and observance of human rights and fundamental freedoms . . . .

NOW, THEREFORE,

THE GENERAL ASSEMBLY

PROCLAIMS this Universal Declaration of Human Rights . . . .

There can be no mistaking the fact that the professed purpose of the instrument, i.e., the Universal Declaration of Human Rights, is to fill the gaps of and elaborate upon the Charter in the field of human rights, hence "related to" the Charter. As such, it constitutes the "authoritative interpretation of the charter of the highest order."[11]

As for the second criterion, the question whether the Declaration was accepted by the other parties to the Charter as being related to the Charter must be answered in the affirmative in view of the fact that the Declaration is subscribed to by all of the parties to the Charter.

The above analysis is confirmed in *Filartiga v. Pena-Ira*,[12] in which the United States Court of Appeals for the Second Circuit held that "although there is no universal agreement as to the precise extent of the 'human rights and fundamental freedoms' guaranteed to all by the Charter, there is at present no dissent from the view that the guaranties include" rights which have "become part of customary international law, as evidenced and defined by the Universal Declaration of Human Rights."

---

11. *See* 6 *Montreal Statement of the Assembly for Human Rights* 2 (New York, 1968, reprinted in 9 JOURNAL OF THE INTERNATIONAL COMMISSION OF JURISTS 94, 95 (June 1968); *see also* Sohn and Buergenthal, INTERNATIONAL PROTECTION OF HUMAN RIGHTS 519 (New York, 1983).

12. 630 F.2d 876, 882.

The Rights of the Elderly as Human Rights

Are the rights of the elderly a part of human rights? What provisions, if any, in the Universal Declaration of Human Rights bear upon the rights of the elderly?

By using such terms as "all," "all human beings," "everyone," and "no one" throughout its text, the Declaration leaves no doubt that the elderly are included among those entitled to human rights. In addition, Article 2 reads in part:

> Everyone is entitled to all the rights and freedoms set forth in this Declaration, without distinction of any kind, such as race, color, sex, language, religion, political or other opinion, national or social origin, property, birth or other status.

But does the term "other status" include that of the elderly?

Significantly, the 124 nations gathered at the 1982 World Assembly on Aging in Vienna adopted by consensus the International Plan of Action on Aging,[13] whose Preamble reads:

> The countries gathered in the World Assembly on Aging
>
>   . . . .
>
> 1. *Do solemnly reaffirm* their belief that the fundamental and inalienable rights enshrined in the Universal Declaration of Human Rights apply fully and undiminishedly to the aging . . . .

Thus, the Plan of Action on Aging is an authoritative interpretation of the purposes of the Charter of the United Nations, albeit indirectly through the Universal Declaration of Human Rights, as based on the two criteria discussed earlier.

A review of the content of the Vienna International Plan of Action on Aging shows that its recommendations in such areas as health and nutrition, housing and environment, social welfare, income security and employment and education frequently aim not at equal rights for the elderly, but at more than equal rights. How is this compatible with the goal of equality or "without distinction"? Did not Sir Humphrey Waldock, later the President of the

---

13. Text reproduced in *Aging in All Nations, supra* note 1 at 45-92.

International Court of Justice, define "human rights" as "rights which attach to all human beings **equally**, whatever their nationality"?[14]

The answer to this question may lie in the fact that the word "equally" may be interpreted either narrowly to mean "identically" or broadly to take into account one's capability in relation to goals. Given the biological differences between men and women, for example, a narrow definition would not make sense. Rather, emphasis should be placed on equal "right to enjoy the fruits of social and economic progress," as well as the concomitant duty to "contribute to it." This interpretation was in fact adopted by the World Plan of Action of the World Conference of the International Women's Year in Mexico City, 1975.[15] The same rationale would justify the differential rights attached to the child, the youth, the disabled and the mentally retarded, as well as the elderly.

While the Vienna International Plan of Action on Aging contains many useful and innovative recommendations to assist and protect the elderly, to enhance their sense of well-being, and to increase their productivity in the society, it is deficient in one important area: namely, a systematic compilation and analysis of each country's laws bearing on the rights of the aged, followed by recommendations for legal reform in the light of human rights principles. Such compilation, review and reform activities have been undertaken in observance and fulfillment of the goals of the World Population Year,[16] the International Women's Year,[17] and

---

14. Waldock, *Human Rights in Contemporary International Law and the Significance of the European Convention*, 11 INTERNATIONAL AND COMPARATIVE LAW QUARTERLY 3 (Supp. 1965) (the paper was delivered at the European Convention on Human Rights).

15. *See* U.N., LAW AND THE STATUS OF WOMEN viii (New York, 1977).

16. *See*, e.g., UNFPA, LAW AND POPULATION (Law and Population Book Series No. 15 (1976)); Cohen, *Law and Population Classification Plan* (Law and Population Monograph Series No. 5 (1972)). More than thirty projects were established around the world based on the Classification Plan. Most of their reports were published in Law and Population Book and Monograph Series, which are available in the libraries of major population institutions.

the International Year of the Child.[18] Regrettably, it was neglect-
ed by the World Assembly on the Aged. Perhaps the sponsor and
publisher of the present volume can, in cooperation with relevant
United Nations bodies, pursue a "principle of action" that will help
fill this gap through the following strategy:

Principle/Strategy for Action

A systematic approach to the problem of the aged requires a
joint and coordinated effort on the part of all governmental
agencies concerned.[19] Such effort should replace the practice of

---

17. *See*, e.g., U.N., LAW AND THE STATUS OF WOMEN (Law and Population
Book Series No. 18 (1977); Carmen Rodriguez de Munoz and Elsa Roca de
Salonen, THE STATUS OF WOMEN IN LATIN AMERICA: LAW AND CUSTOM (Law and
Population Book Series No. 19 (1977)) (a summary of fifteen country projects in
Latin America).

18. *See*, e.g., UNITAR, LAW AND THE STATUS OF THE CHILD (2 vols., New York.
1981) (containing thirteen country chapters based on Cohen, Lee and Stepan, *The
Rights of the Child: A Classification Plan* (Law and Population Monograph Series
No. 46 (1978)). Altogether, 60 country monographs were prepared in observance
of the International Year of the Child involving cooperation among UNICEF,
UNITAR, and the various national commissions on the International Year of the
Child.

19. Thus, both the President's Task Force on Aging in 1970 and the Senate
Advisory Committee of 1971 called for the creation of a White House Office on
Aging to represent the case of the elderly and to build and implement a national
policy on aging effectively. An Action Office on Aging Act introduced by Senator
Church in 1973 would have established a White House-level office, directed by
a Presidential Assistant on Aging. An alternative would be a Secretary of Aging
heading a separate cabinet department. Each of the Cabinet departments having
concern with human resources, such as HEW (now HHS and DOE), HUD, DOT
and Labor should establish the post of Assistant Secretary of Aging. In addition,
there should be cooperation between the new Committee on Aging in the House
and its Senate counterpart. At the state level, appropriate commissions, advisory
committees, and the like should be created to deal with the elderly with authority
similar to that of the federal Administration on Aging. These may be coordinated
by Secretaries of Aging in state government cabinets who would keep the needs
of the elderly before the governors.
  See Robert N. Butler, M.D., *Toward a National Policy on Aging*, in WHY
SURVIVE? BEING OLD IN AMERICA 351 (1975). *See also Society's Responsibilities*

adopting piece-meal legislation or measures focusing on particular services for the aged. In view of its limited amount of resources, each country must construct its own list of priorities from the competing demands of the rights of the elderly in the light of each countries's needs and its social and economic conditions.

Since human rights impose a legal, and not merely a moral, responsibility upon states, there is a legal duty on the part of each state to see that laws and policies which conflict with the goals or implementation of such rights are amended or abolished and that new laws and policies are adopted to conform with and further these rights. Three stages are envisaged in such legal reform on a global basis:

(1) **Law Compilation**. The first step is to compile all the existing laws of a state bearing on the aged in one place. In the interests of completeness and comparability of laws of different states in the same fields, a classification plan for laws affecting the rights of the aged should be developed, perhaps modeled on *The Rights of the Child: A Classification Plan*.[20]

The compilation task may be more difficult than it first appears. Statutes and decrees are often scattered throughout the body of the law. Judicial decisions in many countries are not reported or published. Moreover, customary law is hard to "compile." In a federated state, such as the United States, the compilation work would be even more complicated. Nevertheless, there is no short cut to a systematic legal reform.

(2) **Analysis**. The compiled legal material must be analyzed from the viewpoints of: (a) its conformity with human rights principles, and (b) the extent to which it is complied with by the people. With respect to the former, a list of basic human rights most pertinent to the elderly in the light of the economic, cultural and social conditions in each country should be drawn up to provide standards for comparison with the actual laws.[21] As for the latter, a clear knowledge about what people are actually doing under the law would enable lawmakers to take into account the differences

---

to the Elderly 33 (Hearing before the Select Committee on Aging, House of Representatives, 94th Cong., 1st sess., November 11, 1975 (Washington, U.S. Government Printing Office, 1975)).

20. *See* Cohen, Lee and Stepan, *supra* note 18.

21. For a list of 14 basic human rights to family planning that provided the standards for the Law and Population Projects in some 35 countries, *see* Lee, *supra* note 2, at 318-19; UNFPA, *supra* note 16 at 12.

between the law on the books and the law in actual practice, as well as the reasons therefor, so that the ensuing law reform can strike a proper balance between realism and idealism. An empirical investigation would need to be conducted involving systematic interviews with such groups as physicians, nurses, public health officials, nutritionists, sociologists, psychologists, housing and social welfare officers, educators, religious leaders and legislators. Sample surveys of public opinion should be classified according to age, sex, religion, education, occupation, race and geographic region. Input by sociologists are crucial in the preparation of questionnaires, the conducting of field surveys and the evaluation of results.[22]

(3) **Draft Codes**. Based on the compilation and analysis of the existing laws, a proposed revision of the laws in the form of a draft code should be drawn up aiming at the full achievement of human rights for the elderly.

All of the above tasks may be entrusted to the leading university of each country with demonstrable capability in interdisciplinary research. The fact that such a university is usually a national university has the added advantage in assuring that its findings can receive serious consideration by policy-makers, more so than if the project were undertaken by a private institution. It may be noted that in many countries there is a great deal of interchangeability between law deans and professors, on the one hand, and government officials like ministers of justice, attorneys general, etc. on the other. There is a natural interest on the part of the latter to follow the progress of the work of their university colleagues.

If a university is indeed engaged to undertake the above-mentioned tasks, it may profit from the methodology used by the Law and Population Projects in some 35 countries funded primarily by the United Nations Fund for Population Activities during the 1970's. Transposed to Law and the Rights of the Elderly, a typical two-year project would be based at the law faculty of the leading national university in cooperation with such other related faculties as those of Medicine, Public Health, Nutrition, Sociology, Economics and Public Administration. Assisted by researchers, the project

---

22. *See* Bulatao and Lee, *The Impact of Law on Fertility Behavior: Perspectives of Philippine Influential*, 48 PHILIPPINE LAW JOURNAL 22-53 (1973); Law and Population Book Series No. 9 (1974).

would perform the following functions:[23]

- Searching out, compiling and bringing up-to-date all the legislation, administrative decrees and judicial decisions which affect or may affect the rights of the aged, as described under the "Law Compilation" above;

- Describing customary laws if different from those mentioned above;

- Preparing a country monograph on Law and the Aged, following a uniform table of contents;

- Establishing a Board of Advisors to consist of not only academicians and jurists, but also high government officials from different Ministries to provide guidance to the project as well as critiques on draft codes (see below);

- Offering an interdisciplinary seminar on Law and the Aged during the second year of the project;

- Preparing a set of draft codes on the rights of the aged, based on human rights principles;

- Sending copies of the draft codes to key individuals and government officials, particularly the Ministries of Justice, Education, Health, Social Affairs, Finance, and Transportation, as well as the Attorney General, legislators and educators, for their comments, and integrating such comments into the final draft; and

- Promoting the adoption of the final draft through its widespread dissemination, the holding of national and regional conferences, etc., toward legal reform.

Elderly Refugees

Finally, this paper should not end without drawing the reader's attention to the plight of a particularly vulnerable group of the elderly who have often been overlooked: namely, the elderly refugees.

According to estimates by UNHCR and UNRWA, there were

---

23. UNFPA, *supra* note 16 at 18-19.

450,000 refugees aged 60 and over throughout the world in 1982.[24] Forced to leave their own countries, suffering from ill health and malnutrition, and separated from their relatives and friends, these elderly refugees have the additional misfortune of being less likely to be selected for resettlement in third countries than refugees still in their prime. Recommendation 43 of the Vienna International plan of Action on Aging specifically provides:

> As far as possible, groups of refugees accepted by a country should include elderly persons as well as adults and children, and efforts should be made to keep family groups intact and to ensure that appropriate housing and services are provided.

In addition, the World Assembly on Aging adopted a resolution entitled, "The Aging People in Lebanon." Though addressing the problems faced by the elderly people in that war-torn country, the content of the resolution, when shorn of political rhetoric, should be made applicable everywhere. The resolution "urges Member States to take all necessary measures to ensure the protection and to safeguard all civilian population, including in particular the elderly, during periods of tension and armed conflict." It also reinforces Article 14 of the Geneva Convention relative to the Protection of Civilian Persons in Time of War,[25] by requesting "the General Assembly to take necessary measures which would declare institutions for the elderly as 'immune protected areas' in situations of armed conflict and aggression, as in the case of hospitals, Red Cross facilities, etc."

It may be appropriate to end this paper with a quotation from George Bernard Shaw: "The worst sin towards our fellow creatures is not to hate them, but to be indifferent to them: that's

---

24. According to the United Nations High Commissioner for Refugees, in 1982 there were 300,000 elderly refugees between 60 and 92 years of age. UNHCR, *The Older Refugees: Report of the United Nations High Commissioner for Refugees*, U.N. Doc. A/CONF.113/21, February 17, 1982. This figure, however, did not include Palestinian refugees under the care of the United Nations Relief and Works Agency for Palestine Refugees in the Near East (UNRWA). *See*, U.N. Doc. A/CONF.113/21, Add.1.

25. International Committee of the Red Cross, *The Geneva Conventions of August 12, 1949* (Geneva 1981), p. 153.

the essence of inhumanity." Our indifference to the elderly would be not only inhuman, but also myopic. For sooner or later all of us will become the aged.

A FUTURE LAW FOR THE AGED:
AN ANALYSIS OF THE JAPANESE PROPOSED LAW
AND A PROPOSED LAW REFORM FOR THE FUTURE WORLD

*Yutaka Tajima**
Japan

Introduction

Since Japanese law relating to the problems of the elderly is still in an early stage, it may not be a good model for worldwide application. Japanese society, however, can be a very good object of study for considering the subject matter. Japan, which is a highly industrialized country with a dense population, has all the problems relating to the elderly that most countries of the world are presently facing or will face in the near future. This is the main reason why the present writer, a specialist in comparative law, focuses his attention on Japanese law.

Actually, several problems relating to the elderly are peculiar to Japan. Therefore, before consideration of the law relating to the elderly, it is necessary to state the general situation in Japan and Japanese society. First, demographically, it is important to note that, since the early 1960's, when the first statute on the issue, The Welfare of the Elderly Act of 1963, was enacted, the problems of the elderly have been acute. In 1960, there were about 5,398,000 aged people, approximately 5.7 percent of the whole population. Today these figures are 14,819,000 and 11.9 percent, respectively.[1] By definition, "aged people" means those who are

---

* Professor of law at the Institute for Advanced Legal Studies at the University of Tsukuba in Tokyo; J.S.D.; M. Litt. (Cantab); LL.M.; LL.B; Visiting Professor, University of California at Berkeley, 1979-80; Visiting Professor, Harvard Law School, 1986-87; author of several books.

1. Ministry of Public Welfare, *White Paper on Public Welfare for the 62nd Year of Showa* (1987) 210 (1988). The same statistics show that the percentage of the elderly will be 23.6% in 2020, the highest in the world.

65 years old or older. These figures indicate that Japan is faced with immense societal problems. Although some of these may be unique to Japan, it is worthwhile considering them in light of the aging of populations.

A primary issue in Japan is the accommodation available to aged people. At present, about 25 percent of the aged have no children. A large percentage of the aged people are living alone apart from their children, even though they have children.[2] Unlike many other societies, Japanese society is constructed in such a way that no person can avoid daily contact with neighbors, and indeed, those elderly people living alone normally have good friends in the vicinity. This social structure can help them through various hardships, particularly when they are ill. This is important since public homes for the elderly are scarce and private homes are often too expensive.[3]

The employment of the aged is another serious issue. In Japan, those who reach the age of 60 are expected to retire without exception from their office. In many cases, retirement comes before this age. The retired are treated as disabled persons, and it is extremely difficult for them to find new employment. Although pensions and national insurance systems are available to them, they may need non-material support with which to identify as human beings. Unfortunately, there is not much available to them. There are very few helpers or volunteers to help the elderly. The reason why so many of the aged often go to hospitals is probably that they want to have friends with whom they can talk.

A third issue to be covered is the medical care of the aged and related matters. The problem of senile dementia is the most critical issue. Another critical issue relates to the fraudulent trade to which the aged are apt to fall victim as exemplified by the Toyota

---

2. More than 65% of the aged persons wish to live alone, and those who cannot do so are likely to experience the trouble that will be discussed below. Professor Kazuo Aoi explains in detail why the aged in Japan wish to live alone in his article. Aoi, *Family Problems Related to the Aged*, in SOCIETY OF THE ELDERLY 101-33 (1979).

3. There are about 2700 public homes in which 200,000 aged persons in total are living. *See also* note 15 *infra*. Private homes number about 120 in which 10,538 aged persons are living.

Trading Company case.[4] The sex life of the elderly is another matter which must be considered in connection with their medical care.

Brief reference should be made to the interpretation of the provisions in the Japanese Constitution related to the subject matter. "The aged" is not a distinctive class under constitutional law and is not specifically mentioned there. However, the aged are protected by the Constitution in two ways. First, article 25 of the Constitution guarantees a "high cultural life" to the people, including the aged.[5] Secondly, under article 14 the aged are entitled to equal treatment under the law.[6] Since the implementation of these two constitutional mandates is entrusted to the legislature, rights are not specific and can only be enforced when concrete laws are made by the Diet or when courts recognize the existence of such rights.

Status of the Elderly Under the Civil Code

Who is responsible for the care and support of the aged? Section 877(1) of the Civil Code provides that persons in direct lineal line and siblings are mutually responsible for helping each

---

4. In the Toyota Trading Company case, salesmen of the company solicited many aged persons to make "investments" contracts of gold, diamond, and other precious commodities. The sales were found to be fraudulent, and as a consequence, many aged people committed suicide or suffered extreme hardship. The investigation conducted by the Center for Citizens Good Living after this case revealed the fact that victims of pyramid selling and other wrongful sales are mostly aged persons.

5. Under this constitutional mandate, there are several statutes enacted for the welfare of the aged, which are referred to in the following part of this chapter, in addition to the legislation providing for the national health insurance system and the national pension system.

6. *See* Hirata v. Mayor of Tateyama, Supreme Court Decision of 27th May 1964, 18 Saihan Minshu (no. 4) 676. The Grand Bench held that the original court had erred in its holding that "being aged does not fall under the category of a social status" for which discrimination is prohibited by article 14 of the Constitution. *See also* note 14 *infra*.

18

other.[7] Therefore, children or grandchildren are obligated to take care of and support their aged parents or grandparents. In contrast, § 820 of the Civil Code must be read together with this section of the Civil Code. Section 820 states that "the person who holds parental power, or *parens patriae*, shall have the right and duty to protect and educate children." Thus, the relation and obligation of a person toward his or her children is much stronger than that toward his or her parents. This is significant, since the Supplementary Benefits Act, which is the basis for welfare or for helping the aged, stipulates that those who are obligated to support others by law shall be primarily responsible for guaranteeing the livelihood of those who should be cared for and that all available sources related to them shall be utilized before they receive benefits.

The Supreme Court decision of February 13, 1951 explains in specific terms the duty of children to support their parents.[8] In that case, an aged mother who had been living with her eldest son in a house which her husband had left for the family moved to her married daughter's house.[9] The daughter claimed that her older brother should pay an equal share of the expenses necessary for support and medical treatment of the mother. Payment was refused, and after the mother's death, litigation followed. The brother insisted that he had been truly willing to care for and support the mother but that his sister had prevented him from performing his legal duty. Both the Hiroshima District Court and

---

7. This provision is declaratory and, therefore, it cannot be enforced unless the concrete obligation is determined by the liable persons concerned or by the family court. Quoting the opinion expressed by the late Professor Maki, a moralist, introducing this provision to the legislative committee, Professor Kawashima states that "the obligation set up by this provision can contain the *fides* or service of children toward their parents (i.e. *ko*), and further, special intimacy or service among those relatives living together in the same house." T. Kawashima, FAMILY SYSTEM AS AN IDEOLOGY, 183 (1957).

8. Fujii v. Fujii, Supreme Court Decision of Feb. 13, 1951, 5 Saihan Minshu (no. 3) 47.

9. This is very typical in Japan. The mother of a son is very often critical of his wife and does not wish to be cared for by the wife. This situation is commonly called the *yome-shutome* dispute.

the Hiroshima High Court accepted his argument. However, the Supreme Court reversed and remanded the case to the High Court for determination of the amount of reimbursement.

As a result of this Supreme Court decision, all those liable for support and care of the aged shall equally bear the expenses. Children are undoubtedly among persons liable. A consultation meeting may be held by those liable persons to decide how the liability should be borne by each member.[10] Those not participating in such meeting are impliedly "exempted" from liability under the Civil Code. In general, however, each liable person is expected to bear an equal share. More specifically, each liable person is obligated to contribute to the extent that he or she has a "surplus" after payment of all expenses necessary to support his or her own children. Unfortunately, the treatment of children and parents is not the same. For example, the Civil Code allows a person to supply only a small fish to parents, while the person has a legal obligation to supply the same food (e.g. beefsteak) that he or she actually eats to his or her own children.[11]

This differential treatment is quite shocking to the aged who were brought up under the old family system.[12] That system was heavily influenced by Confucianism, upon which the old civil law was based. Under this old system, a man could make a declaration that he would "abdicate the headship of the family" at any time,

---

10. The family meeting was obligatory under the old civil law but not today. Even under the new civil law, however, the family court must, in fact, hold a consultation meeting when those liable persons cannot make a mutual agreement about the care of their elderly relative.

11. This is a theory proposed by the late Professor Z. Nakagawa which normally has been accepted by family law specialists. It should be noted, however, that it was expressed at the time when the parent, or the family head, had an absolute power under the old law. *See* Osaka High Court Decision, June 19, 1974, 27 Kasai Geppo (no. 4) 61.

12. *Cf.* Ito v. Ito, Court of Cassation Decision of Feb. 29, 1916, 22 Minroku 172, which is quoted in the decisions of the lower courts in Fujii v. Fujii, *supra* note 8. This states that the good morals of respect for parents would be denied if children could sue each other in the court. Professor Kawashima explains this mentality of the Japanese in T. Kawashima, FAMILY STRUCTURE OF JAPANESE SOCIETY 178-82 (1950). *See also* note 7 *supra*.

and thereafter, he could claim his support from the man who succeeded to the headship. A comparison of the old and new family systems is worthwhile, since most Asiatic countries, including China, Korea and Vietnam, still maintain a system similar to the old Japanese system.

Under the old system, the concept of "family" was much wider than that of the new one. A family included several generations. The family head had a special power over the generations and could determine all family matters. A sort of organic force functioned to care for the aged in the whole family, and indeed, they were "respected" by members of the family. This of course was not universally true, since some poor farmers were forced to abandon their parents due to the extreme, unbearable hardship experienced by their families. The new system in contrast is based on the idea of a "single core family." The above-mentioned Supreme Court decision certainly reflects this new idea. That decision set forth that the parent-children relationship, and not the children-parent relationship, is the most significant human tie under the present civil law.[13]

Homes for the Elderly
and the Welfare of the Aged

Accommodation is the most important matter. The central government, as well as local governments with the delegation of power, is expected ultimately to take the responsibility to care for the aged. The Welfare of the Elderly Act of 1963 provides that local governments shall maintain four kinds of homes for the elderly.[14] The problems relating to these homes for the elderly are mainly in urban communities. These homes are very rare in rural communities, because rural life compels the whole community

---

13. *See also*, State v. Aizawa, Supreme Court Decision of April 4, 1973, 27 Saihan Keishu (no. 3) 265. Here, the Supreme Court held that section 200 of the Criminal Code (patricide) was unconstitutional under article 14 of the Constitution.

14. There are (i) special homes for those aged persons who require full attention, (ii) general nursing homes, (iii) small scale homes for the elderly, and (iv) homes which require payment of a small amount because the aged persons have reasonable income.

to take care of the elderly.[15] In agriculture, there are roles that the aged can play and indeed are expected to play so they have a place in society. Governmental subsidies to local governments solve most problems that the elderly may have in rural areas. In contrast, problems of the elderly are very acute in urban communities, especially in Tokyo and in Osaka. There the elderly often live alone and there is a lack of welfare officers to help them. Furthermore, even if an elderly person is put into a home, problems persist.

Homes for the aged are expensive and scarce.[16] In addition, problems with the "privacy, dignity and liberty" of the aged in these homes should not be taken lightly. With respect to privacy, there are normally four persons in one room which inevitably leads to conflicts in personal taste, and can develop intransigent difficulties. Despite this serious problem, it is still considered necessary to keep four people in one room, so somebody will be able to report an emergency to the appropriate authority. Most residents, however, feel that their privacy is oppressively invaded by the system.

The aged person's "dignity" can be compromised in these homes in a number of twisted ways. An educated person may be disliked by his or her co-residents simply because he or she does not watch a popular television program, or if one resident is taking special note of something, the others might feel uncomfortable. Further, an intellectual woman may be offended by the manner of a certain home helper or the behavior of her co-residents. These are only a few examples of the trouble which elderly people experience in such homes.

Most residents of these homes for the elderly wish to have "liberty." Liberty however is narrowed significantly, mostly because "uniformity" is necessary in the community life of such homes. For instance, a novelist who writes throughout the night

---

15. It should also be noted that rural communities have been the supplier of the labor force of the country, and the aged people are responsible for all family affairs while major members of the family are working in industries.

16. The public homes referred to at note 15 *supra* are essentially for the poor people. Private homes are usually more expensive than hotels.

would be forced to give up this habit if he or she wished to enter such a home. At present, homes for the elderly are not rich enough to allow such varied lifestyles and such forms of "liberty."

A special note should be made of the "self-respect" of the elderly. As of September 15, 1988, which is incidentally the national holiday for respect of the elderly, the number of the aged over 100 years old exceeded 2600. One television program on that day reported that most of them had lost "self-respect." In fact, one old woman said in the program that she was alive only for the purpose of going to "hell."

Employment of the Aged

The Security of Employment for the Elderly Act, enacted in 1971, provides that if an employer establishes age for retirement, it shall not be less than 60.[17] Nearly 80 percent of the Japanese companies have adopted a system under which their employees are forced to retire at the age of 60 without exception, though a considerable number of companies allow each individual employee to continue his or her employment on a yearly contract basis until the age of 65. In order to entrench this Japanese labor practice, companies normally stop wage increase at the age of 55 (in some rare cases, at 45) and give each employee the option to retire before 60 at his or her own pleasure.[18]

In most developed countries, the law prohibits discrimination on the basis of age. In the United States, for example, by law, a public employee may not be discharged because of advanced

---

17. *See* section 4 of the 1971 act. This Act provides for the establishment of "the silver manpower center" and various information services for the aged people, including "counseling." How this Act has been implemented is explained in details in *Administrative Inspection Bureau of Department of General Affairs*, REALITY AND PROBLEMS OF THE EMPLOYMENT POLICY OF THE AGED PERSONS (1988).

18. *See*, generally, R. Magota, *Wage, Retirement Allowance and Pension of the Aged People*, in PENSION REFORM AND THE LIFE OF THE ELDERLY (Jurist Special Issue no. 36) 110-17 (1984).

age.[19] West Germany also prohibits compulsory retirement at any age, and in 1983 France established a system to rigidly regulate the retirement system of private companies. In comparison with these advanced legal systems, Japan is very backward in the protection of the elderly.

There are at least two reasons that may justify the present situation of Japan. These factors are in some ways beneficial to the elderly, although they result in the general situation in which the elderly are kept out of the work force. First, private corporations usually adopt a pension system through which employees who have worked for a certain number of years are entitled to receive monthly payments shortly after their retirement. In many cases, corporations take care of retired persons who have worked for them for a long period.[20] Second, the Government has taken a positive step towards advancing the policy encouraging employment of senior citizens by establishing a new agency called "the silver manpower center." The purpose of this new agency is to create new employment opportunities by which the aged may start a new life.[21] It was started only recently and we can hope it will have a successful future.

In reality, this labor system causes many problems for the

---

19. However, those who have completed 15 years of service are in fact encouraged to retire and start receiving their annuity. 5 U.S.C.A. § 8331.

20. *See* M. Nagamachi, *Counterplans of Corporations for the Aged Society*, in PENSION REFORM AND THE LIFE OF THE ELDERLY, *supra* note 19, at 118-25. Large corporations have various subsidiaries and are normally able to find a position for the retired employee. With respect to public employees, private companies in some way connected with the government office in which an employee has served are normally willing to employ him or her after his or her retirement, though this practice was often criticized as "amakudari (employment by influence exerted from above)."

21. The silver manpower center, established under the 1971 Act mentioned at note 20 *supra*, has made efforts to accept consigned projects from various governmental offices. Bureau of Administrative Inspection of the Department of General Affairs, *supra* note 18, at 51-52. This report recommends the promotion of the activities of this center with the assistance and cooperation of related agencies such as the Information Center for the Development of the Aged Persons' Ability and the Counseling Room for the Employment of the Aged.

24

elderly. First, whatever the retired person does with his or her free time will cost a great deal of money. Usually the monthly payment which the retired persons receive is not enough to meet the expenses.[22]

Second, due to the fact that they did not have time to learn how to enjoy life outside of work, many aged people have failed to find an activity attractive enough to make them feel that their lives are worth living. Third, even if an aged person can find a new job, often the kinds of jobs available are not as attractive and pay is relatively low. These factors often lead to frustration and dissatisfaction.

The problems and overall condition of the aged after retirement has created the bedridden aged, "those aged people who keep lying on the bed all the time, though they are not sick."[23] Doing nothing is the easiest way for them to make money and increase their bank accounts, enabling them to make sizable gifts to their grandsons or granddaughters with the potentially false hope that in return they can expect reasonable care. Increased assets also may allow the elderly to take an expensive trip, although this only occurs occasionally.[24] At the extreme, as exemplified by the woman quoted above, some of the aged, bedridden or not, may simply wish to die. Under Japanese law, however, suicide is a crime and the aged do not have a right to die or to "euthanasia."

----

22. The payment is composed of the basic allowance, a fixed amount similar to the British or Swedish elderly allowance, plus a variable amount in proportion to the contribution of each employee for the public fund, and an allowance similar to the American style pension. The total monthly payment is at best 70% of the wages at the time of retirement and in many cases it is much less, though it may be occasionally increased when the growth rate of the national gross income is very high.

23. There are presumably about 570,000 such persons, and the figure is increasing. Bureau of Administrative Inspection of the Department of General Affairs, PRESENT CONDITIONS AND ISSUES OF THE POLICY FOR THE ELDERLY 16 (1986). This report also explains the conditions of the welfare services for the aged such as "short stay," "day service" and other volunteer activities.

24. The aged people enjoy trips to a "hot spa" as the most attractive form of relaxation. In hot spa resorts, they can enjoy variety shows, popular songs, fish dinners, and a bit of adventure.

The labor situation in Japan inevitably creates a great number of retired elderly. Increased numbers wish to enter homes where improvement of facilities and better services are needed. Furthermore, the problem related to the aged's mental and medical care is exacerbated by these increased numbers.

Medical Care and Assistance
in Other Hardships

Modern medical science shows that man starts aging at around 40 years old. This turning point varies with each individual. With aging, a person begins to be vulnerable to illnesses peculiar to the elderly. These include, in order of decreasing frequency, (1) viral diseases, (2) mental diseases, (3) vascular tract problems in the brain, (4) pneumonia (particularly bronchial pneumonia), (5) difficult recovery or bad development after accidental injury, (6) papatitis and gastritis, and (7) hypertension, among others.[25] Senile decay or dementia is not a disease, but it is normally counted among the diseases peculiar to the aged, and it is ranked between 5 and 6 in the above list.

Since the Elderly Medical Treatment Insurance Act was enacted in 1972, the medical expenses of illnesses in the above list are covered by insurance.[26] This insurance system probably has been abused and now the fund for payments under it is bankrupted. In order to deal with the resulting financial problem, the

---

25. M. Yoshikawa, *Diseases of the Adult and Diseases of the Aged*, 60 SOCIETY OF THE ELDERLY (1979). "Mental anguish" and "suicide" are included between items 5 and 6 among the causes of death.

26. The amount of the payment made for the medical care of the elderly varies depending on each local government. At some time, medical expenses were paid in full by local governments with a subsidy from the central government, but this system was amended in 1983. *See* K. Sonoda, *Public Health and Medical Care Administration in Aged Society*, in PENSION REFORM AND THE LIFE OF THE ELDERLY, *supra* note 19, at 158-63. Each aged patient is presently required to pay a nominal fee when he or she visits hospitals. Concerning the bankruptcy and countermeasures of the public insurance funds, *see* N. Maeda, *The Policy on Welfare and Health of the Elderly in Japan*, in WELFARE OF THE AGED AND MEDICAL CARE OF THE AGED 130-43 (Yoshida & Giga ed. 1981).

insurance fund for the elderly was recently linked with other public insurance funds. As a result, the whole public insurance system must be reconstructed in order to meet the financial insecurity of the future.

Beyond the financial crisis in the care for the aged, there are very significant legal problems, especially with respect to senility.[27] Section 93 of the Civil Code provides that "a declaration of intention shall not be invalidated if the other party has reason to believe that it is the intention of the party." Thus, an aged, who may in fact be senile, signs or puts a signet on a legal document, he will be legally bound to respect whatever obligations he has promised in that document.[28] Whereas § 4 of the Civil Code allows a minor, e.g. a 19 year old university student, to rescind a contract that he or she has signed, the aged are not entitled to rescind their contracts. It is questionable why minors and senile persons, who may not have the presence of mind to make proper judgments about their own affairs, should be treated differently. Section 709 of the Civil Code provides that "a person who violates intentionally or negligently the right of another is bound to make compensation for damage arising therefrom." The family member caring for the aged may be vicariously obligated to pay damages under this provision. This imposes a severe burden on the family who must always pay close and full attention to the elderly relative.[29]

The mental hardship of the aged is not necessarily limited to illness. Mental hardship may result from the lack of understanding of the family about the sex life of the aged. Kawabata, Tanizuchi, Shimazaki, and many other great novelists of Japan, who wrote about the life of the aged, illustrated what seems to be an exotic

---

27. Only those who are declared incompetent or quasi-incompetent are exempt from liability. Senile people are, however, not such persons.

28. The victims of fraudulent trade practice have faced hardship mostly because of this rule. *See* note 4 *supra*.

29. Section 714 of the Civil Code, which provides for the liability of the supervisory person, is not strictly applicable to the case of senile persons, but, in fact, the family have conducted themselves as if it were applicable *mutatis mutandis* to them.

sex life.[30] This topic deserves careful study and attention in practice. Indifference to the problem can lead to intense unhappiness and depression, and indeed, in one case, suicide was the unfortunate result.

A Future Law for the Aged

The future of the aged is by no means crystal clear. Problems relating to the aged, discussed in this chapter, can be solved to a considerable extent by changes in the social and mental attitudes held by the people in general, through education and by other means, both public and private. There still remain some problems, however, that cannot be settled without the strong support of positive law.[31]

Several laws must be introduced and adopted in order to achieve a more ideal situation and life for the aged. This would be a situation in which the aged can work as much as they like but can also retire at any time and start receiving public funds sufficient enough to make them feel their lives are worth living. The following presents suggestions for achieving this goal.

Our future law for the aged should prohibit public and private entities from forcing retirement solely on the basis of age. The aged should be able to retire voluntarily without any prejudice after the age of 65. This may indeed help our society. The compulsory retirement system has caused a great loss to our society, since many elderly persons who are more able than the ordinary employee, have been kept out of the work force. Aging is a natural process which the corporation should keep in mind when it makes employment contracts. The corporation should provide for changes in the working role of the employee to a more appropriate one as he or she ages.

---

30. *See* Y. Miyoshi, *Aged Persons and Sex*, in SOCIETY OF THE ELDERLY 221-39 (1979). This essay vividly shows this aspect of the aged persons' life, though it is written from the standpoint of literature.

31. Experience of the British people, who have been active in volunteer activities for the elderly for a long time also shows this. *See* generally, N. Roberts, OUR FUTURE SELVES (1970).

The problem would solve itself without introduction of the said new law, if after compulsory retirement, the aged could easily find new jobs comparable to his or her previous one. As an alternative, a law which established an office under the Ministry of Labor for helping the aged in starting a new life could help solve the problem of comparable employment. The aim of this law and office would be to identify, standardize and implement comparable jobs for the elderly.

The future law must also change the people who are making decisions about the aged. In the past, the welfare administration for the elderly has not worked well in part because the administration is staffed by young people. Officers working for the administration are normally very young, much below 50, and at any rate, they are also obligated to retire by the age of 60 under the present legal system. The aged should make their own decisions about their welfare. Stereotypical responses to problems of the elderly must be eliminated. Forcing free boarding passes on the aged and creating "silver seats" in trains and buses were not good ideas, since they merely reinforced the stereotype of the weak, frail and poor elderly person. Each aged person should have the freedom to make his or her own decisions within the welfare system. In order to attain this, it is necessary to give wide discretion to welfare officers and social workers who are sensitive to the needs and issues concerning the elderly. Further, it is imperative to create a new judicial system for the supervision and proper management of the administration described in this treatise.

THE OBLIGATIONS OF THE ELDERLY

*David Thomson**
New Zealand

Many things have contributed to real and imagined shifts in the nature of elderly populations in western societies - their swelling numbers, the maturing of mid-century public and private pension programs, improved education amongst the aged, expansion of private savings and assets, a willingness to organize politically in tapping public sympathies or unease, a new sense of the leisure and comfort appropriate to age, the emergence of counter-voices of protest such as Americans for Generational Equity, and more. We shall look further into these presently: what interests us for the moment is the appropriate reaction for gerontologists, and for all who are concerned to understand what is happening to our societies.

I note several current reactions. One has been an understandable confusion: how can people say or believe these things, when they run so counter to what we have known for so long to be true? A second has been defensiveness: we must work harder and talk louder in securing more for the aged. A third, and one I share fully, has been to welcome the changes, for they are exhilarating as well as unsettling. Social gerontology is being invited to center stage, to cast aside its marginal status and intellectual lethargy. Communities and individuals are beginning to sense, perhaps rather sooner than the scholars who specialize in these things, that population aging is rapidly reshaping their worlds - not just for the aged, or for themselves in their last years, but for everyone at all stages through life. The two year old of 1990, just as much as her 30 year old mother or 60 year old grandmother or 85 year old great-grandmother, is caught up in this vague and ominous-sounding

* Senior lecturer in history at Massey University in New Zealand; Member of the Aging Unit, Cambridge Group for the History of Population and Social Structure; M.A., University of Canterbury; Ph.D., University of Cambridge.

process of aging. What it all means, for individual, family or wider society, is something being asked with mounting urgency. The moment has truly come for those who study aging in all of its manifestations.

How are we to respond? First, we must grasp the opportunity to be heard, to influence and to lead. Second, we must display flexibility and open-mindedness, admitting that we too are feeling our way into a new and unfamiliar world. Old dogmas about the rights and desserts of the elderly will not go down well, unless balanced by an awareness of powers and freedoms, and hence of the obligations and restraints that lie upon the late-twentieth century aged.

Third, we will have to take an expansive view of our subject. For too long the aged have been treated as special and distinct, as standing aside from the mainstream: they are not of us. This sidelining has taken various forms. One has been to make the aged into children: we must do things for them, without expecting an input from them in return. Another has been to ignore the wider impact of what we do for the aged. Discussions of their health care needs, for instance, have taken place in isolation from tougher questions of the correct or appropriate distribution of a society's health resources. This made our lives simpler: an approach that allowed us to avoid arguing about whether hip replacements should have priority over maternity services was appealing.

But this will not be possible or acceptable from here on. The aged now form a substantial block of all voters, investors and consumers. Their decisions in each role affect not just themselves, but all of their fellow citizens, for now and well into the future. They cannot be given an "exempt status" - able to "need" or "want" without limit, but not called to account for the effects of their actions. That was once possible, when the aged were fewer and much poorer: their claims were of little overall consequence. It can no longer be the case, as the aged come to command major fractions of political and economic power. Studies which continue to foster this sense that the aged are out of the mainstream, and so not bound by the normal obligations of voting adults, will enjoy less and less credence.

Fourth, we will find ourselves giving new meanings to old terms, and should not shy from the challenge. In particular, the varied concepts of "aging" will have to be reassessed. "To age" or "to grow old" have until now referred to what were essentially individual processes. Individuals aged, but societies, economies, politics or value systems did not. In turn, gerontology or the study of aging centered upon the experiences of persons - their health, bodily or mental capacities, housing requirements and the like. However, "aging" now refers to much more vital shifts in the nature of economies and societies, rather than of individuals. We are already living through the first phases of "demographic aging," "political aging," "economic aging" and more. Each, as it develops, will come to affect the life-course of the individual at least as much as will the individual's own personal aging.

What it means to say these things is as yet unclear, for our imaginations fail to make the necessary leaps. My own physical aged phase will occur in the 2020s and 2030s. I will then be one of the globe's first "mass elderly," and that fact will have to mean that my personal experiences of being old will be very different than if I had grown old in the world of my father or my grandfather. The nature of saving, investment, distribution of resources through time, perhaps even of economic growth or the future of capitalist economies, are all being remade by the processes of aging which are now in train. The intellectual challenges to students of aging are of an immense and exciting order.[1]

Generations in Time

One further ingredient in a successful new study of aging will have to be a sensitivity to "generation," and this last I want to expand upon in the remainder of this essay. The historian's contention here is that a study of generational experiences holds the key to understanding much recent social, economic and political history, the reasons why images of the aged are now altering rapidly, and the likely future shape of political debates within aging electorates. By generation we shall mean neither "old and young," nor "parent and child," nor "a span of about 25 years," nor "the people alive at a particular moment." The

---

1. An important recent contribution to this opening of wider issues is Laslett, A FRESH MAP OF LIFE (London: Weidenfeld and Nicolson 1989).

everyday usage coming closest to our intentions is "the people born in a certain era"; generation here means a birth cohort. Membership of a generation is thus fixed from birth, and all of a generation age together, accumulating common experiences along the way from the fact of passing through the same life-phases in the same historical moments.

A central failing of aging studies - indeed, of our intellectual traditions more generally - has been a persisting unwillingness to grapple with notions of cohort or generation. All sense from their daily lives that generation is of vital importance: my own birth in 1953 has to mean that however like my father or grandfather I might be in terms of occupation, education and much else, I cannot but move through life acquiring a different set of experiences, one more akin to those of my contemporaries than of my predecessors or successors. Yet, while we recognize this as individuals, as scholars we remain happier dealing with social class, gender, nationality and the like, rather than with experiences deriving from date of birth.

A brief historical survey will help illustrate the significance of generation for aging studies in the 1990s. The issue to be explored is as follows. Modern welfare states bind all citizens in an elaborate and compulsory pooling of resources and risks, freedoms and powers. The justification for this pooling is that all generations will benefit, with the resources and freedoms lost in some life phases being rewarded amply in others. Such is the "implicit welfare contract between generations" which makes a welfare state possible, and citizens of all birth dates have to assume that it exists and is observed by others, if a massive pooling based upon "pay as you go and have faith in future rewards" is to hold much attraction.[2]

The question for the historian - and us all - is whether societies do, in fact, behave in this way. Members of successive generations join, participate and leave the pooling at different points in time: what are their lifetime histories of participation, of member-

---

2. Thomson, SELFISH GENERATIONS? THE AGING OF THE WELFARE STATE (Wellington: Allen and Unwin 1991).

ship of modern society and state? And, do differences in these histories help illuminate current confusions about the nature of old age, as well as the ongoing larger processes of aging? The focus here will be upon New Zealand - a small, early and modestly-developed member of the collective of mature welfare states. Questions of its typicality or representativeness must lie open for now, though I have elsewhere and on many occasions argued that my country's experiences betray a deeper, universal pattern of aging.[3]

This "aging of the welfare state" as I have called it bedevils all modern states, delivering successive generations highly contrasting experiences of what a lifetime within the modern state is to mean for them. The New Zealand example, I will hold, provides an excellent example of a worrying wider phenomenon.

The implicit contract between generations, which all must assume to exist, sets up powerful expectations of consistency and reciprocity through time. That is, the participant in this obligatory pooling has to believe that actions today oblige others to reciprocate later, and that there will be some consistency about the whole exchange as it runs decade after decade. Citizens who are forced to pool with unknown millions of others do so in the faith that their current sacrifices will be rewarded and their futures thus secured: selfless altruism and a blind disregard for personal consequence are not the bases upon which we collectivize risk and resource in mass societies. Expectations of reciprocity and consistency underpin the whole exchange.[4]

What must strike the historian however, is that welfare states have not operated according to these essentials. Nor do they seem even to have recognized them or their importance, or to have

3. Thomson, *The intergenerational contract - under pressure from population aging*, AN AGING WORLD - CHALLENGES AND DILEMMAS FOR LAW AND SOCIAL POLICY (Eekelar & Pearl (eds) Oxford: Oxford University Press 1989); Thomson, *The welfare state and generation conflict: winners and losers*, WORKERS VERSUS PENSIONERS: INTERGENERATIONAL JUSTICE ON AGING WORLD (Johnson (ed) Manchester: Manchester University Press 1989).

4. A useful discussion of the moral commitments which underpin a welfare state is Room, in Mommsen, THE EMERGENCE OF THE WELFARE STATE IN BRITAIN AND GERMANY, 1850-1950 (London: Croom Helm 1981).

intentions of observing them in the future - plans all run in the opposite direction. The results, amongst much else, are the current dramatic loss of confidence in public solutions to welfare problems, a growing sense of personal insecurity, the resurgent respectability of individualism and self-help, and significant shifts in perceptions of the aged and their rights.

That welfare states have ignored the imperative to deliver consistency and reciprocity through time is at once apparent. Tax rates rise and sometimes fall, so that individuals passing through the same life phases in 1950 or 1970 or 1990 are forced to pay very different contributions into the pool, even as they lead identical lives. At the same time taxation exemptions for children or school fees, house-buying or overtime work, employment-related expenses or superannuation savings have expanded and contracted, emerged or disappeared: the price of participation in the pool depends upon being born in one year rather than some other.

In similar fashion, family allowances come and go, old age pensions rise or fall in real or relative value, health services are extended or contracted and gain or lose free status, indirect education charges creep into "free" public schooling, unemployment benefit rules are tightened and loosened, and so on. Beyond that, governments use the extensive powers which individuals have surrendered to them to fix or modify interest rates, to protect local employments from foreign imports or to expose all to unfettered competition, to manage inflation up and down, or to determine investment patterns or returns on savings. Relations between individual and state, as identical citizens follow identical lives separated only by date of birth, prove anything but consistent.

This obvious historical point leads to a further question: has the inconsistency and lack of reciprocity been random and patternless? Can I, set to live my way through this maze of ceaseless change by being born in 1953, expect nevertheless that the inconsistency of it all will not work against me over a lifetime? For if the individual can have that faith, then a sustainable public pooling between generations might still prove possible: if not, the future of the welfare state looks bleak, and the attractions of individualist welfare solutions will gather apace.

The answer to this is unequivocal - inconsistency has not been random or unstructured through time. Instead, the constant changing of the rules of participation has produced a striking historical pattern, one emerging moreover in all modern states. The changes work to the persisting advantage of particular generations, making successive life-stages attractive habitations as they move into them and punishing ones as they move on, relinquishing them to successors. In New Zealand's case, the winners from this are the "welfare generation" as I have described them. These are those born between about 1920 and 1945, with those born in the 1930s forming the most privileged core. The losers were their predecessors, and to a greater extent their successors: the further one's date of birth lies from the 1930s the greater the likely lifetime penalty. Elsewhere, the bounds of the welfare generation will vary because of the timing of local historical events such as the introduction of certain social security measures. But in each instance, the key lifelong beneficiaries are those who were children or young adults at the formation of the modern welfare state, around or soon after World War II.

Why welfare states should behave through time in this way is a complex matter - as fairy godmothers to some generations, and vengeful stepmothers to others.[5] The issue goes beyond our concerns here, but it cannot be ignored entirely because of its inherent great interest and because of its significance to our present purposes.[6] The explanations seem not to lie in demographics: the shifting of welfare priorities in step with the personal aging of favored generations precedes rather than follows demographic aging. Nor is it a result of electoral aging. Between 1950 and 1980, for example, all electorates in welfare states either remained stable in age-composition or became slightly more youthful, and yet an aging of welfare interests took place.

---

5. My thinking on this draws upon the writings of many, including Hardin & Baden, MANAGING THE COMMONS (San Francisco: W. H. Freeman 1977); Hirsch, SOCIAL LIMITS TO GROWTH (London: Routledge and Kegan Paul 1977); Hirschman, SHIFTING INVOLVEMENTS: PRIVATE INTEREST AND PUBLIC ACTION (Oxford: Martin Robertson 1982); Thurow, THE ZERO-SUM SOLUTION (New York: Simon and Shuster 1985); Wynne, SOCIAL SECURITY: A RECIPROCITY SYSTEM UNDER PRESSURE (Boulder: Westview Press 1980).

6. Thomson, SELFISH GENERATIONS? THE AGING OF THE WELFARE STATE, Chap. 6 (Wellington: Allen and Unwin 1991).

Nor should we stress a conscious or deliberate process of "capture," of knowing manipulation of the welfare state by some cohorts to their own advantage. There have been elements of this. For example, New Zealand political leaders in the early 1970s justified a substantial expansion in old age provision on the grounds that "our generation, the children of depression and war, are owed it." A conspiracy view is also tempting, given the comprehensiveness through time of the redesigning of welfare concerns: the shape of plans emerging now to curtail provision for old age, once members of the welfare generation have passed on, points further in this direction. Nevertheless, these are elements I would not highlight. The aging of the welfare state, and with it the creation of deep and lasting generational inequities, is rooted in the very nature of the modern welfare state.

By creating compulsory poolings at mid-century, societies unwittingly set up dynamic processes of welfare evolution which would henceforth run largely outside of their control, and would in time erode and negate the original intentions and achievements. The problems of the 1990s, in other words, were already inherent in the ideals and structures of the 1930s and 40s. What we established then were blind, mass poolings involving millions of people unknown to each other, to be operated by popularly-elected governments whose prime mandate would be to maximize immediate living standards. The whole was, in effect, a giant chain-letter.[7] The first benefits were to flow to those present at the outset, and thereafter all were to pass and receive gifts through life, but without the possibilities of opting out or of knowing how any other was playing the game. Personal secrecy and a lack of individual records of contribution and benefit have been insisted

---

7. The image of the "welfare state as chain letter" is not original; it was invoked in the 1950s by Samuelson and others. Samuelson, *An exact consumption-loan model of interest with or without the social contrivance of money*, LXVI J. OF POLITICAL ECONOMY 467-82 (1958). A useful introduction to its early employment is Burbridge, SOCIAL SECURITY IN CANADA: AN ECONOMIC APPRAISAL (Toronto: Canadian Tax Foundation, Paper No. 79 1987).

upon.[8]

This has its merits, but it does place the citizen-voter in an unanticipated and invidious position. Each is under a mounting corrosive sense of suspicion towards others, and an exchange founded to foster security, community and redistributive instincts ends by promoting the very opposite. A consequence for the person who is made to participate in doubt and ignorance, through decade after decade, must be a growing sense of insecurity, and a "rational" desire to minimize contributions while maximizing drawings as soon as possible. To do this may be ruinous for the whole exchange over time - and may be recognized as such by those involved. But not to do so is for the individual to risk loss of position to more grasping or less scrupulous fellows, since consistency or honesty of behavior on the part of all others cannot or is seen not to be guaranteed.

The outcomes for a population caught in this slow spiral of suspicion is the aging of the welfare state, a complex phenomenon which includes the following as some of the means to sustain an expanding redistribution program through the lifetimes of the welfare generation:

- a loss of confidence in collective activity;

- an increased anxiety that a system of social organization designed to deliver future security cannot do so, even if it can deliver rising standards of living at the moment;

- a growing indifference to the plight of "the poor," as unease about one's own future circumstances takes precedence;

- a demand to have the prizes of pooling made immediate, in the form of cash or services rather than invested in future goods;

- a drive to have the prizes placed always ahead of one in life, the penalties behind and on successors;

- an insistence that one's successors pool their resources more heavily than did oneself in similar circumstances, and that these pass forward to

---

8. Some social security funds maintain partial individual records of contribution, but not of lifetime benefits; no nations record the larger flows of resources to and from individuals.

predecessors;

- and the increasing use of public and private debt, environmental depletion, non-maintenance of infrastructure, or the decline in the quantity and quality of human investment.

I have elaborated these ideas elsewhere and will explore them further below: what concerns us here are three consequences. First, the aging of welfare priorities through the last few decades has created a generation which has and is accumulating unusual privilege. Second, this generation is the aged of the 1990s and 2000s, and no discussion of their rights or obligations, as individuals or as a group, can ignore this historical fact, disturbing as it may be. And third, we have suggested that their peculiar history of participation in the exchange with predecessors and successors has not been of their own making for the most part: the winners from the welfare state are in a curious sense the victims of a process as much as are the losers. This will further complicate all consideration of what is right or appropriate or possible with regard to the aged in the 1990s.

Creating a generation of privilege

It is time to move closer to the historical evidence: just how has a generation of privilege been created? In their early years, and through the 1960s, the modern welfare states were overwhelmingly welfare states for youth. In many instances the aged were granted limited pension advances in the 1930s and 40s, but these were not repeated during the next quarter-century. Much greater stress was placed upon the needs and interests of children and young adults - and the fact that many now find this hard to accept is a measure of how far we have moved from those earlier concerns. The reasons for this initial youth emphasis were several. They include obvious ones, such as the desire to guarantee employment, especially for family men, after the experiences of the 1930s; a belief that recent war veterans must be well rewarded; anxiety over population decline and the need to boost growth by making the circumstances of young families attractive; and the requirement of investing heavily to replace war damage or to counter the long-term effects of infrastructural under-investment in the 1930s and 40s.

Other factors were less obvious but equally critical. An exchange between young and old such as exists today, with the largest benefits and in many cases the best incomes now secured for the aged, could not have been introduced at the outset. An electorate with little experience of mass pooling, and in which half of the voters were under about age 40, would not have accepted it. At that point, all had to be won at once to a new exchange relationship between generations, that is between earlier and later born, as would not again be the case once compulsory pooling had been set in motion. A consequence of these peculiar "start-up" constraints was an exchange between generations which stressed youth rather than age, public services rather than instant cash handouts, investment rather than spending, and growth rather than current consumption. The balance was one which held attractions for all ages and generations.

The rights or wrongs of that balance are not germane to this discussion, though they are of course highly relevant to issues such as economic growth, the roots of population aging and much more. What matters here is that a particular balance was struck, in turn setting up powerful expectations about the continuing nature and purpose of the welfare state. An implicit welfare contract between generations requires that the exchange be of no particular nature - only that, once the rules have been agreed, they be observed with consistency. One community could decide to work its exchanges to advantage all as they came into old age. Another might choose youth as the prime time of benefit. In either case consistency thereafter would ensure that members of each generation could have faith in the exchange, with all accepting the price of participating at some points in life in order to gain in others. "Generational equity," or justice for successor generations, would lie not in any particular set of redistributive arrangements, but in the consistency with which the rules of give and take were applied over time.[9]

---

9. This point is well recognized by philosophers of justice: Rawls, for instance, notes that ideal legislators would have to be oblivious to their own personal ages, and could not be allowed to revise their judgments of right as they themselves aged. Rawls, A THEORY OF JUSTICE (Cambridge: Harvard University Press 1971).

These simple requirements have not been met, and any discussion of age or generational rights in the 1990s will not be able to ignore this. "Generational inequity," of which talk is growing, has something to do with the aged now having or being seen to have incomes and security not available to nor intended for the later-born. But the phenomenon goes much deeper, is rooted in history, has been structured into the institutions of modern state and society, and will be especially difficult to debate or resolve because of this.

* * * *

The switch from youth to aged priorities in recent decades has taken common forms in Europe, North America and Australia, and the New Zealand experience offers important insights into the many interwoven aspects of this process. Amongst the most obvious have been changes in social security spending. Until the 1960s, cash payments to younger adults, through family allowances and war pensions for the most part, matched and outstripped total payments to the aged. In 1951, for instance, cash benefits for the aged absorbed 2.8 percent of New Zealand's gross domestic product (GDP), alongside family allowances at 2.2 percent and other grants to adults under the age of about 40 at a further one percent. This "balance" was maintained until the end of the 1960s, with age benefits still accounting for just over three percent of GDP by the beginning of the 1970s.

But in the 1970s and 80s change has been dramatic, and had little to do with demographics or any shift in the numbers of old and young. In the mid-1970s a new old age provision was introduced. The age for full entitlement was lowered to 60 years; all incomes and assets testing was abolished; no contributions histories were required; pension payments to all were lifted substantially; an indexing procedure very favorable to the aged was put in place; and no "phase-in" period was included. Meanwhile the family allowance paid to the parents of every child - New Zealand's only other universal welfare programme - was allowed to wither. By the end of the 1980s, cash benefits to the aged absorbed around eight percent of GDP, family allowances just half of one percent. Other non-universal payments to the younger half of the population did grow, including unemployment, sickness and single-parent allowances, though by 1990 these together were equivalent to about one-quarter of the amounts paid to the aged in total, and were smaller as a fraction of national income than had been family allowances alone in earlier decades.

The amounts received by individuals under these schemes further reflect the revision of age priorities. In 1945, when the universal family allowance scheme was introduced, the mother of each child received an automatic, tax-free weekly payment equivalent to about three-quarters of a day's pay for a laborer: today it is less than one hour of comparable pay. The average family formed in the 1940s or 50s had close to four children: four children brought to their mother family allowances considerably greater than an old age pension at that time, and child income tax reliefs were available to all. But, by the later 1980s a family allowance was worth just five percent of an age benefit, compared with 31 percent when the family allowance scheme was started. Tax reliefs for children have been eliminated.

Additional evidence of this revision of priorities is given in Table One, which records the relative incomes for various social groups and movements in these through the past four decades. This shows that the net "real" or after-tax old age pension adjusted for inflation - the minimum income guaranteed by the state to all aged persons - rose only slowly during the 1950s, and remained of fixed value in the 1960s. Meanwhile the real purchasing powers of younger adults, with or without children, rose sharply. But since 1971, and more especially in the 1980s, these experiences have been reversed. Real net incomes have risen sharply for the elderly, so that the state pension now has about half as much purchasing power again as it did in 1971, or nearly twice what it had in the 1950s. For the non-aged, and more especially for younger adults and for males, real incomes have been falling. Men in their 20s and 30s, for instance, now have on average a 1950s purchasing power. Moreover, this comparison considers all sources of income for the non-aged, but only the state-guaranteed portion of that of the elderly: the expansion in private resources in old age has been considerable. The diverging experiences of old and young are striking.

My reading of the international literature indicates that this inversion of social security priorities has been universal. The erosion or elimination of family allowances is reported widely, as is the expansion in spending upon the aged.[10] No exceptions are known to me, although critics in a couple of countries have entered protests to the contrary. In particular, Sweden is proud of its "family-friendly" policies of the 1970s, which have given both direct cash and indirect service assistance to young families. However, national accounts reveal that even there total spending upon "family policy" has been one of the slowest growing of expenditures, that it does not match the expansion in resources diverted to the aged, and that neither of these has paralleled demographic movements (Nordic Council, annual). A switch in priorities is unmistakable.

* * * *

A second aspect of this shift is the redirection of public spending more generally. In New Zealand in 1951, for instance, total government expenditure upon cash benefits, health, housing and welfare services for the population over sixty absorbed about 3.5 percent of GDP. At the same time, spending on those under

---

10. Clark et al., INFLATION AND THE ECONOMIC WELL-BEING OF THE ELDERLY (Baltimore: Johns Hopkins University Press 1984); Council of Economic Advisors to the United States President, ANNUAL ECONOMIC REPORT OF THE PRESIDENT (Washington: transmitted to Congress February 1985); Field, FAIR SHARES FOR FAMILIES (London: Study Committee on the Family, Occasional Paper No. 3 1980); Flora & Heidenheimer, THE DEVELOPMENT OF WELFARE STATES IN EUROPE AND NORTH AMERICA (New Brunswick: Transaction Books 1981); Guest, THE EMERGENCE OF SOCIAL SECURITY IN CANADA (Vancouver: University of British Columbia Press 1985); Harrington, THE NEW AMERICAN POVERTY (New York: Firehorn Press 1984); Ismael, THE CANADIAN WELFARE STATE: EVOLUTION AND TRANSITION (Calgary: Univeristy of Alberta Press 1987); Jones, THE AUSTRALIAN WELFARE STATE (Sydney: Allen and Unwin 1983); Lister, *Income maintenance for families with children*, FAMILIES IN BRITAIN (London: Routledge and Kegan Paul, Rapaport (ed.) 1982); Mendelsohn, AUSTRALIAN SOCIAL SECURITY FINANCE (Sydney: Allen and Unwin 1983); Patterson, AMERICA'S STRUGGLE AGAINST POVERTY, 1900-1980 (Cambridge: Harvard Univeristy Press 1981); Preston, *Children and the Elderly: divergent paths for America's dependents*, 21.4 DEMOGRAPHY 435-57 (1984); Questiaux, in Eisenstadt & Ahimeir, THE WELFARE STATE AND ITS AFTERMATH (London: Croom Helm 1985).

about age forty, through cash allowances, health and welfare services, war pensions, subsidized housing and education, was three times as great, at around 10-11 percent of GDP. This remained the case until the early 1970s, when the new aged priorities became evident. At the end of the 1980s spending upon the same set of services to the aged stands at about 12 percent of GDP, upon the population under 40 still at 10 percent.[11]

What these figures mean can be debated of course, and we might all want to argue that money spent in providing a service does not represent money spent to the full or exclusive advantage of the supposed end-users. Nor are we arguing the rightness or wrongness of spending upon old or young, or suggesting that the removal of most of the aged from poverty in the last two decades is not a signal achievement. But what cannot be mistaken here is a crucial reversal of social priorities, the destruction of consistency of experiences for successive generations, and the creation of "winners" who have been in the right life-stage to gain much under one spending regime, and later to do the same under the revised rules of redistribution.

Little of this has been peculiar to New Zealand. National accounts reveal a widespread expansion in education spending in the 1950s, 60s and early 70s, but stalled or shrinking fractions of national income being devoted to this in the later 1970s and the 1980s.[12] Studies of health spending indicate a companion shift, from modest spending on the aged to a heavy expenditure upon them in the 1980s. In Britain, for instance, persons of pensionable age absorbed about one-quarter of all public health spending through the 1970s, according to the standard conventions for counting national end-users of a public service as actual end-beneficiaries. By the mid-1980s this fraction had jumped past 40 percent, and experiences in Australia, the United States and

11. Thomson, SELFISH GENERATIONS, *see supra* note 2, at Chap. 2 and 3.

12. OECD, NATIONAL ACCOUNTS (Paris).

44

elsewhere have been similar.[13]

A new unwillingness to invest public money in housing is even more manifest, and points very clearly to the swing away from spending which favors the young. In Britain, North America and elsewhere, investment in public housing has plummeted in the 1970s and 80s to small fractions of former levels.[14] In New Zealand, case governments in the 1950s and 60s invested two and more percent of GDP a year - that is, more than the total old age pension program - in the construction and subsidized rental of family homes, and more especially in giving low-interest loans and interest-free grants to young home buyers. Now the fraction of GDP invested in this way is one-quarter or less of what it was two or three decades ago, even though young adults seeking homes now form a larger fraction of the total population. The turn against housing spending is perhaps not surprising: it was directed to young adults, and is not a public expenditure that will have lasting appeal to older voters, once most own their own homes. But in making such a switch consistency is lost: a substantial benefit taken from the pool by one generation is not made available to successors.

* * * *

Taxation is a third critical area of revision. The priorities of mid-century ensured that substantial tax contributions were not asked of the young. The middle-aged, the self-employed and companies were the prime financiers of the welfare state for youth, and this helped further to fix an expectation of how successive generations were to pay for their participation in the collective give and take as they aged through life. In the early welfare state, income tax rates on individuals were kept low, and personal and dependents exemptions ensured that whole generations would make minimal

13. COMMITTEE ON THE ECONOMIC AND FINANCIAL PROBLEMS OF PROVISION FOR OLD AGE (Phillips Committee 1954); Central Statistics Office, SOCIAL TRENDS (London: CSO); Wroe, *The Elderly*, SOCIAL TRENDS 3 (London: CSO 1973).

14. OECD, NATIONAL ACCOUNTS (Paris: OECD).

payments in their early adult years. But in the last 25 years these protections have been stripped away. Exemptions for self and dependents were cut during the 1970s, and eliminated altogether in New Zealand in the 1980s. In parallel has come a narrowing of exemptions claimable by individuals for work-related expenses, life insurance payments, superannuation savings and much more. The result has been to make young adults major funders of the welfare state. This had not been expected of their predecessors.

In this regard, the New Zealand experience is of considerable interest because of the system's relative transparency and simplicity. All government activity, including health, education, welfare and social security, is financed out of a single national income pool: no separate social security or any other taxes are earmarked or put into special funds, and no records of individual contribution are maintained. The analysis, and the politics, of redistribution, in other words, is uncluttered by federal/state/local divisions, the tying of certain forms of contribution to particular benefits, or pretensions of "insurance." Tracing individual and generational contributions through time is thus comparatively straightforward.

Even so, this unusual simplicity seems not to have produced distinctive or unusual taxation patterns in New Zealand: trends evident here are apparent elsewhere. The decline of family taxation exemptions, for instance, has been reported from Britain, Canada, Australia and the United States. The ending of significant taxation payments by companies and by the self-employed, leaving most direct funding of the pool to wage and salary earners, is widely apparent, and a steep rise in personal income tax rates in recent decades has been universal.[15]

Several New Zealand analyses throw light on shifting taxation priorities. One analysis, concerning individual income taxation experiences is reported in Table Two. This shows part of a larger study and in this example focuses only upon the changing levels of taxation faced by males aged 25-34 years. Studies of other age

---

15. The decline in tax payments by companies has been reported from many countries: *see, eg.*, Page, WHO GETS WHAT FROM GOVERNMENT (Berkeley: University of California Press 1983); Pechman, WHO PAID THE TAXES, 1966-85? (Washington: Brookings Institute 1985).

and gender groups point to similar if generally less extreme patterns of change. In the first step the median gross earnings (excluding social security benefits) for the whole cohort are calculated from census returns, and these are "taxed" at the standard rates for single men. (Personal taxation exemptions are taken into account, but all others are ignored: the results present maximal estimates of likely income tax rates, most especially for the 1950s and 60s.) The tax rate, as a percentage of gross income, is reported in Column A and shows (not unexpectedly) that for single men or married ones without dependent children the price of participating in the welfare state has increased substantially through time. Moreover, this two-to-threefold increase in the fraction of income demanded in income tax was experienced across the whole income range - low paid laborers, middling level clerks and high-pay professionals faced similar increases. It will be recalled, too, that the rising price of participation was being imposed upon "real" incomes which were falling.

Column B shows income tax rates calculated for these same young men, if instead of being single they had each supported a "Standard Family" - a model unit consisting of a wife with no paid employment of her own, and two small children. In this case the change over time in the costs of belonging to the welfare state is even greater: it is now thought appropriate that a Standard Family of median income should contribute to the pool three times as large a share of its income as an identical family, of similar or better real income, 20 or so years ago should have done.

In Column C is recorded what I have called "effective income tax rates," where income taxes are offset against automatic cash benefits received. For many of those born in the 1920s or 30s this gave nil or negative income tax rates through early adult life. But the price of participation in the welfare state is now many times greater. In the 1950s, for instance, a two-child, single-income family of median income would pay "effective" income taxes equivalent to just two percent of gross earned income, according to our maximal estimate. Earlier still, the rate had been negative, and now it is at least nine times as great.

Column D gives one further variation on "effective" income tax rates. The majority of families formed in the 1940s, 50s and 60s included closer to four than two children, and Column D gives a closer approximation to the taxation realities experienced by New Zealand families. Again the patterns are striking. At almost all income levels, tax rates are many times greater for the later-born than they were for the earlier-born, even though all had incomes of similar purchasing power and moved through identical life-phases. Generational consistency is not being observed: prizes and penalties have been rationed by date of birth and little else.

A second analysis concerns what might be termed a "generational tax rate." A generation is at any one moment a mixture of individuals in and out of paid work, facing single tax rates and family ones, receiving and not receiving social security payments. Model income or tax units such as those traced in Table Two capture little of this complexity, or of the obvious point that the mixes change over time. What, we might wonder, have been the "effective income tax rates" for whole generations, rather than individuals?

Published census, taxation and social security data permit calculations of likely maximal income tax rates for whole cohorts, since we can estimate from these sources the total gross income of a cohort or generation, the likely tax changes being faced, the personal and dependents' taxation exemptions available, and the social security income being received. (Once again, the full range of tax exemptions cannot be assessed, and the calculations must over-estimate the true levels of income taxation for the earlier-born but not the later-born.) Some figures on this appear in Table Three and they again confirm the inconsistency of treatment of earlier-born and later-born. At least two things should be noted here. First, the price of belonging to the pooling of income shifts rapidly and substantially over time. Those who were aged 25-34 in 1981, for instance, were at a conservative estimate paying four times as large a fraction of their collective total income in net or "effective" income taxes as did predecessors when at the same age in 1961.

Second, not only individuals but whole generations appear perhaps to have gone into deficit to the collectivity during the early decades of the welfare state. For example, those who were aged 25-34 years in 1951, and so aged 35-44 years in 1961, had a maximal "effective" income tax rate through those 20 years of around three percent. In return for this, together with an unknown amount of indirect taxes, they were granted full citizenship, including the "use" of the many services of a modern state such as policing and defense, access to free education and health services for themselves and their children, special rights to housing - and perhaps most critically for the history of the welfare state, the expectation of transfer payments from successors in later life. They were, in short, drawing more in early adult life than they were paying, and so created a requirement that the same would be true for successor generations. The assumption was further that all would in later life-phases take up their obligations under the implicit contract, by paying heavily in middle-age and by accepting few payments or services in old age, just as those born before about 1920 had done.

This all begs a third form of measurement - a lifetime tally sheet of contributions to and drawings upon the pool - and here very little has been attempted hitherto. I suspect this will change, and that many will soon tackle the tricky technical and philosophical issues involved. A population myopically enjoying benefits much greater than contributions has not sought measurement of such things, but generations sensing a mounting disadvantage and compounding lifetime loss will demand new measures, new data and new forms of enquiry. My own endeavors in this area are modest and experimental and are offered in illustration of what might be done and uncovered.

In pursuing the question "what might a lifetime of contribution and benefit amount to for identical members of successive generations," I have sought to trace a selection of individuals through "typical" life-courses. This poses immediate problems. The actual as opposed to our earlier theoretical maximal income taxation payments are unknown; end-users of general government services such as justice or foreign relations have to be assumed to be all persons equally; the benefits of health or education spending have to be assumed to flow to the individuals for whom the service was designed; and these beneficiaries are held to enjoy a personal gain equal to the full cost to government of providing the service. Beyond lie further difficulties in assessing individual contributions and benefits when these may be spread far apart in time, and when inflation as well as general economic growth alters all values. And what of unpaid or voluntary contributions throughout life?

Even so, the problems are not insurmountable since our

challenge is to explore relative rather that absolute experiences. The same procedures are applied to each generation and will distort the results similarly in each instance: the differences revealed between one generation and another remain significant. Nor are the difficulties of accounting over time intractable in my view. One possibility in counting lifetime contributions and benefits is an "investment" approach - totting up taxes at a compounding rate, to be set against benefits. However, this is inappropriate, since it soon emerges that the welfare generation was probably collecting more than they were contributing from the outset. Indeed, such an approach would suggest that their annual deficits rather than their contributions is what must be compounded over time. This would produce findings very unfavorable to the earlier-born, and that alternative has been ignored here.

Equally unacceptable is a simple counting of annual contributions and drawings in unadjusted dollar values, or in inflation-adjusted currency. This, too, would reflect badly upon the earlier-born, who paid in small amounts decades ago but to whom, in a world of lower general living standards, those small contributions might nevertheless have represented significant sacrifices. My preference is for a moving unit of account, one that gives maximum advantage to the earlier-born in the calculation of possible lifetime contributions and drawings. All annual financial contributions and benefits are calculated here as so many fractions of "average pay" in the years in which they were made, and the results are summed to lifetime totals.

The underlying assumption is that a year's tax contribution equivalent to, say, 25 percent of average pay in that year represents a comparable degree of sacrifice for similar individuals whether made in 1950 or 1990, if the individuals paying had comparable levels of real income. This means that an individual's "units of sacrifice" may be tallied over a lifetime, and that this tally may be compared with the total "units of sacrifice" of an identical individual, who happened to be born a decade or two earlier or later. In similar, fashion benefits are calculated for each year of life in units of average pay, and are totalled over a lifetime to give an estimate of lifetime "units of benefit." The experiment is tentative at this stage: my hope is that others will follow, being encouraged or stung or enraged into further work in this vital area.

The results are striking, even when the method has been designed quite deliberately to play down contrasts between earlier and later-born. Table Four gives a summary of the "average" experiences of those born in the 1920s and the 1950s, who are in each case treated through life as having had the median income for their generation at every stage in life, and the experiences of employment, family, retirement and the like typical of their cohort. An "average" couple born in New Zealand in the 1920s - let us call them the Earlys - look set to collect at least 40 units of benefit through their lifetime membership of the welfare state. That is, the cash benefits they will receive, together with the various services which they (and their minor children) might use, will have cost the nation taxes to the equivalent of about 40 units, or 40 years of the average gross pay of male adults.

Their contributions to that pool of taxes will be much smaller. At most, lifetime income taxes for the two will total six or seven units of average pay, covering about one-sixth of their lifetime gains. Their old age pensions alone, costing the pool about 12 units or years of average gross pay, will be twice as large as their total lifetime income taxes when assessed in this way. Indirect taxes for them are unknown, but are arguably considerable. The assumption made here is a maximizing one: we hold that every tax or duty paid by a company in New Zealand, and every tax or duty paid through consumption or production taxes, is ultimately a tax upon individuals such as the Earlys, and should be counted as part of their lifetime contributions to the pool. This method suggests a possible indirect contribution during a lifetime as high as 13 or 14 units, or a total tax contribution of perhaps 20 units. Even so, it appears still to be half or less of what the pool will pay to them.

Consider now the companion experiences of the Lates - an "average" couple born in the 1950s. Their income taxes, if the rates in force in the 1980s hold for the rest of their lives, will reach about 15 units or years of average pay, and their indirect taxes a similar amount. But their drawings from the pool, should public expenditures continue at current levels for the next 40 or so years, can be projected at no more than about 25 units of average pay. In other words, their gains at every stage in life are already, or are planned to be, less than for their predecessors as they moved through similar lives and had comparable or greater real personal incomes.

Moreover, we can be certain that 1980s levels of taxation and benefit will not, and cannot, continue as projected here. Population aging in the early twenty-first century makes it unavoidable that overall tax contributions, whether direct or indirect, will have to rise for the Lates, and that benefits in their later lives will have to be cut still further. Our projections here of what the Lates may expect in the years ahead take a few of the announced changes into account - for example, the lessening of retirement pension next century - but make no allowances for those that must yet come.

In short, our method gives a minimal picture of the Earlys' gains, and of the losses the Lates will face. The welfare state simply does not function in comparable manner for the two, and I predict that the tensions generated by this inconsistency will become a major force in all societies in the coming years. It will make sense for us all - citizens and scholars alike - to recognize that in each nation we have not one but several welfare states, each operating at the same moment and yet evolving separately through time. These are not the welfare states of rich and poor - those also exist as variations of these others - but are the welfare states of different generations. This is an historical reality which will have to be confronted in the 1990s, as older citizens insist that their expanding expectations of comfortable retirement be met, and younger ones look hard for reasons why a distorted exchange between generations should be prolonged, to the mounting detriment of themselves and their children.

* * * *

Thus far we have concentrated upon government taxation and spending. This is a conventional approach, but it also makes good political sense. It is to taxes - and to income taxes in particular - that each of us appeals when insisting that we have participated fully in the collective pooling, that we have paid our way in life, or that we have given much and so are deserving of all we get in return. It is social security benefits or health and similar social spending which we have in mind when asserting that we have cost government little through life, have received minimal assistance to date, or are owed something better now. Any measurements which bring into question these powerful myths, and so attack vital concepts of self-worth as much as more obvious political positions, or which suggest that the fates of individuals are in large part being determined simply by the chance of when one was born, will have major implications for us all.

But focusing upon taxes and benefits alone is to narrow attention unduly. The powers which all citizens ceded to the collectivity when the modern welfare state was formed have been used much more widely to advance the interests of some generations, and to retard those of others. Worrysome, too, is the gathering pace and nakedness with which the state is now assisting and holding back successive generations through these various mechanisms.

One area in which the changing uses of power are evident is employment. A prime reason for bringing about the modern welfare state was to protect and foster employment - to improve the education and skills of the work force, to ease transitions from school to work place, to secure continued employment at good wages for all who sought it, to banish dangerous working conditions or the struggle to retain earnings and position in sickness or old age. In other words, the modern welfare state had two principal thrusts to it. The first - for that was the order of priority - was to provide full and secure employment at substantial rates of pay.[16] From the moral and material rewards of that would flow well-being for most citizens. Second, the welfare state would provide supports for all in employment, through public health and education services for instance, as well as giving income protection to those who could not find well-being through paid employment.

The means to guaranteed employment were varied, but all nations relied upon heavy doses of state control: freedoms were sacrificed for rewards to the employed. In New Zealand, as elsewhere, the freedoms lost were for the most part those of consumers and investors, the gains those of producers and borrowers. From the end of the 1930s to the 1970s, extensive import controls were imposed through an elaborate licensing system. The aim was to encourage manufacture and hence jobs within New Zealand, and to free workers from the dictates of

---

16. Thurow, THE ZERO-SUM SOLUTION (New York : Simon and Shuster 1985).

foreign interests - a clear reaction to the 1930s. Immigration policy was controlled, quite deliberately and explicitly, to the same end. The result for 30 years was "over-full employment" (or more vacancies than people seeking work); free tertiary education and generous trainee allowances; rapid promotions; rising real earnings; and increased worker and union bargaining power. The negative consequences included limited choice for consumers, indifferent product design and quality, and higher prices since local manufacturers were sheltered from competitive imports. Securing full employment was the over-riding concern.

Once more, the rights or wrongs of using shared powers in this way need not distract us here. But the results were not age or generation-neutral, and that is significant. Moreover, the fact that this particular balance of producer and consumer interests was kept to rigidly for more than 30 years placed lasting obligations upon successive generations. Employment, and its rewards and costs through life, became an integral part of the implicit welfare contract between generations. Older persons in general suffered under the policy of import control. Secure or well-paid employment was of little use to them, while high prices and limited choice meant that their small state pensions and other incomes bought even less than they might have done. The gains for younger persons were much clearer: earnings rose faster than did prices, and were guaranteed to do so while the welfare state held to these founding principles. An expectation of consistency and reciprocity was reinforced: advantages enjoyed early in life were to be passed to successors in turn, and the penalties accepted later.

In fact, little has turned out that way. In the 1970s, and more especially in the 1980s, New Zealand along with much of the western world has switched to an enthusiastic embrace of "liberal economics." The former protection and subsidization of producers has been abandoned, and consumer interests given maximum freedom. Import licensing, quotas and the like have gone or are being dismantled, and with that one of the fundamental raison d'etre of the modern welfare state. The employment needs of younger persons are not now a central concern, even while political rhetoric still extols the importance of work. Governments see themselves as having little active role or obligation in this area: the best "employment protection," it is now held, lies in letting private business freely create "real job" at whatever rates and remunerations it sees fit. The consumer is to enjoy the lowest costs and greatest choices available.

This abandoning of a central set of initial principles goes further, however, for it has taken many other forms. New Zealand has in the last years reduced the rewards and securities of younger workers, while extending those of older ones (that is of aging members of the welfare generation). In the aftermath of war and depression, a range of formal and informal employment practices grew to complement the macro-policies of import substitution and full employment. For instance, the central government, by far the nation's largest employer, furnished lifetime guarantees of employment to all employees, together with cheap housing loans, generous transfer allowances, and an elaborate unfunded superannuation scheme which was to be carried by the later-born.

Outside the state sector, private employers bent to government, union and individual worker pressures in the face of labor shortages, and conceded training allowances, trade union control of employee selection, generous revision of employee superannuations, and informal agreements to lifetime employment through "last-on-first-off" policies in hiring and firing. Occupancy of a position in the labor market came to grant a "squatter's right" to it, and the longer the incumbency the greater the right to retain or "sell" that possession. Nor did many question this, for such things were underwritten by a widespread consensus that providing secure employment at rising levels of reward was a right and proper use of collective power - the very purpose of the welfare state.

In the last 20 years this consensus has gone, and with it many of the uses of state power to foster employment and rewards for younger workers. Young trainees for either government or private employments now receive little assistance. Student teachers or nurses and trade apprentices, for instance, were salaried until the 1970s, but now must meet their own costs: university and polytechnic students now face fees on a scale unknown to their predecessors. Employment at the end of training is no longer guaranteed as it once was; government does not undertake to employ any of its staff for life; short-term contracting without fringe benefits or protections is replacing salaried employment in both the public and the private sector; promotion channels have been narrowed and constricted very deliberately; youth unemployment benefits have been cut; privileges on holiday or sickness leave have been withdrawn; and subsidized employer loans for buying homes have gone.

Equally significant is that little of this has counterparts for older workers. Instead, during the same period greater effort and expenditure than ever before has gone into protecting those in the last years of a working career, and to rewarding exit from the labor force. "Retirement packages," "golden handshakes," "superannuation top-ups," "redundancy deals," "giving everyone a few years in a top job so as to bump up superannuation" and the like have become the new features of the late-twentieth century work place. The move to outlaw mandatory retirement ages can be seen as one further element in this: the freedoms of choice of aging workers must be maximized.[17] The priorities of the welfare state have been inverted: where once most expenditure went in getting people into the work force, it now goes to rewarding them on the way out - and the same cohorts benefit in each case. A new term has entered the New Zealand vernacular to describe this process. It is "grandparenting," or the continuation of privileges for those who have already had them and expect them to continue, but the denial of them to later-comers. It is an apt and disturbing metaphor for the late-twentieth century state.

The effects of this turn against the employment interests of the young are varied. A first has been a widespread rise in youth unemployment. In New Zealand, those under age 25 have borne about one-half of all unemployment in the 1970s and 80s, while levels of unemployment fall steadily as age rises. Amongst those under age 35 unemployment levels are now worse than they have ever been for any age-group in our recorded history - they are worse, for example, than any in the 1930s (Eichengreen, 1989). Some insist that this result is "sad but inevitable," an unavoidable consequence not of social choice but of demographics, or the

17. Eekelaar & Pearl, An Aging World - Challenges and Dilemmas for Law and Social Policy (Oxford: Oxford University Press 1989); Ginsburg, *Flexible and partial retirement for Norwegian and Swedish Workers*, Monthly Labor Review (Oct.) 33-43 (1985).

56

arrival of too many "baby-boomers" in to the job market in one short crowded span of time.[18] But this must be open to question.[19]

Heavy youth and young-adult unemployment is a new phenomenon historically - it has few precedents. Nor is it clear that in a late-twentieth century economy it is the young who have the least to offer employers in the way of energy or new skills. In the past it has always been the middle-aged and older who have suffered in the labor markets on these counts, and have formed the bulk of the unemployed as a consequence. The new youth unemployment cannot be dismissed as a "natural phenomenon." It is a consequence of social choice, of a collective decision to ration employment in certain ways. Further, even if youth unemployment were unavoidable, the responses of societies to it - cutting youth training expenditures, stopping youth unemployment benefits, raising rewards and protections for older workers - cannot be explained away as inevitable. They tell much of the underlying shift in age or generational sympathies.

A second striking consequence has been the fall in earnings of men aged under 40 years, relative to those of older workers. The changes for women have been more complex, yet in the same direction. Some New Zealand evidence on this appears in Table Five. This table refers only to those in full-time employment: the low pay of the unemployed is not being counted here.[20] A

18. Easterlin, BIRTH AND FORTUNE (London: Grant McIntyre 1980); Easterlin, *The New Age Structure of Poverty in America: Permanent or Transient?* 13.2 POPULATION AND DEVELOPMENT REVIEW 195-208 (1987).

19. Bradbury, *The Shrinking Middle Class*, NEW ENGLAND ECONOMIC REVIEW (Sept. 1986) 41-55; Samuelson, in Feldstein, THE AMERICAN ECONOMY IN TRANSITION (Chicago: Chicago University Press 1980); Thurow, THE ZERO-SUM SOLUTION (New York: Simon and Shuster 1985).

20. The fall in relative earnings of the young has been noted in several countries: Bradbury, TRENDS IN THE DISPOSABLE INCOMES OF AUSTRALIAN FAMILIES, 1982/83 to 1989/90 (New England Economic Review (Sept. 1986) 41-55; David & Smeeding, HORIZONTAL EQUITY, UNCERTAINTY AND ECONOMIC WELL-BEING (Chicago University Press 1985); Denison, TRENDS IN AMERICAN ECONOMIC GROWTH, 1929-1982 (Brookings Institute 1985); Levy, DOLLARS AND DREAMS: THE CHANGING AMERICAN INCOME DISTRIBUTION (New York: Russell Sage Foundation 1987).

number of points emerge. First, the relative earnings of men in their twenties and thirties have been falling since the early 1970s. Second, the fall has been greatest among the youngest workers. Third, older ones have not experienced this same loss of earnings.

And beyond lie other disparities not captured in the census. Income tax levels upon younger workers as a whole have risen more steeply in the last 20 years than have those on older workers, so that the gap between after-tax rewards for younger and older persons will have widened still more. "Fringe benefits" or non-cash rewards such as housing loans have declined, and the remaining ones been focused towards older employees. And while immediate returns to younger workers have been falling, so have their prospects of lifetime remuneration. Their pays, for example, do not increase as they get older at the same rates as did those of their predecessors. Their pension entitlement are not as generous as those of their earlier-born colleagues, while the demography of their society makes further cutbacks and disappointments later in working life inevitable. The simple age relativities expressed in Table Five incorporate little of this widening gap in remunerations.

A third measure of the change in age and generational fortunes which stem from the shift in employment priorities lies in the detailed records of household income, expenditure and saving (NZ Department of Statistics, annual). In the last 20 years persons under about age 40 - and especially women - have taken on growing amounts of paid employment, despite the difficulties many face in finding and keeping it. In 1971, for example, 64 in every 100 persons aged 25-34 were in the full-time labor force - by 1986 it was 71 in 100. But persons past about age 50 had at the same time been abandoning employment for retirement and leisure. Among those aged 55-64, 51 in 100 were in full-time employment in 1971, just 41 in 100 by 1986: past age 64 the levels dropped from eleven to four in 100.[21]

---

21. The rapid decline in employment amongst the middle-aged in the last 20 years has been reported in, for example, Britain (Johnson, THE LABOUR FORCE PARTICIPATION OF OLDER MEN IN BRITAIN, 1951-81 (London: Centre for Economic Policy Research, Discussion Paper No. 284, 1988)); France (Cribier and Guillemard, in Johnson, WORKERS VERSUS PENSIONERS - INTERGENERATIONAL JUSTICE IN AN AGING WORLD (Manchester: Manchester University Press 1989)); the United

58

These counter-trends might have been expected to raise the overall incomes of younger cohorts, and to depress those of older, more especially since by the end of this period the young were collecting many more unemployment, sickness and single-parent allowances than ever before, in addition to their more numerous earnings. But that has not happened. The underlying shifts in economic fortunes have been so powerful that these contrary moves in employment have served only to slow, not to counter or reverse them. During the 1970s and 80s the total real or inflation-adjusted incomes, spending and saving of those in their twenties and thirties has been falling while those of older persons and especially of those aged 50-64 has been rising.[22] One result is that the lowest per capita incomes, spending and saving for any age cohort are now the dubious preserve of those in their thirties, after modest account is taken of the costs of their dependent children.[23] The aged on average do better. All this is a recent and historic development, the significance of which has yet to be reckoned politically, economically, psychologically or culturally[24].

Moreover, to assess the age distribution of resources in this standard way is to miss many of the larger and more lasting changes taking place now. Current incomes and expenditures are only symbols of the wider shifts in generational fortunes. This is

States (Rones, *Using the CPS to track retirement trends amongst older men*, MONTHLY LABOR REVIEW (Sept. 1985) 46-49).

22. Bradbury, TRENDS IN THE DISPOSABLE INCOMES OF AUSTRALIAN FAMILIES, *see supra* note 20; Council of Economic Advisers to the US President, *see supra* note 10 ; Levy, *see supra* note 20.

23. Thomson, SELFISH GENERATIONS, *see supra* note 2, at Chap. 4.

24. Similar trends are commented upon in the non-New Zealand literature: Bradbury, *The Shrinking Middle Class*, *see supra* note 19 ; Bradbury, TRENDS IN THE DISPOSABLE INCOME OF AUSTRALIAN FAMILIES, *see supra* note 20; Council of Economic Advisers to the US President, *see supra* note 10; Levy, *see supra* note 20; Ruegg, in Eisenstadt & Ahimeir, THE WELFARE STATE AND ITS AFTERMATH (London: Croom Helm 1985).

so for a number of reasons.[25]   First, these studies take no account of the costs of the things which younger or older persons
actually buy, rather than of things in general.   For instance, few
older persons have large mortgages, or have to spend substantial
portions of their incomes on housing or superannuation. The young
must spend on these to acquire what the elderly already hold.
Furthermore, the elderly enjoy concessionary pricings not available
to others - on public amenities such as transport, but also from
private businesses selling insurance, theatre tickets, air fares,
holidays and much more.   None of this is taken into account in
these incomes and expenditures calculations. The "discretionary"
portion of spending for older and younger households, could we
pinpoint it in the official surveys, would probably favor the aged by
a significant margin.

Second, our conventional accounting methods reveal little of
changes in quality of purchase. They show only that those under
age 40, for example, are receiving and spending less now per head
in inflation-adjusted dollars than did persons of a similar age 10 or
20 years ago: they do not show that they achieve the same quality
of purchases for the same amounts of money spent.   There are
good reasons for suspecting that they do not. A study of housing
costs affords important insights into this, for the cost of buying a
home brings together many of the important changes impacting
upon younger citizens today - changes in taxation rates and
exemptions, earnings, house prices, interest rates, repayment
terms, government loans, social security supports and more.

A model of the first-home buying process has been constructed
for this study in New Zealand, and it indicates that the expense of
buying a modest first home has multiplied several times in the last
20 years. For example, a Standard Family (single income, adults
aged 25-34 years, with two children) of median income could have
bought a basic or 'model' new home in the 1960s or early 1970s
by investing 15 percent of its total net income in annual mortgage
repayments.   An identical family buying the identical house by
1986, and making use of all the government assistance still
available to it, would pay 84 percent of its income in repayments.

---

25.   Useful discussions of some of these wider issues are in David and
Smeeding, *see supra* note 20; Kristol, in Feldstein, *see supra* note 19.

That is, the true cost of the house had multiplied several times in relation to youthful incomes, although little of this will be revealed in existing income-assessment procedures. It might be noted, too, that during this same period the older half of New Zealanders came to occupy a greatly expanded quantity and quality of housing, while the Standard Family of the model did not, and that New Zealanders past age 40 spent a smaller fraction of their incomes on housing by the late 1980s than they had done in the 1960s or 70s.

Increases in the relative costs of a first home of at least this five-fold order were suggested by the model for young persons of all income levels, and an array of responses and adaptations have become evident. Young adults now delay marriage as their predecessors did not; postpone having children; have few children; the women amongst them take up paid employment in addition to raising children; buy smaller, older or cheaper houses; move to poorer neighborhoods; acquire rundown houses which require expensive renovation later but are more affordable at the outset; and in New Zealand's case, at least, they emigrate in large numbers. Costing analyses are needed which can trace the substitution of quality for price, or the shifting of current costs into the future. When we have them they will show gaps between the experiences of older and younger consumers rather greater than those showing up already.

A third factor which must enter an improved measure of resource allocations between age groups or generations is the contexts in which incomes are received and spent. Just what are different groups expected to buy out of those incomes? This matter has been touched upon already, but deserves further discussion. The true purchasing power of $100 for a young family, for instance, is dependent not only upon price or the availability of special concessions to that age group. It is determined further by the range of goods which the family is expected to buy, and in this regard the incomes of young adults have worsened significantly in recent years, both relative to those of older persons and to those of young adults before them.

For instance, free health and education services for children have disappeared in recent years, and young adults must now make their falling incomes - as revealed by the standard approaches

- spread further and more thinly to pay for items once not part of the expenses of a young household. State old age pensions available to older persons today are not to be given to the present young when they reach old age next century. Out of their diminishing incomes, the young are now pressed to purchase private health and superannuation insurances, although their predecessors did not and were not expected to spend their better incomes on these things when in similar circumstances. The context of supports amidst which incomes are spent determines further that the true incomes of young adults are falling fast.

A fourth aspect of this loss is dwindling "future prospects," and in this the experiences of generations diverge perhaps most of all. Conventional accounting traces only that fraction of the rewards of employment which are received immediately, and even that fraction only poorly. But a large portion of one's remuneration lies in what is promised for the future. For example, a weekly pay of $100 has a "true" worth which is much enhanced if it comes along with the assurance that it will be repeated next week and every other week, than if the same $100 brings no such "future prospect." The same is true if it is collected along with an expectation of future promotions, mounting pension entitlement and a substantial state old age benefit, or if it is received in conjunction with many other public benefits which mean that the $100 need only be used on certain things (the others coming free). The experiences during working life for the Earlys have been of substantial and growing "future prospects," but those of their successors are already very different.

* * * *

Our discussion of lifetime employment experiences touched upon various other ways in which generational interests are being handled inequitably by the modern state. These deserve drawing out a little more, for they reveal further the inversion of priorities which has occurred in the last couple of decades. Financial deregulation has paralleled the unleashing of imports. From the 1930s to the 1970s, New Zealand operated a highly regulated economy - many locals decried it as the most controlled outside of the Eastern Bloc. Foreign exchange rates were, of course, determined by government, but so were all transactions between

New Zealanders and others. Individuals or businesses could not move money into or out of the country except with government approval, and travelers going abroad were rationed small daily spending allowances. Non-New Zealanders could not move money into the country as they might choose, or invest freely in local assets.

Internal financial regulations mirrored the external. Tight fiscal control ensured, for instance, that interest rates were fixed at low levels. Mortgage terms and rates were not to be amended once set, even if later inflation should alter values radically. Banks and other savings institutions had to put set portions of their portfolios into low-yield government stock. The state was a major lender, thus enabling it to force the competition to its terms. And disgruntled investors could do little to escape this regime, since the export of money was not permitted.

But in the 1970s, and more strikingly in the 1980s, both internal and external fiscal controls have in large part been abolished, as they have through much of the world in this same era. Foreign exchange rates now float free of direct government control, to find whatever levels buyers and sellers may determine. Restrictions upon the movement of money in and out of the country have gone, as have formal controls upon borrowing and lending or the requirement to hold government stock. The state has ceased to be a major lender, and what little it still lends is at "market rates" rather than in competition with private institutions. Mortgage terms and interest rates are now revised incessantly, at the sole instigation and ruling of the lending partner. None of this was permitted 20 or 40 years ago.

Not quite all has changed in this area however. The one thing not to be "deregulated," in an ironic sort of way, is interest rates. Formal controls have gone, but rates have not been freed to float according to market dictates. Instead, in a fundamental reversal of former actions, governments in New Zealand and elsewhere now force interest rates much higher than the "market" might choose, as a deliberate means of combating inflation. Where once the aim of government was to beat down interest rates, it is now to force them up.

Our purposes, once more, are not to debate the rights and wrongs of one fiscal regime over another. But the implications of a switch between them must be evident, for generations and for the implicit welfare contract between them. The rigid controls of the first 30 or 40 years were not accidental, but an expression of a widespread social consensus. This was that locals must be sheltered from the intrigues of monied foreigners; that growth, fostered actively by the actions of the state, was the primary goal; and that lenders must be protected against borrowers. This meant, in turn, that younger persons were to be protected against older, since young adults do most borrowing and older ones lend.

The result was that older persons were forced to lend their savings to young persons at rates very favorable to the young, and to stick with these terms even as prices and wages rose and so reduced to insignificant the returns to lenders. There was no apology about this: it was deliberate, and appeared to capture a popular notion of what was the right and proper use of state power. But fiscal deregulation has once again undermined crucial expectations of consistency and reciprocity. A generation which benefited heavily under one regime in earlier life has proven unwilling, for whatever reasons, to have these advantages pass to successors.

The changing management of inflation has been related and not dissimilar. Until the late 1960s, inflation in New Zealand as elsewhere was low, wages grew faster than did prices, and lending rules and conventions meant that gains from inflationary creep, though modest, flowed to borrowers. This remained the pattern into the 1970s, and as the rate of inflation climbed the gains accruing to those in "mid-career" multiplied, at the expense of older persons. This was so because the old consensus and the rules it had bred remained in force, even though circumstances were changing. Superannuation and pensions were still not index-linked; mortgage interest rates remained "sticky" once set; and wages continued to rise faster than did prices.

But since the later 1970s, inflation has been handled very differently. State, and a good many other pensions, are now indexed to both prices and wages, giving older persons a protection not available to younger. And interest rates are held high, while inflation falls. As one senior business figure put it in a recent private correspondence, it is as if having 'robbed its own parents' by means of one inflationary regime in the 1960s and 70s, the welfare generation is now intent upon "robbing its own children" through the opposite.

The results of the new priorities in inflation management are various, and not easy to measure with conventional techniques. Some are fairly obvious: high youth unemployment, for instance, is a clear and conscious "trade-off" in the 1980s battle to lower inflation and raise returns to older persons. So, too, may be the falling incomes and expenditures of the population under about age 40, while those of older persons rise. Even more significant and lasting, for the life-chances of successive generations, may be the effects of these policies upon investment. With few, and only partial exceptions, all modern states have switched from being heavy investors in both human and fixed capital goods prior to about 1970, to low investments in both now. In other words, they have chosen now to maximize immediate consumption at the expense of longer-term income, and to direct that spending increasingly towards the aged.[26]

The implications of this for different generations are again markedly uneven. Those born in the 1920s and 30s, and so aged or soon-to-be-elderly by the late twentieth century, gain from policies which maximize consumption today. The consequences, in limited human resources for the next century (aging and poorly maintained infrastructure, damaged environments, depleted public assets or poor productive capacities) cannot have an impact upon their lifetime incomes. But, their successors do face those, even as they now receive a falling share of the immediate rewards which are being bought at the expense of those lasting costs.

One further aspect of this complex (new use of state power) should be noted. Until the late 1960s, New Zealand, like many nations, had little foreign or internal government debt. Investment was, in general, generated internally, that is, by New Zealanders of the day foregoing current consumption in order to build assets. In

26. American writers emphasize the declining quality of human investment now, as well as its falling quantity, with falling education and health standards of the young attracting widespread attention: *see, eg.,* Kuznets, in Feldstein, *see supra* note 19; Mead, BEYOND ENTITLEMENT: THE SOCIAL OBLIGATIONS OF CITIZENSHIP (New York: Free Press 1986); Thurow, *see supra* note 5. This concern finds relatively little expression elsewhere.

most years, external trade ran in broad balance, with the country not buying more than it could pay for with earnings at the time, and government finances were maintained similarly so as to keep incomings and outgoings in step.

In the last 20 years all this has changed, and with it both the current and the future prospects of successive generations. Major foreign debt has been accumulated, by both government and private borrowers, even as the society's investment ratios have fallen.[27] In other words, the limited investing now done is not at the expense of consumption foregone by New Zealanders today, so much as by stacking up debt against the consumption of New Zealanders to come. Internal government deficits work to comparable inequitable ends. These are financed at present through borrowing on the local markets.

This means that the unwillingness of New Zealanders to be taxed to finance the services they demand causes not only burdens to fall to the voiceless later-born, but that older citizens of the present make substantial additional profits through funding the deficit in the meantime. In deficit financing, as I am by no means the first to remark, late-twentieth century societies have found a powerful way of binding successors to pay for that which they themselves have not been willing to forego. That those successors will be few in number, poor and multiply-burdened by actions taken today adds to the potential for inter-generational tension which is now building.[28]

One last comment: to talk of conflicting generational opportunities and limitations in these ways is to run both into and across the conventions of much twentieth century economic thinking - I have here been sketching multiple research agendas for the coming decade. But the demand for fresh thinking goes further. The aging - or perhaps better, the many forms of aging - which modern

---

27. The rise of indebtedness of the United States is well known, but it is also a feature of many European welfare states as well: OECD, *see supra* note 12.

28. American readers will find in this many echoes of the current debates concerning the bail out of the 'savings and loans' at the expense of future generations; British readers will find echoes in the problems of their building societies; and all will find echoes in the bad debt provisions pending throughout the international banking system.

societies are now undergoing cast us all into the unknown, and our thinking about it remains trapped in the past. Aging, we too often still assume, can be countered by the old remedies - more saving, more investment, more production, more economic growth. What needs to be explored are new environmental constraints, the very different implications of burgeoning populations in some areas of the globe and retreating and aging ones in others, or how and why such saviors as savings and growth should reappear in welfare states which are so far along the aging path.

How, for example, do we again achieve low interest rates, when to do so will cut swiftly into the incomes of the older half of voters, through lessening the returns and destruction of the viability of personal savings, pension funds, property holdings and the like? Are low rates no longer a viable political option or an attainable goal, and if not, then what implications does this have for investment, production and the prospects of successive generations? Can populations entrapped in multiple forms of aging forswear immediate consumption for the sake of a long-term future that cannot be part of the lives of large numbers? Are the "time-horizons" of youthful and aged societies fundamentally different?

And what of saving? Aging threatens to subvert all customary notions on this. The individual's attempts to move income out of one life-stage and into another are a fiction. Resources "saved for a rainy day" are not moved through time, but are given to fellows for use in the current moment, in return for pledges of a share of the incomes of others later: the modern welfare state operates similarly. But what individuals and whole societies have counted upon unwittingly in such "saving" is being succeeded by genera-tions larger and more affluent than themselves, ones willing moreover to redeem whatever pledges have been entered in their name and before their time. Should any of these three fail, then "saving" as most understand it will break down, and consumption delayed will prove consumption lost. All three essentials look set to be frustrated in the early twenty-first century, and in the realization that private saving offers no fail-safe alternative to public social welfare programs lie some of the most potentially divisive and disillusioning of all generational issues. In short, aging throws out the greatest of challenges to our senses of imagination, proportion and humanity. We all have a duty to address them.

Old Age at Century's End

Debating the rights and obligations of the aged is not going to be easy. Confusion, anger and deep personal hurt are probably unavoidable, and emotions will run high. My own contribution here will have demonstrated this already: one reviewer, speaking for others, has written that "[Thomson's work] is as much a moral protest as a report on social investigation," and in that he makes a fair point.[29] We confront here some of the thorniest moral and political issues of our times, since many of the ethical issues which preoccupy us for the moment - abortion or genetic engineering, environmental degradation or global warming, race relations or "positive discrimination" - are all parts of the larger question of generations and what it is that they owe to one another. My writing has not sought to disguise the emotional nature of any discussion of generational justice, for these feelings will have to be confronted and managed by us all.

Learning to talk of these things will prove necessary but difficult, and I am under few illusions about the attack, evasion and mind-closing which such probing as mine here will induce. For one thing, we have little prior experience in thinking seriously about generations, or even about language for articulating these matters. Second, generational analysis confronts all with both moral and practical matters of an unfamiliar immediacy. Conventional social analysis is of battles played out between anonymous forces - rich and poor, black and white, capitalist and worker, north and south, town and country. The enemy is always a faceless other, distant and not known as a person. But discussions of generation strip away this protective distancing, and arguments about right and wrong, the best or the necessary distribution of shared resources and the like, must be worked out within ourselves, or with those closest to us physically and emotionally.

Third, the fact that the aged of the 1990s are those who appear to have a particularly unsatisfactory history of participation in the exchange between generations will be especially troubling. Two powerful issues are being conflated at this particular historical juncture, and existing beliefs about the social position or dues of

---

29. Laslett, A Fresh Map of Life, *see supra* note 1.

old people will mix uneasily with newer and perhaps more urgent views on their place as members of a special historical generation. And fourth, the current circumstances and future prospects of their successors make especially fraught the conditions in which the 1990s debates about old age will have to take place. Behaviors during the last half-century, and more especially in the last 20 or so years, mean that the later-born now have poorer immediate incomes and more shrunken "future prospects" than did the earlier-born in similar life-phases. None of this will make for personal or collective ease, and the pressures to ignore and deny the validity of generational discussions will be intense.

In an essay which is already long the space for raising new issues must be limited. Nor do I wish to press any particular case, other than that for a clear and honest addressing of the issues. Neither the most desirable nor the most practicable ways forward are apparent to me. I have no simple answers as to how the current growing disenchantment with collective action is to be halted, or on whether the exchange between generations through large scale public pooling of resource and risk can now be saved. Instead, I want to end by helping push aside a few of the many distractions which will threaten an open assessment of our options.

Several types of response to talk of generations and their histories may be anticipated - indeed, have already shown forth. A first is abuse: "don't talk of your elders like that, young man!" A second is to derogate: "Why does this scholar so hate his own mother?" Another is wishful evasion: "If we don't talk of such unpleasant things they might not be true." Exhortations for reasonableness and silence form a fourth: "These issues represent a threat to democracy and our way of life, so let us leave them alone." A further one is denial of responsibility: "Future generations can look after themselves, I owe them nothing." Another will come from fellow social scientists anxious to defend territory: "Don't try grabbing the agenda for a generation, when we know class conflict to be the dynamic of history." Conspiracy seekers will have their say: "Is there anything here other than a younger group seeking to slip its very reasonable duties to the aged?" And the current favorite is the slave of economic growth: "None of these issues actually need to be faced, since economic growth and ever-rising prosperity will make them melt away."

These evasions enjoy little credibility, and do not deserve our further attention. A second cluster of responses includes what we might call the more legitimate objections, and these will merit closer attention from us all - sadly I cannot give it here. There will be objections to numerous technical aspects of generational studies: How we are to measure lifetime incomes benefits or contributions? For instance, are all open to challenge and refinement? There are many philosophical and ethical points to be sorted out. Do generations have a corporate existence? How do we define their bounds, or allot responsibilities to them for past, present or future actions? As Peter Laslett has noted already, questions of generation and their contrasting histories expose a glaring hole in western philosophy - the failure to define justice through time.[30] There will be queries, too, around the suggestion that aging is taking many interlocking forms, or that it necessitates for all a serious reconsideration of notions of economic growth, the nature of saving, or the options of generations in sharing the costs of demographic decline.

A third form of response will be to insist upon the "rights" of the aged. That is, many will be tempted to see in talk of generations and their histories little more than a thinly-veiled and not-very-sophisticated attack upon the aged of today, and will move to defend the gains they have made or hope yet to make. This will be done by urging "rights," and it is understandable and reasonable that this should happen. We all grow old, and want comfort and security in the long span of life now stretching from retirement to death. But the resort to "rights" will need to be pursued with care: too often "rights" are but "wants" in fancy garb.

In particular, it will no longer be acceptable to argue the "rights" of the aged in opposition to or even divorced from the rest of society. The reality now is that those past about age 60, the age at which most in the late-twentieth century have ceased employment, now command substantial fractions of total wealth, income and political power, such that exercise of these strengths has major immediate as well as lasting consequences for their successors. The "right" to wield these powers must carry

---

30. Laslett, *The retired versus the rest*, TIMES LITERARY SUPPLEMENT (Jan. 26, 1989) 100.

commensurate obligations of restraint in doing so.

This will require important shifts in perspective for most older persons, as well as for social gerontologists, since considerations of obligation or impact upon others have, too often, not been part of past ways of thinking. Among the most familiar of "rights" of old age of which one hears are those to a decent standard of living, security and dignity. But just what these do and can mean at the end of the twentieth century will have to be pondered closely. What is a decent standard of living in old age? Does it mean an income a little short of, equal to or somewhat ahead of, that of a non-elderly person? Is a "right" to a decent standard of living from successors related solely to the resources of those successors, or to the living one was willing to provide to elderly predecessors in turn? At what point does a decent standard of living for the old become a drain upon the future prospects of successors, and what is the appropriate response in that case? Does a "right" to security in old age mean facing the same, more or fewer vicissitudes than do others. What "right" can a third of the electorate have to be protected from adversity? And what is involved in a "right" to dignity? Can such be built upon myths or worse about participation in the exchange between generations, or upon an ignoring of consequences for successors?

Overlaying all discussion of "rights," too, will be one inescapable complication: it is not intended that the "rights" claimed for the aged of the 1990s will pass to their successors. They are, in other words, to conform to the historical pattern -to be vouchsafed for a particular generation but not for others. Two things make this clear. The first we have commented upon already: lifetimes of improving health services, income and more for the aged of the present have only been possible because of a peculiar and unsustainable redistribution of resources between generations in the twentieth and twenty-first centuries. The consequences, in low investment of many forms, mean that in the next century the few young will not be able to give shares of their income to the many aged on a par with what is happening at present. "Rights" are in reality contingent upon circumstances rather than absolute, and must relate to the possibilities: they cannot transfer from one generation to another.

Second, it is clear that all governments intend this loss of "rights" in old age in the future. This is evident in the whole process of "political aging"' which has been discussed here. In the 1970s and 80s, as populations have become unable or unwilling to pay for the welfare state which they demand, the response has been to whittle away the programs which will favor the later-born, while protecting and enhancing those for the earlier-born. In many instances, the belief which underlies this has been made quite specific: the aged or soon-to-be-elderly have a "right" to be protected against any retreat in living standards or loss of expectation, since they have played their part honorably and are now in no position to alter their lot: the later-born still have some chance to affect their own futures. The greatest injustice, it is often said, is to strip an aging person of any of the benefits they have come to expect.

Nor is there anything theoretical or speculative about this redefining of the "rights" of the aged of the future, for it is happening already. To return to New Zealand one last time, it has been announced here in the last couple of years that in the next century age for entitlement to retirement benefit is to be raised by five years; pensions of the retired are to fall by about 30 percent in relation to wages of younger persons; private superannuation contributions and payments are to be taxed much less favorably than for the current elderly; and that all will pay for health services which are still free to the aged of today. "Rights" in old age, in other words, are the preserve of particular aging generations, not of a life-phase through which all will pass, and this must cast all debate about "rights" of the aged under a dark shadow.

ADDENDUM

Revised June 29,1990

THE OBLIGATIONS OF THE ELDERLY
New Challenges for Gerontology

Until very recently all who worked with or for or wrote about the elderly could be confident of their task. Purposes and assumptions were clear and shared widely, if seldom made explicit. The aged were poor and helpless, lacking in power, status or rights. Their needs were for more money, visibility, services, comforts and protection. The function of the gerontologist was to provide these, and he or she could expect a good measure of unquestioning public support in going about this task.

One result has been major gains for the aged during the past few decades. Another was an intellectual inquiry too often marred by vacuous complacency, an unwillingness to challenge, and a failure to place aging and the elderly within the context of larger societal developments. The aged were in endless need and deserving of whatever extra they could get: what more was there to say? Agendas were set, career paths mapped out - and wider social and intellectual opportunities missed, energy and drive lost, as we failed to define a substantial role for ourselves. The Cinderella status of gerontology, and the ceaseless competition for research funds and talent from a low ranking in the priorities pecking order, was at least in part a self-inflicted wound.

All this is now changing fast, to the discomfort of many. Accepted verities are under attack from many quarters. The elderly of the 1980s and 1990s are perceived increasingly as too numerous, affluent, leisured, privileged, demanding, grasping and irresponsible. A demure, silent, marginal and powerless minority has in many eyes been replaced by a self-centered, politically-astute and self-aggrandizing mass of insistent elders, who think little of securing fast-growing incomes for themselves while the young face retreating standards of living.

Table 1

Real Net Income of various income units
1945-86

Income Unit

	1 Elderly Pensioner	2 Single Parent two children	3 Single Man 20-24	4 Single Man 25-34	5 Single Man 35-44	6 Single Woman 20-24	7 Single Woman 25-34	8 Standard Family 2 children
1945	66	58	55	62	71	-	-	72
1951	86	80	66	66	69	60	68	71
1956	90	87	82	84	86	82	82	85
1961	101	98	92	92	94	83	93	95
1966	98	95	101	100	100	95	101	100
1971	100	100	100	100	100	100	100	100
1976	130	114	99	98	99	114	115	98
1981	149	113	95	97	100	116	123	98
1986	139	116	77	82	90	98	114	85

Column 1. Net rates of standard age benefit (or National Superannuation after 1977) to single elderly persons, after taxation deductions at the rate for a person who had little additional income.

Column 2. Net incomes from family benefits and widow's benefit (or domestic purposes benefit), for women with two children and no other income from any source. Movements in sickness and unemployment benefits to adults with children were on a similar scale through this period.

Column 3. Net incomes for the median income earners amongst all males aged 20-24 years who were in full-time employment, assuming that they were taxed as single men.

Column 4. Net incomes for the median income earners amongst all males aged 25-34 years, assuming that they were taxed as single men.

Column 5. Net incomes for the median income earners amongst all males aged 35-44 years, assuming that they are taxed as single men. The patterns for older males were almost identical.

Column 6. Net incomes for the median income earners amongst all women aged 20-24 years who were in the full-time paid work force, assuming that they are taxed as single women.

Column 7. Net incomes for the median income earners amongst all women aged 25-34 years who were in the full-time paid work force, assuming that they are taxed as single women.

Column 8. Total Net Income for a Standard Family of two children. Income consists of two family benefits and Family Care in 1986, together with the after-tax income for the median income earners amongst all men aged 25-34 years, assuming that those earners received the tax deductions for a dependant spouse and two children.

Table 2
Income Tax Rates for Men Aged 25-34 Years
(at the median point in the income range)
1945-86

	A	B	C	D
1945	+11	+ 5	-11	-26
1951	+17	+10	- 1	-14
1956	+15	+ 9	+ 2	- 6
1961	+15	+10	+ 2	- 9
1966	+16	+11	+ 5	- 3
1971	+20	+15	+11	+ 1
1976	+25	+21	+16	+ 8
1981	+27	+23	+18	+13
1986	+29	+27	+18	+ 9

Column A. Income tax as percentage of gross income for man at median income for all men aged 25-34 years, if he paid taxes at a single person rate.

Column B. Income tax as a percentage of gross income for man at median income for all men aged 24-34 years, if he paid taxes for a 'Standard Family', that is assuming he had a wife without earned income of her own and two small children.

Column C. "Effective income taxes," that is income taxes as assessed in Column B, but with the two automatic Family Benefits being set against the taxes to be paid. A positive sign indicates that the total income taxes payable were greater than the total family benefits received, a negative that total taxes were less than total family benefits received.

Column D. "Effective income taxes" as for Column C, except that the family is here assumed to include four children rather than two.

Note: No account is taken of the various income tax exemptions available in the 1950s and 60s, other than the personal and dependents exemptions.

Table 3
"Effective" Generational Income Tax Rates
1951-81

		1951	1961	1971	1981
Cohort	25-34	7	4	12	16
	35-44	4	3	11	17

Note: The table shows the percentage of a cohort's total earned income which would go into income taxes, after the taxes assessed of the cohort have been reduced by the total amount of social security cash benefit which the cohort would receive at the same time.

Table 4
Lifetime Balance Sheet for Two Successive Cohorts

	Earlys (born 1930)	Lates (born 1955)
Contributions		
I. Personal Income taxes paid between ages		
17-24	1.1	2.3
25-34	0.8	1.6
35-44	1.5	4.0
45-retirement	3.8 or 5.3	7.9
Total lifetime income tax contribution -		
maximal estimate	7.2 or 8.7	15.8
"more realistic estimate"	6-7	15
II. Total possible lifetime "other" taxes	14	14
Total possible lifetime contributions	20-21	29
Benefits		
Social Security Cash Allowances -		
Family Benefit	1.6	0.7
Old Age Pension	12.6	8
Education	4	2-3
Housing	1.1	1
Health	3	3
"General Government Services"	15	12
Total Benefits	37	27

Table shows contributions and benefits measured in units of "average pay."

Note: The sources and methods are explained in the text. The procedure has been conservative, seeking to play down the contrasts between the experiences of the two couples.

Table 5
Relative Earnings of males
1951-86

	20-24	25-34	35-44	45-54
1951	70	90	100	98
1956	69	92	100	99
1961	71	92	100	98
1966	74	94	100	96
1971	71	94	100	96
1976	71	93	100	95
1981	66	90	100	95
1986	63	87	100	95

Table shows median gross incomes for each age group as a percentage of those for the 35-44 age group.

THE OBLIGATIONS OF THE ELDERLY:
A COMMENT

Dr. Eric Midwinter[*]
England

A prominent British gerontologist strode into my office at the Centre for Policy on Aging, London, and asked: "Are there two David Thomsons?" The question was genuine enough to cause me actually to check that but one, in this field, exists. Why had several of us felt that we were watching one of those 1940's Hollywood dramas, where Bette Davis or Olivia de Havilland played twins of contrary dispositions? We were confused as between the David Thomson who concluded, contrary to popular belief, major redistribution of resources towards the elderly has not occurred[1] and the David Thomson who wrote of the refashioning of once youth-centered welfare states into mechanisms for benefitting the aged ahead of others[2] in a piece which is the base of his current essay, and which I have discussed already elsewhere.[3]

Change of mind provides no moral dilemma. Indeed, cussedness is the more likely academic posture, and perhaps we should admire so diametric a switch in belief. No, the question is an intellectual one: borrowing David Thomson's own question about generational equity, "has the inconsistency and lack of reciprocity

---

[*] Director of the Centre for Policy on Aging in London; Social Historian; Policy Analyst; and author of numerous books and reports on old age; M.A.

1. D. Thomson, *The decline of social welfare: falling state support for the elderly since early Victorian times*, 4 AGING AND SOCIETY 451-82 (1984).

2. D. Thomson, *The Welfare State and Generation Conflict: Winners and Losers*, in WORKERS VERSUS PENSIONERS: INTERGENERATIONAL JUSTICE IN AN AGING WORLD 3556 (P. Johnson, C. Conrad and D. Thomson, eds., Manchester University Press (1989)).

3. E. Midwinter, *Workers Versus Pensioners*, 23.3 SOCIAL POLICY AND ADMINISTRATION (1989) 205-10.

been random and patternless?" Do these two opposed views represent, perhaps for some professional purpose, a disinterested ordering of two sides of the issue, or do they represent some evolution toward a completely different truth, based on more recently acquired evidence? If the latter, then one might reasonably expect a demolition job on the previous, to me, very convincing testimony. Literature is full of dualisms and conflicting faces, and it is cheering to find something of this in gerontology. Borrowing another of David Thomson's ausages, is the "Early" or the "Late" Thomson the more reliable - which the Jekyl and which the Hyde?

My observations are those of a Little Englander, and based entirely on scrutiny of the problem in the United Kingdom, and I remain the adoring fan of the unreconstructed David Thomson, whose earlier research I shamelessly plundered, persuading myself that the cruder examinations underpinned his sophisticated findings. In my own study of matters[4] I think I confirmed his trenchant resolution that "an aged pensioner of mid-nineteenth century Britain was favored more under the "harsh" new poor law than has been any twentieth century pensioner of the state . . . as British society has grown richer it has not become more willing to make up the standard of living of its poor members to the levels enjoyed by those in employment.[5]

Perhaps one of the differences is that, in his earlier work, David Thomson was less inclined to regard welfare statehood as a post-1945 phenomenon, and to recognize, if only implicitly, its longer-standing nature. For example, the much vaunted invention of the British old age pension, implemented in 1909, was, in effect, the "nationalization" of locally administered poor relief - and at an immediate very similar cost which had a tradition traceable to the late sixteenth century. Similarly, intergenerational strife is no new aspect of society, and, in most communities, the younger approach to the older has been at best equivocal. These generational and

---

4. E. Midwinter, *The wage of retirement: the case for a new pensions policy*, 4 POLICY STUDIES IN AGING (Centre for Policy on Aging (1985)).

5. Thomson, *The decline of social welfare, see supra* note 1.

state/individual dichotomies are not of sudden vintage, and it is unhelpful to suggest they are.

If there has been change, it has been in the collapse of work which, over nearly two hundred years in the UK, has sloughed off two echelons, the younger and the older, replacing their work with schooling and retirement respectively. These are not simply, or even primarily, social goods proferred the dependent by a good-natured work-force. They are forms of social control to combat the anxieties of non-work. To think otherwise is to ignore the basic motif of social stability and preservation, for, as Jeremy Bentham argued, "security and subsistence" are two of the chief "subsidiary ends of legislation." Governments which fail to observe this rule might risk the property and well-being of their well-to-do citizens.

The other, and allied change, has been in the demographic reversal of the dependent cohorts, but, in Britain, without changing the overall pattern. As is well-known, the main reason why the proportion of older people has increased is because the proportion of younger people has decreased. This gives rise to the intriguing formula in approximate order of magnitude.

% Aged	0-14 Years	65 + Years	Total Dependents	15-65 Years
1841	36	4	40	60
1911	31	5	36	64
1980	21	15	36	64

This suggests that the non-work problem, if problem it be, has not altered in toto, and that proportionate shifts of resources might be in order. Similarly, because work remains the essential key, productivity, not numbers, must be marked. The question of older age, as of younger age, would be much less bothersome if, as in days of yore, work dominated lifestyles much more emphatically.

As it is, and as David Thomson the First proved, millions of older Britons exist in a relative poverty no better than their fore-bears, and, as a consequence, are denied access to the everyday comings and goings of ordinary citizenship. That is sad for them and wasteful to their community.

A sharper line of inquiry might be a more individualized one. To adopt David Thomson's caricature, let us assume two people born in 1930 who, for reasons accidental or otherwise, emerge as teenagers from the Second World War, one becoming a shop assistant and one a civil servant. To avoid any internal argument about talents and contributions, make that a conscientious shop assistant and an indolent civil servant. One earns a wage and lives in municipal housing; the other draws a salary and becomes an owner-occupier. Eventually, they retire, and, in 2010, aged 80, their quality of life is barbarously distinct. The shop assistant exists, in dire pauperdom, on a meager state pension, still in municipal accommodation, probably in an impoverished and woebegone environment. The civil servant lives, on an index-linked pension, owning an expensive property in a pleasant area, and maybe with savings or inheritance to add a plush cushion. This is how they spend, for twenty or more years, their Third Age - their life-style determined by that post-war mix of accident and design which directed one down one route and one down another. If we are to evoke the spirit of John Rawls, then it might be more profitable to examine transfer across generations, not between them.

Much of this leads to the general point that few really regard the world as does Thomson the Second. Most people understand that "all is flux," or, in the phrase of Heraclitus, "man steps but once in the same river." It scarcely needs a very long essay to convince us all of that. David Thomson recognizes that emotion must play a part in this discussion. Right, then, what about the millions of this generation, including New Zealanders, who, far from basking, as he describes it, in unwonted luxury, were killed in the Second World War? How do you legislate for war, and recession, and other savage or, for that matter, pleasant disruptions in the negotiation of generational contracts and the like?

There may be an even tenor in, say, the fictional Narnia of C.S. Lewis, but, in reality, people comprehend a life of kicks and ha'pence. Take taxes. Of course people grumble occasionally at paying them but, in general, they accept some version of the collective kitty, and, for a surety, they don't analyze it with a sort of chronological geography. They recognize that taxes go backwards, forwards and sideways. Older people pay for schools at which they have no children; middle aged people pay for fire engines they hope to God they'll never need; younger people pay for health care for older people, and so on. David Thomson never quite realizes that most people prefer to pay for health care rather than be in the hospital: he somehow makes it sound as if taxpayers feel cheated if they are not lying, drugged, supine and amputated, in some hospital cot. Who prays for a burglary so that they may get their money's worth out of the police?

The rougher truth was described some years ago by Aneurin Bevan, one of the architects of the reformed welfare state of Britain's "silent revolution" in the post-war years. He claimed that, for reasons which are not discernible to the smartest researchers or most adept politicos, societies, large and small, swing from dog-like to cat-like. The canine mood is a more cheerful, cooperative one, all hands to the pump and amicable fellowship; the feline mood is more selfish and private, less concerned with collective action. If anything makes a difference as to how people fend for themselves and other during the life-span, this is probably as near an explanation as one might commonsensically find.

There is only one guess for which domestic pet represents the mood in the United Kingdom over the last ten years.

SUPPORTING THE AGED:
THE PROBLEM OF FAMILY RESPONSIBILITY[*]

Robert J. Levy[**]
United States

Following the precedent set four hundred years ago in the "Elizabethan Poor Law,"[1] most states of the United States enacted some form of financial support program for the dependent aged.[2] The state programs were regularized and made much more uniform in 1935 when the Social Security Act[3] made the federal government the dominant financial and administrative partner in the operation of these "cooperative" welfare endeavors. The same statute enacted the completely federal "insurance" scheme now officially described as the "Old Age, Survivors, Disability Health

* This paper was originally prepared as a presentation at the Sixth World Conference of the International Society of Family Law, Tokyo, Japan, April 8, 1988. It was published originally as a chapter of the proceedings of the Conference, AN AGING WORLD (Clarendon Press and Nihon Kajo Publishing 1989). Research assistance was provided by Karen Wasserman, Esq. Financial assistance was graciously provided by Space Centers, Inc., St. Paul, Minnesota.

** Dorsey & Whitney Professor of Law at University of Minnesota; Reporter for the Uniform Marriage and Divorce Act; co-author of CASES AND MATERIALS ON FAMILY LAW (3rd ed. 1984); Fellow at the Center for Advanced Study in the Behavioral Sciences, 1968-69; B.A., Kenyon College, 1952; J.D., University of Pennsylvania, 1957.

1. For a general discussion, see tenBroek, *California's Dual System of Family Law: It's Origin, Development and Present Status*, 16 STAN. L. REV. 257 (1964).

2. Lopes, *Filial Support and Family Solidarity*, 6 PAC. L.J. 511 (1975).

3. *See* 42 U.S.C. § 301 (1935).

Insurance" program[4] and always known popularly as "Social Security."[5]

This is not the place to review the ancient English and American tradition of "relief" and the "relative responsibility" policies which have been its constant companion; the history has been traced frequently and well by others.[6] It is clear that continuing expansion and enrichment of welfare programs is the common experience of industrialized societies. Yet, governmentally financed welfare programs have customarily included provisions designed to recover at least some of the expenditures from persons related biologically and/or familially to the welfare benefit recipient. Even as governments have recognized their responsibility to protect old people from the consequences of abject poverty, they have also followed the Elizabethan Poor Law's original initiative to share that financial responsibility with close relatives of aged fund recipients. Which "responsible relatives" are required to support their aged kin, the nature of the financial partnership to be established between the government and the responsible relative, the nature and scope of the "defenses" to support liability which the financially responsible relative may claim -these and many other issues have been variously resolved from state to state and from time to time. But the basic policy has been observed uniformly: parents are required to support those children and children are required to support those parents, who are recipients of government financial aid.

---

4. The program was amended to include medical and hospital benefits ("Medicare") in 1965. *See* Pub. Law 89-97 (July 30, 1965), codified in 42 U.S.C. §§ 1395, 1396 (1982).

5. The OASDHI program does not provide actuarially based insurance benefits based on invested premiums, of course, because younger workers (and in the medical provisions, government funds) subvent payments to retired workers and their survivors. Perhaps the description indicates that distinguishing "insurance" from the "categorical welfare" programs which provide subsistence to the poor provides an important but symbolic support for public acceptance for an additional tax on workers. *See* note 91 *infra* and accompanying text.

6. *See generally* Riesenfeld, *The Formative Era of American Public Assistance Law*, 43 CALIF. L. REV. 175(1955); tenBroek, *supra* note 1; Lopes, *supra* note 2.

I

A. Methods of Enforcing Family Support Obligations

We can begin by describing the various ways that "family" or "relative" responsibility for the support of indigent persons can be "enforced."

1. Direct Enforcement

It is possible to find in recent American judicial reports cases in which an indigent person has tried to obtain support directly from a relative made liable by a state statute of apparently universal application.[7] Indeed, one can even find cases in which the support obligation has been enforced by use of the criminal sanction. In *State v. Kelly*,[8] for example, a son was convicted of failing to support his 72 year old, "infirm and semi-invalid" mother. The court held that the mother fit the statutory description of a person "who is destitute of means of subsistence and unable either by reason of old age, infirmity, or illness" to support herself. Mrs. Kelly was receiving a small old age insurance benefit under a federal statute, but lived with her daughter and son-in-law and received direct payments from the couple for "hospitalization insurance, doctor and medicine" bills as well. The court held that the term "destitute of means of subsistence" in the statute did not exclude aged persons who were being supported by the defendant's sibling.[9] Behind the arid statutory analyses in opinions like *Kelly*, of course, lurk human and family tragedies whose dimensions are difficult to determine. Yet, despite the cases imposing a

---

7. *See, e.g.*, Pickett v. Pickett, 251 N.E.2d 684 (Ind. App. 1969) (civil suit by divorced mother against her son for support after death of former husband; son had received $238,000 from father's estate plus a house which he transferred to his mother-in-law; mother brought suit for support after being evicted from the house transferred to mother-in-law; support award affirmed).

8. 2 Ohio App.2d 174, 207 N.E.2d 387 (1965).

9. For a similar holding under the same statue, *see* Beutel v. State, 36 Ohio App. 73, 172 N.E. 838 (1930).

direct relative support responsibility, a search of the appellate cases suggests that direct enforcement, whether accomplished by civil or criminal process, is commonly limited to the fathers of your children.[10]

2. Indirect Enforcement

Expansion of government responsibility for the poor has led to great increases in indirect enforcement of such relative support obligations - by means of welfare benefit denials and benefit diminutions. Consider the only non controversial family responsibility program - compelling support for dependent children from their fathers. Suppose that a statute provides income supplements to poor children and their mothers. (In the United States the program is Aid to Families with Dependent Children, or "AFDC.") The federal statute (or its accompanying regulations, perhaps, or a state law which is required by the federal statute) may demand that both the mother and the father contribute to the child's support. The resulting "family responsibility" can be "enforced" indirectly in the administrative process of benefit determination. If the child's father earns more than the welfare program's eligibility minimum, the child may not be guaranteed benefits, but part of the purpose of the support requirement, to limit the expenditure of government tax dollars, is nonetheless served. The result is the same if the child is eligible for a benefit whose size is decreased in accordance with a parent's income. Family responsibility is "enforced," government expenditures are saved, even if the child's income flow is not necessarily increased.[11]

B. Indirect Enforcement: The "Needs" Test

---

10. For some of the difficulties with any kind of enforcement of support against fathers in the United States, see Chambers, MAKING FATHERS PAY (1979).

11. Given impetus by a recent federal statute, parental support of children has become a favored policy in the United States; and a variety of direct enforcement techniques have been adopted and are being used with greater frequency. See generally United States Senate Finance Committee, REPORT NO. 98-387, TO ACCOMPANY H.R. 4325, CHILD SUPPORT ENFORCEMENT AMENDMENTS OF 1984, 98 STAT. 1305 (April 9, 1984).

So long as welfare programs are based on delivering subsistence income to recipients, on a "needs test," some form of relative responsibility is inevitable: unlike a "social insurance" program which guarantee benefits to all members of the covered class, welfare benefits are designed for and limited to the needy - that is, those whose current income is insufficient to cover current expenses. And if the government must determine the recipient's "needs," it must take account of "resources" (whether income or assets) of the recipient which could be used to reduce the recipient's benefit.[12] Moreover, the government will look as well to the resources of those persons whose familial relationship is sufficiently close to the recipient that it seems natural or appropriate to assure that they would help the recipient if the government benefit were not available.

1. Resources of the Welfare Recipient

These features of welfare programs based (let me reemphasize) on "need" have produced a host of complex and difficult issues for welfare administrators even when the issues are limited to the resources of the recipient himself or herself. A few examples should suffice.[13] Should an aged person be deemed eligible for welfare despite the fact that she has an unencumbered residence which, if sold, would provide her ample support for a limited or substantial period? The issue is one of determining which *assets* an applicant for welfare must "spend down" to the welfare

---

12. The Social Security Act required "state plans" to "take into consideration any other income and resources" of an applicant for public assistance. *See generally* Levy, Lewis and Martin, SOCIAL WELFARE AND THE INDIVIDUAL 68-85 (1971). *See also* notes 14-29 *infra* and accompanying text.

13. The most complex issues require courts to determine the extent to which state-created private law doctrines determine rights and responsibilities under welfare programs created by the federal government. The issues are similar to those which commonly arose under the Internal Revenue Code before the United States Congress began to provide specific federal definitions of common property concepts. Similar problems are sometimes created in the "insurance" provisions of the Social Security Act. *See, e.g.*, Capitano v. Secretary of Health and Human Services, 732 F.2d 1066 (2d Cir. 1984).

eligibility level.[14]

Or suppose that an applicant for old age assistance has transferred his home to his children before entering a nursing home, thus assuring his poverty and entitlement to welfare benefits. To what extent should the asset transfer be deemed fraudulent and therefore ignored in determining the applicant's eligibility? This issue alone produced a flood of state court litigation during a period when most state rules differed with the prevailing federal mandate.[15] It then occasioned a complex amendment to the federal statute permitting (and another, subsequently, requiring) the states to ignore such transfers. The amendment no doubt became politically acceptable (perhaps essential?) when it became clear to the Congress that many state and federal tax dollars were being expended by allowing families to strip their aged parents of funds before placing them in government supported nursing homes.[16] The federal statute was followed by a round of federal court suits brought by legal services lawyers for the aged poor, attacking the constitutionality of the federal statute.[17]

---

14. *See, e.g.*, Dept. of Social Services v. Barbara M., 474 N.Y.S.2d 195 (Fam. Ct. 1984); Lee v. State Dept. of Pub. Health & Welfare, 480 S.W.2d 305, 309 (1972); Matter of Welfare of C.S.H. 408 N.W.2d 225, 227 (1987); DeJesus v. Perales, 770 F.2d 316 (1985).

15. *See, e.g.*, Haight v. Kandiyohi County Welfare Board, 291 Minn. 538, 191, N.W.2d 559, (1971); Downer v. Dept. of Human Resources, 705 P.2d 144 (1985).

16. *See* 42 U.S.C. § 1396p (1982). See, e.g., Lewis v. Hegstrom, 767 F.2d 1371, 1374 n.2 (9th Cir. 1985) (Oregon's administrative rule defining a period of ineligibility for benefits for Medicaid applicants who have transferred their homes for less than fair market value within two years of application does not conflict with Social Security Act's federal standards). *See also* note 43 *infra* and accompanying text.

17. Schweiker v. Gray Panthers, 453 U.S. 34 (1981); Randall v. Lukhard, 709 F.2d 257 (4th Cir. 1983); Synesael v. Ling, 691 F.2d 1213 (7th Cir. 1982); Fabula v. Buck, 598 F 2d 869 (4th Cir. 1979). *See also* Note, *The Asset Transfer Dilemma: Disposal of Resources and Qualification for Medicaid Assistance*, 36 DRAKE L. REV. 369 (1986-87); Note, *To Deem or Not to Deem: Evaluating and Attributing Available Spousal Income to an Institutionalized Medicaid Applicant*,

It is a short step from direct determinations of a welfare
applicant's available resources to the administrative task of
arranging continuing determinations of recipient eligibility. Suppose
that a recipient's resources suddenly increase - because of a
worker's compensation or a volunteer fireman's award, perhaps.[18]
Or suppose the state seeks to "recoup" its welfare expenditures
from a recipient who is now ineligible because of an unpredicted
increase in wealth? As might be expected, the legislative responses to this problem, as well as the judicial interpretations of resulting
ambiguous statutes, have varied with the condition of the economy
and the community's toleration of welfare expenditures. One form
of "recoupment" was standard for many years - the imposition
upon the estates of aged recipients of an obligation to reimburse
the government for welfare benefits.[19] The reimbursement
obligation was often imposed by way of a lien on the estate of the
recipient.[20] The requirement has produced even more complex
legal issues. For example, when a recipient dies owning a joint
estate with his wife in residence, may the state impose a reimbursement obligation on the residence despite the fact that under
state law a joint estate passes automatically at the death of one
joint owner to the other?[21] The constitutionality of the reimburse-

---

67 VA. L. REV. 767 (1981).

18. *See* note 22 *infra.*

19. Levy, Lewis & Martin, SOCIAL WELFARE AND THE INDIVIDUAL 129 (1971);
Estate of Hinds v. State. 390 N.E.2d 172, (1979). For an impressive empirical
study and brilliant examination of reimbursement policies, as well as an analysis
of the problems which parallels the approach adopted in this paper, *see* Baldus,
*Welfare as a Loan: An Empirical Study of the Recovery of Public Assistance
Payments in the United States*, 25 STAN. L. REV. 127 (1973).

20. *See* State Board of Social Welfare v. Teeters, 258 Iowa 1113, 141
N.W.2d 581 (1966): Thomas v. State, 241 Iowa 1072, 44 N.W.2d 410 (1950);
Goff v. Yauman, 237 Wis. 643, 298 N.W. 179 (1941).

21. *See* Application of Gau, 230 Minn. 235, 41 N.W.2d 444 (1950).

ment obligation was affirmed in *Snell v. Wyman*[22] even during one of those occasional periods of "welfare liberalism" in the United States. The "Medicaid" program, enacted during the same period, barred the states from establishing liens against the estates of recipients prior to their deaths and from claiming reimbursement for benefits except from the estates of recipients or their spouses.[23] As the Boren-Long Amendment indicates,[24] however, the trend toward protecting relatives from liability for the aged (if it was in fact a trend) was short-lived.[25]

2. Resources of the Recipient's Spouse

It is another easy, but by no means inevitable, step from determining continuing eligibility and insisting on "recoupment" to a requirement that a recipient's family expend its "available resources" on the recipient. The justification for making some classes of relatives liable is obvious. Few disagree with the proposition that fathers who are absent from the home should support their children to the extent of their ability whether or not the government provides the children's mother with supplementary support; under these circumstances, using the welfare administrative structure as an enforcement aid reinforces a community and

---

22. 281 F. Supp. 853 (S.D.N.Y.). aff'd 393 U.S. 323 (1969). The New York statute was also upheld against an Equal Protection claim despite the fact that it exempted from reimbursement workers' compensation and volunteer firemen's awards. Three forms of repayment obligation authorized by state law were approved: liens on potential and actual recoveries by the recipient for personal injuries; liens on interests in real property owned by recipients; assignments of the interest of an insured recipient in life insurance policies (in cases where the estate of the insured is named as beneficiary and where no beneficiary is named). Each of the several plaintiffs had been required as a condition of continued benefits to make an assignment to the welfare agency of his interest in one or another of such assets.

23. 42 U.S.C. § 302(a)(11)(E) (1969).

24. *See* note 16 *supra*.

25. *See also* note 55 *infra* and accompanying text.

moral norm even as it saves tax dollars.[26] Community consensus may not be as clear for the liability of other relatives - but their responsibility flows inevitably from the needs and resources principles of welfare administration based on "need." Consider the income and resources of spouses of recipients. Should a wife be permitted to profit from governmental welfare largess while married to a man whose income or resources are such that he is not also entitled to welfare? Even a very strong state commitment to spousal financial independence[27] would not persuade most state legislators that spouses are completely separate actors when welfare benefits are at stake. Indeed, in an important sense, this problem of financial responsibility seems akin to the problem of aged parents who give their assets away to family before seeking government welfare aid - a situation which led, eventually, to the Boren-Long Amendment and federally mandated imposition on the aged of responsibility for their "phantom assets."[28]

3. Resources of Children and Other Relatives

It is a much more substantial stride from notions of spousal responsibility in welfare administration to requiring that a larger group of relatives help the government pay for the dependent aged. Although some state statutes (once again following the precedent set in the Elizabethan Poor Law) have imposed liability on siblings and grandchildren,[29] the most common class held liable for

---

26. The statement is true so long as the enforcement effort does not cost more administratively than it returns in collections from absent fathers. For some indication that a cost-benefit analysis which includes non-monetary costs of enforcement is appropriate in determining issues of relative responsibility, see note 58 infra and accompanying text.

27. Bruch, Management Powers and Duties Under California's Community Property Laws: Recommendations for Reform, 34 Hastings L.J. 229 (1982).

28. See note 14 supra and accompanying text.

29. See, e.g., Ill. Rev. Stat. ch. 23 § 3-1.2 (Smith-Hurd 1967), Iowa Stat.Ann. § 249.6 (1969). Both statutes are cited in Levy, Lewis & Martin, supra note 20, at 125. The Iowa statute has been repealed. See generally tenBroek,

support of the aged is children. Yet attributing to parents the income and resources of their children, closely related though they may be, causes problems in defining the proper scope of liability.

a. Which Children Should be Liable?

Does a child who offers to support her aged and poor parents by providing them with housing in her own home become exempt from direct financial contribution if the government provides cash benefits? The answer obviously depends upon the specific language of the statute as well as on the policy the court determines the welfare program was designed to promote - but judicial attitudes toward filial support for parents will obviously also play a role.[30]

Of this there can be no doubt: imposing support responsibility on children entails finding solutions to agonizingly difficult legal issues in embarrassing, sometimes even tragic, factual contexts. In some states, for example, a child who was abandoned by his parent is not required to support that parent.[31] In *Lasher v.*

California's Dual System of Family Law: It's Origin, Development and Present Status, 16 STAN. L. REV. 257,258 (1964).

30. *See, e.g.*, Los Angeles County v. La Fuente, 119 P.2d 772 (Cal. Ct. App. 1942) (daughter's offer to house her parents with her family no defense to suit by welfare department for contribution where statute authorized suit against spouse or adult child pecuniarily able to support aged person and purpose of Old Age Security Act was to leave considerable freedom of action to those receiving aid). *But see* Nichols v. Social Security Commission, 349 Mo. 1148, 164 S.W.2d 278 (1942) (applicant living with child denied eligibility because legislature had recently amended statute to make ineligible a person with income or resources sufficient to provide reasonable subsistence "whether such income or resources is received from some other person or persons"; Commission cautioned to investigate carefully financial ability of such children lest dutiful children be penalized while children who lack "pride of family and filial affection" profit from refusing to support their parents).

31. *See* Mandelker, *Family Responsibility Under the American Poor Laws*, 54 MICH. L. REV. 497, 517-518 (1956). For some indication that exceptions similar to this one are not unique, *see* 45 C.F.R § 232.12(b)(2)(1979) (Social Security Act's requirement that mother "cooperate" with law enforcement authorities to establish father's paternity is subject to a "good cause" exception where

Decker[32] an application by the local welfare commissioner to obtain support from the adult child of an old age assistance recipient, the trial judge interpreted ambiguous statutory language to permit refusal to order support when the parent had abandoned the child during his infancy.[33] But judicial interpretation of ambiguous legislative language cannot always carry the day. In *Mitchell v. Public Welfare Division*,[34] the recipient's son was resisting a support action because during his minority his mother had "deserted or abandoned" him, a defense specifically provided by the relative responsibility statute. The trial judge's imposition of liability was affirmed. When the defendant was born, during the Great Depression and in another state, his father was married to and living with another woman - and his mother left him with his stepmother when he was a year old because she could not afford to care for him; but the mother moved in with the family when her son was four and lived there until the defendant went into the army twenty years later. The son later brought his mother to Oregon to live near him - but did not want to contribute to her welfare benefits. The court quoted the mother's testimony concerning her initial departure from the defendant:

I wasn't able to take care of him, carry about the place and work.

---

establishing the child's paternity would result in the likelihood of physical harm to the mother or to her child, where the baby was conceived as a consequence of forcible rape or incest, or where the mother is considering placing the child for permanent adoption). *See also* Cass County Welfare Department v. Wittner, 309 N.W.2d 320 (Minn.1981) (county welfare boards have right to appeal state public welfare department's decision that mother need not identify alleged father).

32. 43 Misc.2d 211, 250 N.Y.S.2d 615 (Family Ct. 1964).

33. The statute, N.Y. Fam. Ct. Act §415, read: "In its discretion, the court may require any such person [an adult child] to contribute . . . . "For an instance of the creation of an abandonment exception by California administrators, *see* Bond, Baber, Our Needy Aged 319 (1954): "One county director reported that the district attorney refused to prosecute children who claimed that the parent-recipient would not support them as children - although the California statute contains no 'abandonment' exception."

34. 528 P.2d 1371 (Ore. App. 1974).

... I didn't just give him away, but I just left him.

No, I didn't have money to ...

Nothing but a birthday gift or Christmas package or something like that.

... I did see him every once in a while.

The court found that since the mother's work on the farm, "small as it might have been, contributed to the food raised for all of the farm's occupants,"[35] the mother had neither "deserted" not "abandoned" the defendant and he was, therefore, liable to the government for a share of her welfare benefits.[36] It is not obvious how these issues should be handled legislatively or in practice: it seems unfair to impose support liability on a child for one who has mistreated that child in the past; but the standard defenses are inevitably vague and the marginal cases present an unpleasant and unedifying spectacle - especially those in which an ungrateful child (or one who simply wants to share support for his parent with the government "as other taxpayers do") tries to take legal advantage

---

35. *Id*. at 1372

36. For a sample of the kinds of unpleasant factual squabbles about ancient family history to which such defenses can lead, *see, e.g.*, Cheatham v. Juras, 502 P.2d 988 (Ore. App. 1972) (son liable for mother's nursing home care despite fact that she had placed him and his belongings in the street and placed younger brother for adoption because mother's medical record indicated she was mentally ill and not responsible for her actions due to a case of progressive Multiple Sclerosis); Drugg v. Juras, 501 P.2d 1313, 1315 (Ore. App. 1971) (relative responsibility proceeding reversed for findings of fact as to whether parents had been responsible for son's dependency as a child, a defense to liability; son was oldest of six children and compelled to work and to give his earnings to drunken father; son left home and took full-time work at eleven years of age; younger sister corroborated son's testimony, reporting that "his father gambled away much of the family's meager income, the family was hungry much of the time, the [son] had inadequate patched clothing, and as a result of these things he (as well as she) was the object of ridicule at school to the extent that he was ashamed and truant"); Denny v. Public Welfare Division, 483 P.2d 463 (Ore. App.1971) (son liable for welfare benefits to mother despite statutory exception for child whose parent "without good cause, was responsible for the child's being 'dependent'"; mother had placed defendant in foster homes only to enable her to try to earn a living).

of actual or perceived ancient parental neglects. A statute proposed for New York by a private social welfare research commission indicates some of the difficulties:

> No relative of a recipient of, or applicant for, public assistance and care, who would otherwise be legally responsible shall be liable for such support if the recipient or applicant shall have been found by a court of competent jurisdiction, whether civil or criminal, to have committed an act equivalent to any of the violations of law set forth below (or their equivalents in any other jurisdiction), according to the terms of which the relative was a victim or subject of such violation (The sections referred to . . . are those of the New York Penal Law): Abandonment; Abduction; Assault; Bigamy; Carnal Abuse of a Child; Compelling Woman to Marry; Compelling Prostitution by Wife; Endangering Life or Health of Child; Incest: Kidnapping; Maiming; Non-Support of Child; Prostitution; Rape; Robbery; Sodomy.

> Provided, however, that the above protection against liability shall not apply to any relative of full age and legal capacity who, by his or her conduct subsequent to the commission of the violation of law by the recipient or applicant, has voluntarily forgiven the recipient or applicant for the commission of the violation of law.[37]

The specification of offenses and the requirement of a judicial finding certainly provides greater certainty than the traditional statutes. But societal ambivalence about these issues reappears in the "condonation" provision; and that provision, however logical, will reintroduce just the unpleasantness that cases like *Mitchell* have always encouraged.

But are aesthetic considerations relevant? If relative responsibility is seen simply as a direct tax measure, as a convenient means of saving government revenues by imposing upon a narrower (but by no means an arbitrarily chosen) class than taxpayers generally, a true public policy dilemma can be avoided. It may still be unfair to impose support on children who were once abandoned or maltreated by their parents, but tax policy, like life itself, is not always fair.

Even if there is no dispute about the general policy of imposing liability on children, difficult doctrinal and administrative judgments

---

37. *See* Community Service Society of New York, FAMILIAL RESPONSIBILITY AND PUBLIC WELFARE: ISSUES AND RECOMMENDATIONS 15 (1964).

must be faced. Should the liability of sons with working wives be the same as the liability of working daughters with working husbands? In *Page v. Welfare Commissioner*,[38] the Connecticut relative responsibility statute was held to violate the Equal Protection Clause:

> The plaintiff's mother was, in 1973, a recipient of public assistance. The commissioner's financial investigation revealed that the plaintiff was married, living with her husband, and the mother of four minor children. Both the plaintiff and her husband were employed, with gross monthly incomes of $481 and $649.50, respectively, In determining the amount of the plaintiff's monthly contribution to the support of her mother, the commissioner allowed her an exemption of $325, which was then the exemption for a single person living outside the home of the public assistance recipient. No exemption was allowed the plaintiff for her four children. The support contribution was computed by taking one-half of the difference between her gross monthly income and the exemption allowed.[39]

Because the statute as interpreted by the commissioner allowed working male children of welfare recipients an exemption for their minor children while denying such an exemption to married working females, the court held that the statute discriminated unconstitutionally against women:

> The regulations here in question clearly differentiate between working married mothers and working married fathers. The earnings of the latter are granted significantly greater exceptions in the financial determination of ability to contribute to the support of a needy parent than are the earnings of the former. As a result of this distinction, working mothers married to working husbands are able to contribute only a disproportionately small share to the support of their immediate household. The benefits which flow to the immediate household of a working parent who is also liable for the support of his or her disabled parent, therefore, depends upon the sex of the working parent. This is precisely the situation which the Supreme Court ruled unconstitutional [in an earlier

---

38. 170 Conn. 258, 365 A.2d 1118 (1976).

39. *Id*. at 1121, 365 A.2d at 1121.

case].[40]

b. Administrative Problems

If children are to be liable, the legislature must make difficult choices about the amount of their liability. The alternative, of course, is to leave local welfare administrators and prosecuting attorneys discretion to make their own choices.[41] Some picture of the complexities can be gathered from the matrix (Table 1) developed by California welfare officials to guide the discretion of local officials in administering filial responsibility provisions.
or, consider the impact of the Boren-Long Amendment's effort to deny welfare benefits to those whose spouses have assets sufficient to support them. The federal and state statutes and the controlling federal and state regulations are too long and complex to report here.[42] But consider *Manfredi v. Maher*,[43] one of a series of federal cases brought to test the Constitutionality of the Boren-Long amendment's provision for interspousal income attributions in determining eligibility for Social Security Act Title XIX (Medicaid) benefits where one of the spouses is confined for a long term at a nursing or convalescent home. Notice how complex the administration of even a spousal resources provision

---

40. *Id.* at 1124, 365 A.2d 1124. The Connecticut Supreme Court's sex discrimination - Equal Protection analysis might be explained in part by the Court's opposition to the very notion of a family responsibility scheme.

41. As to the problems of discretion, *see* the note 62 *infra*.

42. Consider the remarks of Judge Friendly in DeJesus v. Perales, 770 F.2d 316, 321 (2d Cir. 1985) (upholding as consistent with the Social Security Act a New York regulation that requires an applicant to "spend down" his resources to qualify for Medicaid): "This appeal requires the interpretation of a statute of unparalleled complexity. . . . The Supreme Court has characterized the Social Security Act as 'among the most intricate ever drafted by Congress' and has quoted our observation . . . that the Act is 'almost unintelligible to the uninitiated.'"

43. 435 F. Supp. 1106 (D. Conn. 1977) (regulation requiring interspousal income attribution in determining eligibility for Medicaid benefits violates Social Security Act).

100

Table 1
The Relatives' Contribution Scale of the Welfare and Institutions Code[44]
Number of Persons Dependent Upon Income

Net Monthly Income	1	2	3	4	5	6 or more
$ 400 or under	$ 0	$ 0	$ 0	$ 0	$ 0	$ 0
401-450	5	0	0	0	0	0
451-500	10	0	0	0	0	0
501-550	15	0	0	0	0	0
551-600	20	0	0	0	0	0
601-650	25	5	0	0	0	0
651-700	30	10	0	0	0	0
701-750	35	15	0	0	0	0
751-800	40	20	0	0	0	0
801-850	45	25	5	0	0	0
851-900	50	30	10	0	0	0
901-950	55	35	15	0	0	0
951-1,000	60	40	20	0	0	0
1,001-1,025	65	45	25	5	0	0
1,026-1,1050	70	50	30	10	0	0
1,051-1,075	75	55	35	15	0	0
1,076-1,100	80	60	40	20	0	0
1,101-1,125	85	65	45	25	5	0
1,126-1,150	90	70	50	30	10	0

44. This matrix appears in Swoap v. Superior Court of Sacramento County, 111 Cal. Rptr. 136, 148, 516 P.2d 840, 854 (1973). The statute read in part: "For purposes of this chapter, income of an adult child is defined as the sum of the income constituting the separate property of the adult child, the income (excluding earnings) of the adult child, and the earnings of the adult child but not of his or her spouse. In computing net income, a flat 25-percent allowance shall be permitted for the cost of personal income taxes, disability insurance taxes and social security taxes, expenses necessary to produce the income, including the cost of transportation to and from work, meals eaten at work, and union dues, and the cost of tools, equipment and uniforms."

can become; and notice as well the evasive efforts such a provision can produce:

Arthur O: Guertin is a retired person in his seventies. His wife, Lucy Guertin, 66, resides at the Hamilton Pavilion nursing home . . . having entered that institution on May 14, 1974. Arthur Guertin has exhausted his savings and borrowed against his insurance policies to support his wife in the home. After these resources were used up, Lucy Guertin applied for and began to receive Medicaid benefits.

Arthur Guertin's total current income consists of a state pension of $179.62 per month, plus $271.90 in Social Security old age benefits. Of the $451.52 per month thus received, Arthur Guertin must contribute $229.52, or somewhat more than half of the total amount, toward his wife's support in the nursing home. Should he refuse to make such contributions, Lucy Guertin would be denied Medicaid assistance, with the result that she would ultimately be forced to leave the state (to find the care she needed). Thus, Arthur Guertin is left with $222 per month out of which he must meet all personal and household expenses.

The impact of this financial privation upon Arthur Guertin's life style has been pronounced. Guertin testified before the court that he has been obliged in recent months to subsist on the equivalent of one and one-half meals per day (coffee and toast in the morning, a "light lunch" during the evening, and sometimes a sandwich at noon). He has been unable to afford the cost of a low-salt diet, and a doctor has ascribed a recent illness to the plaintiff's failure to maintain such a diet. In order to conserve on energy costs, Guertin reportedly restricts himself to one bath a week, and uses a single 60-watt bulb for illumination in the evenings when needed, but he also sits in the dark for long hours with no lighting at all. Despite these measures, Guertin is unable to meet utility payments. Indeed, his various expenses are such as to leave him perpetually in debt, dependent on such help as he occasionally receives from relatives. It has been suggested to Guertin that he could solve his financial problem by divorcing his wife, but he refuses to do so, and thereby continues to be subject to the state's income attribution rule.[45]

---

45. It is not clear that a dissolution of marriage will always be allowed in cases of this type. In *In re Bennington*, Cause No. 576-260 (Super. Ct., Lake County, Ind. May 26, 1976), the court ordered further hearings on an attempted marriage dissolution by a couple faced with a state welfare regulation of the type promulgated in Connecticut, stating that "should [the state's] regulations be valid it is not clear that the parties should be permitted to circumvent [them] by going through a dissolution." Slip Op. at 3. [Court's footnote.]

Or consider the situation of one of the plaintiffs in another "spend down" case, *Norman v. St. Clair*:[46]

> At the time of the suit, 79-year-old Troy Norman was institutionalized in a skilled nursing home in Mississippi. According to affidavit testimony, Mr. Norman's health was such that he could not receive the proper nursing care from his wife at home. He received a monthly Social Security disability check for $160.50. He had no other source of income and was eligible for Medicaid.
>
> Troy Norman's wife, Nonne Mae, lived in the community with their 14-year-old son Thomas. . . . Mrs. Norman had a monthly employment income of $298.26 (excluding taxes, social security, and employment-related expenses) and received monthly social security checks for $47.90. Their son Thomas also received a social security check of $47.90. Mrs. Norman was not eligible for Medicaid. Application of the state's calculation of Medicaid eligibility and Medicaid income yields the following:

Net monthly income of ineligible spouse	$346.16	
Less standard allowance for spouse's needs	78.00	
Less allowance for minor child ($65.00 - $47.90)	268.16	
Deemed Income		17.10
	$251.06	

> The deemed income from Mrs. Norman is added to Mr. Norman's income (minus the $7.50 disregard) producing a total income available to Mr. Norman of $404.06. Since this is less than $450, Mr. Norman is eligible for Medicaid.
>
> To determine how much of his medical expenses Mr. Norman must pay himself, the state calculates as follows:

New monthly income of Mr. Norman	$153.00	
New monthly income of Mrs. Norman	346.16	
Total net monthly income		

46. 610 F.2d 1228, 1233-34 (5th Cir. 1980).

of both   499.16

Less allowance for
Mr. Norman   -34.00
                                  465.16
Less allowance for
Mrs. Norman   -140.00
                        325.16
Less allowance for unmet
needs of Thomas
($65.00-47.90)   -17.10

Equals "Medicaid Income"
to be paid by Normans to
nursing home $308.06

The state's allowance of $140.00 for Mrs. Norman's living expenses is a uniform amount which does not vary.

As these figures suggest, $189.06 of Mrs. Norman's income is deemed available to Mr. Norman to be used in paying his nursing home medical expenses. . . .

My purpose in providing such detail of these sad chronicles is not to bias consideration of the wisdom of relative responsibility provisions, but simply to emphasize that the policy calculus must include an estimate of the administrative cost of creating as well as enforcing relative responsibility.

II

It seems clear to me that a rational public policy decision as to the wisdom of enacting or maintaining legislation requiring adult children to support their aged parents requires careful weighing of a number of broad considerations. Those considerations are quite different from each other and are difficult to quantify or to compare. I will address each of the relevant considerations in a summary fashion.

A. The "Moral" Issue

No relative responsibility program would last without some community consensus as to its fairness. The ancient lineage of relative responsibility laws suggests that there is a consensus that adult children should support their aged parents. Thus, commentators have spoken of "strengthening family bonds," the "obvious fairness" of such a requirement, or the "moral responsibility" involved, in defending filial support programs.[47] Judges often appear convinced that such provisions are just:

> It seems eminently clear that the selection of the adult children is rational on the ground that the parents, who are now in need, supported and cared for their children during their minority and that such children should in turn now support their parents to the extent to which they are capable. Since these children received special benefits from the class of "parents in need," it is entirely rational that the children bear a special burden with respect to that class.[48]

But in recent, years social welfare theorists, as well as moral philosophers and legal commentators, have claimed that the consensus is changing. The 1961 White House Conference on Aging (whose conferees did not necessarily represent a spectrum of interests and attitudes on such issues) concluded that:

> Laws and practices which enforce or assume support from adult children, and in many places with little or no regard for the needs and responsibilities of adult children and their young, weaken family relationships and family responsibility, and are destructive to older persons and the families of their adult children. Such requirements should be remove from State laws and

---

47. *See* Lopes, *Filial Support and Family Solidarity*, 6 Pac. L.J. 27. 508, 525 (1975), *quoting* other commentators. *See also* Community Service Society of New York, *supra* note 38; Bond & Baber, *Our Needy Aged* 316 (1954).

48. *See* Swoap v. Superior Court of Sacramento County, 111 Cal. Rptr. 136, 147, 516 P.2d 840, 851 (1973) (majority opinion). The Court added in a footnote that the rationale is supported by the inclusion of an "abandonment" exception. *Id.*

practice.[49]

Most arguments against filial support laws begin with a description of demographic changes which are thought to drive ethical values: the number of aged persons in the population is growing rapidly and aged people are living ever longer; the imposition on their children of a support obligation, therefore, has become and will continue to be a more onerous burden than it was in the past:

> Filial obligations were far less likely to be called upon at the turn of the century; they were likely to be burdensome over a much shorter period of time, and they were more likely to be shared by a greater number of children per aged parent.[50]

> [A]lmost all observers agree that the social effects of the challenged relative responsibility provisions are harsh and self-defeating. "[A] large body of social work opinion [has long maintained] that liability of relatives creates and increases family dissension and controversy, weakens and destroys family ties at the very time and in the very circumstances when they are most needed, imposes an undue burden upon the poor . . . and is therefore socially undesirable, financially unproductive, and administratively infeasible." . . . As Justice Friedman, writing for the Court of Appeal in the instant case, observed, "[The challenged provisions] strike most aggressively and harshly at adult children occupying the lower end of the income scale. The enforced shift of subsistence funds from one generation to the other distributes economic desolation between the generations. It injects guilt and shame into elderly citizens who have made their contributions to society and have become dependent through life's vicissitudes."[51]

---

49. REPORT OF THE WHITE HOUSE CONFERENCE ON AGING, *The Nation and Its Older People* 173 (1961). *See* also Community Service Society of New York, *supra* note 38, at 6, listing a variety of union, professional and political groups favoring the elimination of relative responsibility in the Medical Assistance to the Aged Program.

50. Daniels, FAMILY RESPONSIBILITY INITIATIVES AND JUSTICE BETWEEN AGE GROUPS, LAW, MEDICINE AND HEALTH CARE 153, 154 (September, 1985). Professor Daniels, a philosopher, constructs a strong case against a moral obligation on the part of children.

51. Swoap v. Superior Court of Sacramento County, 111 Cal. Rptr. 136, 160, 516 P.2d 840, 864 (1973) (dissenting opinion). *See also* Baldus, *supra* note 19.

And the widespread rejection, in the literature if not the cases, of the policy underpinnings of the Boren-Long amendment suggest a stirring of the intellectuals to support nonreimbursable government welfare expenditures.[52] Moreover, in recent decades there has been some retreat from adult child-relative responsibility provisions.[53] Yet no matter how exquisitely the philosophers analyze the issues, the "moral" consideration may best be captured by the emotional expressions of those parents who object to impositions on their children. Consider the arguments of Jennie Baxter, a 75 year old Californian receiving old age welfare benefits who opposed the subsequently abolished California relative responsibility program:

> No one is born into this world with a debt to their parents for their birth and contributions until their maturity. That is the parent's contribution to life and society. When the child reaches maturity, he starts a new separate unit and in turn makes his contribution to life and society as did his parents, carrying on the generation cycle through eternity. The children should not be saddled

---

52. *See* Daniels, *supra* note 50; Lopes, *supra* note 47; Note, *Relative Responsibility Extended: Requirement of Adult Children to Pay for Their Indigent Parents' Medical Needs*, 21 FAM. L.Q. __ (1988): Patrick, *Honor They Father and Mother: Paying the Medical Bills of Elderly Parents*, 19 U. RICH. L. REV. 69 (1984); Note, to *Deem or Not to Deem: Evaluating and Attributing Available Spouse Income to an Institutionalized Medicaid Applicant*, 67 U. VA. L. REV. 767 (1981); Acford, *Reducing Medicaid Expenditures Through Family Responsibility: Critique of a Recent Proposal*, 5 AM.J. LAW & MED. 59 (1979-80); Note, *Pennsylvania's Family Responsibility Statute - Corruption of Blood and Denial of Equal Protection*, 77 DICK. L. REV. 331 (1972); Van Houtte and Breda, *Maintenance of the Aged by Their Adult Children: The Family as a Residual Agency in the Solution of Poverty in Belgium*, 12 LAW & SOC. REV. 645 (1978). *But see* Garrett, *Filial Responsibility Laws*, 18 J. FAM. L. 793 (1979).

53. *See* Cal. Stats. 1975, c. 1136, p.2811, § 1. *See* CALIF. WELF. & INS. CODE § 12350. *Cf.* Estate of Hinds, 390 N.E.2d 172 (Ind. App. 1979) (statute terminated support liability of adult children of parent for adult child institutionalized for a continuous period of more than twelve months). *Cf.* Baldus, *supra* note 19, at 216: "After the enactment of the Social Security Act in 1935, recovery was adopted in OAA and AB programs throughout the country. However, a repeal trend began in the South in the late 1930's and spread to the Southwestern and Border States in the 1940's and 1950's."

with unjust demands that keep them at or near the poverty level with no hope to escape it, just because a parent still breathes. And aged parents should not have to live their remaining lives facing the heartbreaking experience of being such a burden to their children. Many would prefer death but are afraid of retribution for taking their own lives. Their grief - a living death.[54]

But if the moral consensus is changing, what explains the subtle shift toward more relative responsibility provisions, a trend recognized even by opponents of such programs?[55] And there can be no doubt as to the powerful support for new initiatives compelling parents to support their children.[56] Wisconsin even passed a statute requiring support of a dependent child by the child's grandparents if the parent of the child is also dependent.[57] It is doubtful that the moral consensus in the United States favoring support of parents by their adult children has disappeared.

B. The Administrative Issues

A fair assessment of "relative responsibility" cannot be accomplished without evaluating the administrative problems such a program would entail. A homely example should suffice to illustrate the point. If it cost more to identify, find and "prosecute" responsible relatives than could be collected from them, establish-

---

54. *See* note 51 *supra.*

55. *See* Daniels, *supra* note 50, reporting new initiatives in three different states. *See also* the description of the Boren-Long amendment, notes 16-17 *supra. See also* Ackford, *supra* note 52, describing a Massachusetts Welfare Department initiative to impose responsibility on adult children with taxable incomes over $20,000 per year to contribute to the cost of nursing home care for their parents receiving Medicaid. Massachusetts had repealed its family responsibility law when the original Medicaid statute circumscribed the states' ability to collect from parents and children. *See* note 23 *supra.* The Department's proposal, which antedated Boren-Long, was submitted to the Department of Health, Education and Welfare pursuant to a Social Security Act provision allowing formal waivers of the federal requirements of the Act.

56. *See* note 11 *supra.*

57. *See* WIS. STAT. ANN. § 49.90(1)(a)(2) (1985).

108

ing or retaining such a program would undermine the tax saving purposes it supposedly serves. Some people would urge that the program be retained in any event because it asserts and reinforces a moral norm. But legislatures which have eschewed all concern with efficiency in the pursuit of morality have often found their policy efforts defeated.[58]

To devise the complex reimbursement formulas many states have adopted [59] requires personnel time and money; finding "responsible relatives" and obtaining money from them requires even more. And if the responsibility provisions contain discretionary exceptions such as those for abandoned or maltreated children described earlier, [60] the costs of administration and enforcement will inevitably be even higher. There is no need to reemphasize the administrative difficulties and costs produced by the very complexity of the statutes and their policies. On the other side of the ledger, very little is known, nationally or for any state, as to the real return which might be realized from a fully enforced relative responsibility provision. One study in California, more than thirty years ago, discovered that although county officials believed by more than two to one that the programs cost more to administer than they produce in revenue, at least one county director who gave figures reported almost $6 collected for every dollar spent.[61]

---

58. *See, e.g.*, Skolnick, JUSTICE WITHOUT TRIAL: LAW ENFORCEMENT IN DEMOCRATIC SOCIETY (1966). *But see* the text following note 83 *infra*.

59. *See* the matrix once adopted in California, note 42 *supra*. Other states have similar schemes.

60. *See* notes 29-37 *supra* and accompanying text.

61. Bond & Baber, OUR NEEDY AGED 201 (1954). Yet the numbers were quite small; experience in one county may not be generalizable and there was no check on the accuracy of the figures reported. *See also* Community Service Society of New York, *supra* note 37, at 9, reporting that although a prior study of New York had found a similar 7 to 1 return ratio, collections from relatives had been lumped with recipient reimbursements and the cost figures had ignored the fact that expenditures required to establish existence of relatives and their ability to contribute. Chambers, *supra* note 10, reported data that suggested that criminal enforcement of fathers who do not support their children may improve performance generally.

More recently, Baldus reported that in 1969 reimbursement provisions returned approximately seven-tenths of one percent of welfare transfers in that year. National gross savings, including savings from deterred applications, were estimated to be between $80 and $90 million and the administrative cost of collection was approximately thirty percent.[62]

Even if more complete national or state collection figures were available, the cost-benefit ratio question might not be answerable because of the tradition of discretionary administration of relative responsibility. No one seems to doubt that local welfare officials, as well as prosecutors, in fact fail to insist on support in some cases. One study concluded:

> Despite a great deal of talk about "making responsible relatives live up to the law," [relatively few counties bring suit]. Boards of supervisors are generally willing, after the registered form letter has failed to produce results, to have the county attorney write an official warning threatening a suit, but, all being elective officials, neither he nor the supervisors have any stomach for forcing people to support their aged relatives against their will. As politicians, they figure - and no doubt correctly - that they would lose more votes than they would gain through such proceedings. In the last analysis it would seem that the vigor and, to some degree, the success with which this provision is administered depend heavily on the attitude of the board of supervisors.[63]

The same study reported that some prosecutors refused to seek funds from those adult children who claimed that their parents had not provided them with support as children, despite the absence in the statute of an "abandonment" or "nonsupport" exception. Moreover,

---

62. Baldus, *supra* note 19, at 133-36. Although reimbursement return for OAA, the welfare program for the aged, was considerably higher than for other programs, reimbursement amounts declined precipitously in states which did not employ post-death liens. *Id.* at 190. Since decedents' homes are easier to find than relatives, and liened estates are easier to collect money from than unwilling children, it seems likely that collections from relative responsibility laws would produce less return than would reimbursement laws. Baldus reports that federal cost analyses and welfare officials agree. *Id.* at 197 note 261. *See also id.* at 196-98 (describing how little is known about reimbursement collection costs).

63. Bond & Baber, *supra* note 61, at 201.

one director told of a professional man whose income was [at the top of the payment scale matrix]. But he is reported to have told the district attorney that if he made him pay he would force [the prosecutor] to press charges against all the others who had been notified of obligations but had not paid. The district attorney could not face the prospect of making so many political enemies, so nothing more was done. . . .[64]

No proper cost-benefit analysis can be undertaken if we simply do not know the amounts which should be placed on either side of the equation.

But discretionary administration is not conceived by welfare administrations as an evil to be eliminated or at least controlled. Rather, social welfare theorists see much discretion as a virtue. Public welfare programs are seen as social services "providing preventive, rehabilitative and family strengthening services (and not merely a 'dole')" through the services of professional social workers who view relative responsibility not in a "narrow economic sense" but "in its broadest social and psychological context."[65] The most recent policy study recommended clear and fair rules which leave a discretionary "residue of manageable size." The exercise of discretion presupposes, the study claimed, deployment of an adequate number of "professionally qualified and experienced social workers" supervised by "adequate and professionally qualified supervisory personnel in key welfare center positions."[66] The scope of discretion and reasons for providing for it were described with specificity:

[The view that the public welfare program is a social service agency] introduces considerations which cannot be measured in dollars and cents, may never be expressed in such terms and, in fact, may have to be ignored insofar as the legally responsible relative is concerned. . . .

Likewise, the gift of the adult to his aged parents, expressed by regular visiting and interchange, a continuing affectionate contact, the meeting of extra needs not regularly included in the Department of Welfare budget, has

---

64. *Id*. at 319.

65. Community Service Society of New York, *supra* note 37, at 27.

66. *Id*. at 26.

a meaning far greater to the maintenance of strong family ties and a sense of responsibility of family members for each other than the insistence by the Department, under the law, for a specific amount of support.

Enforcement may easily result in lessening rather than strengthening significant family relationships.

On the other hand, a professional evaluation of family relationships may lead to the conclusion that a non-supporting relative, financially able to contribute, should be helped to see the psychological meaning and value to the economically dependent relative and to himself that a financial commitment would symbolize. . . .

The use of discretion, therefore, would make it possible for the professional worker to move either way, to recommend waiver of the support requirement or to help the relative see the social and psychological values that in some instances money payments can represent.

The exercise of professional discretion, as it pertains to familial responsibility, is a subtle, complex matter. This is so because it requires placing in the fore and not the background the social and psychological considerations which need to be evaluated by a professional social worker. Yet it is the proper estimate and balance of all these factors which determine whether family life is strengthened or weakened by legal insistence upon support.

The freedom to use professional discretion, properly exercised, could well result in a major advance in reducing the cycle of dependency because the emphasis would be placed on social, not merely economic, values. If family ties are being or have been continuously and badly weakened over a long period of time, moral obligations tend to fade into non-existence. Even a sincere attempt at legal enforcement is then not only economically costly and socially destructive but often becomes a mockery and a farce. But . . . when money can be used to restore poor relationships to healthy ones or to maintain good ones, the professional worker with discretionary powers can use social work skills to help the responsible relative understand and achieve this.

When responsibility for economic support is not voluntary and resort to the law seems necessary, it suggests the possibility that some breakdown in family relationships has already taken place or that superior value is placed by the responsible relatives, and often by the applicant for assistance himself, on the long-term aspirations and goals of the responsible relative for his own family. Therefore, such cases require the judgment of qualified social workers in public welfare programs.[67]

---

67. *Id.* at 28-29.

No more persuasive paean to professional discretion could be devised. But such commendation ignores the extent to which professional discretion built into public programs - in the schools, in juvenile courts, in mental institutions, in prisons - has both failed and either delayed or obstructed desperately needed social reform. The movement toward "determinate sentencing" is the most notorious, but by no means the only, contemporaneous effort to escape the tyranny of professional discretion.[68] Because of the "lower status professionals accord to public agency employment (impeding the employment of highly qualified professionals) and the civil service protection afforded public employees (impeding elimination of professionals who perform poorly),"[69] there is no reason to believe that discretion will be exercised any more wisely in public welfare-relative responsibility administration than it has been in other fields where administrators have some power to coerce clients. In fact, anecdotal evidence, some of it reported above,[70] suggests that in this field of endeavor, as in others, studies of official discretion will turn up a significant number of abuses. Indeed, the federal government itself has turned away from professional social worker management of public welfare case-loads.[71] (On the other hand, if efforts to achieve uniformity are of

---

68. *See, e.g.*, Feld, *Criminalizing Juvenile Justice: Rules of Procedure for the Juvenile Court*, 69 MINN. L. REV. 141 (1984).

69. Levy, *Custody Investigations in Divorce Cases*, 1985 AMER. BAR FOUND. RES. J. 713, 719.

70. *See* notes 64 and 65 *supra* and accompanying text. *Cf.* Handler, *Controlling Official Behavior in Welfare Administration*, 54 CALIF. L. REV. 479;, 493-95 (1966) (social worker discretion in determinations of which mothers were to work and what they had to do). *But see* Handler, *Discretion in Social Welfare: The Uneasy Position in the Rule of Law*, 92 YALE L.J. 1270 (1983) (recommending a return to structured discretion).

71. The former categorical assistance programs are now merged in the federally financed (although the states can supplement federal payments)and administered program known as "Supplementary Security Income" (or "SSI"). *See* SOCIAL SECURITY AMENDMENTS OF 1972, PUB. L. No. 92-603, § 301. Even the AFDC program, still segregated because, it seems, its recipients are less worthy, is now administered mechanically rather than by professional clinicians.

the kind indicated in the Manfredi and Norman cases,[72] where collections are placed at a level which can be attained only at great personal expense for many families and with a substantial inducement to relative evasion, evasion through administrative discretion may be both inevitable and healthy.)

C. Of Deterrence and Individual Dignity

The progression of federal policy - from Medicaid's 1965 prohibition of relative responsibility[73] to the 1980 Boren-Long amendment's authorization of state plans containing "transfer of assets" punishments,[74] to the permission given in the 1982 Tax, Equity and Fiscal Responsibility Act for state plan provisions imposing eligibility sanctions for pre-application transfers of family homes[75] - suggests an unpleasant possibility. It may well be that as the expense of welfare programs increases, legislators (and perhaps the public as well) will demand greater financial accountability from recipients and a wider net for catching alternative resources - simply to save money. No doubt, responses to current fiscal exigencies play a role in such developments; and it is also likely that these changes have something of a tidal quality.[76] But

---

72. *See* notes 44-46 *supra* and accompanying text.

73. *See* Conf. Rept. No. 682, July 26, 1965, to accompany H.R. 6675 (Social Security Amendments of 1965), 105 CONG. & ADMIN. CODE, 89th Cong., 1st Sess. 2147 (1965).

74. *See* note 16 *supra*.

75. The later events in the story are told in Lewis v. Hegstrom, 767 F.2d 1371 (9th Cir. 1985).

76. For a description of the legislative trends toward and away from repeal of lien and reimbursement provisions, *see* Baldus, *supra* note 19, at 176-77. Baldus also reports reimbursement legislation variations from region to region based upon political, economic and property value considerations. *Id.* at 135. Yet "trends" are fairly gross phenomena. One example should suffice. The years of the Reagan Administration have obviously not produced liberalizations of welfare. But see *Expanded Right to Medicaid Shatters the Link to Welfare*, N.Y. Times, March 6, 1988, p.1, col.5 (describing expansions achieved in coverage during the

at bottom a social norm may be lurking: government subsidy of the poor cannot be too large or too generous - and relative responsibility enforcement is seen as a way of avoiding both evils.[77]

It certainly seems clear that relative responsibility provisions have not been designed (and may not be operated) exclusively to raise money. Rather, they operate at least in part to deter increasing welfare rolls. Some of the cases[78] and many of the commentators[79] recognize the matter explicitly. But little is known empirically about the deterrent efficacy of relative responsibility. The usual illustration, the experience in Maine during 1948, is not altogether clear. When the State revived its relative responsibility law by requiring all children of assistance recipients to submit detailed financial data, more than 2,000 cases were

---

last eight years by provisions "hidden" in comprehensive budget reconciliation bills).

77. That judges are subject to these tidal changes is indicated by the California courts' adventure with the constitutional invalidation of relative responsibility provisions. The story is told in a majority opinion which backs away from the precipice, validating the adult child responsibility statute. *See* Swoap v. Superior Court of Sacramento County, note 48 *supra*.

78. *See, e.g.*, Lewis v. Hegstrom, note 75 *supra*, at 1378: "We believe that in enacting section 1396p(c)(2)(B), Congress sought to reduce budget outlays and to create a strong disincentive to the transfer of homes for less than fair market value. . . . By pegging the period of ineligibility to the average amount the state actually pays for medical services to Medicaid recipients, government moneys are spread the furthest. A longer ineligibility period results through such a computation; a longer ineligibility period creates a stronger disincentive to the transfer of a home for less than fair market value."

79. *See e.g.*, Lopes, *Filial Support and Family Solidarity*, 6 PAC. L.J. 508, 522 (1975): "By far the most important cost saving aspect of filial support laws lies in their inhibitory effect on applications for public assistance." Baldus, supra note 20, at 155-56, found a statistically significant relationship between both reimbursement and relative responsibility policies and the percentage of old age assistance recipients receiving support from one or more adult children. *See also id.* at 176-77 (significant negative relationship between home ownership and OAA explained by deterrent effect of reimbursement law). The budgetary savings produced indirectly by the deterrent effect of reimbursement provisions is analyzed separately. *Id.* at 198.

closed.[80]   Detractors of relative responsibility point out that 40 percent of these closings were due to a failure by children to submit financial statements.[81]   In one sense, of course, this deterrent success is exactly what we want to accomplish: the costs of relative responsibility enforcement are minimized and the largest possible tax saving has been accomplished because no welfare payment at all, rather than a welfare payment reduced by the relative's reimbursement, is paid.   But neither defenders nor detractors of relative responsibility can claim victory here. We do not know what group of applicants, otherwise eligible, has been deterred from applying for benefits. If poor aged parents whose children are also poor but proud have not applied, we have saved tax dollars but only at what many would consider too substantial a cost to the aged poor **and** their poor adult children. But suppose the relative responsibility program has instead deterred from applying those poor aged parents whose adult children can afford to support them but are unwilling to do so because of the availability of an alternative source of support, government welfare benefits? In the second case, our deterrent policy has singled out just the group whose behavior we wanted to affect.   In the absence of much more reliable information than we have had in the past, is it safe to make any assumptions about targeted groups? The most realistic assumption is that some of both groups will be affected. And yet, considering the size of welfare benefits in most states, even today,[82] and relying (in a different fashion, for this purpose) on the belief that there is a national consensus that adult children should support their aged and dependent parents, doesn't it seem likely that a deterrent policy might affect a larger portion of "false positives," of parents of poor but proud children, rather than

---

80. *See* Stevens and Springer, *Maine Revives Responsibility of Relatives,* 6 PUB. WELF. 122 (1948), reported in Lopes, *supra* note 79, at 527.

81. *Id.* at 527.

82. Consider the amounts at stake in the *Norman* and *Manfredi* cases, quoted in the text accompanying notes 44-46 *supra*.

parents of wealthy but crass children?[83]

The deterrence rationale justifies intrusive investigations by welfare personnel of all families in order to deny or diminish subsistence funds to that small proportion of the welfare applicant and recipient population who are getting a "free ride" - that is, those who are living on government largesse when they could be living on the largesse of their children. Phrasing the matter in this fashion makes it difficult to ignore the unresolved issues of welfare applicant and recipient dignity: to prevent "cheating" by a few we are imposing on all the indignity of an investigation of their children's resources.   (Investigation of the resources of relatives may not occur until after the applicant has been declared eligible - but that administrative refinement postpones but does not change the essential nature of the indignity.) Can such intrusive governmental forays be justified? They are certainly a familiar aspect of the American tradition.[84] This tradition has had vocal opponents - and their voices have been heard: the "categorical assistances" were combined into "SSI," a substantially less fully investigated, less socially stigmatized, program;[85] eligibility

---

83. In addition, Baldus, *supra* note 19, at 156-57, provides data strongly suggesting that adult children who support their "deterred" aged parents do not provide as much support as a welfare grant would. *Cf. id.* at 163 (following passage of Washington statute limiting estate reimbursement liability if heirs prove their inability to support welfare recipient during lifetime, reimbursement collections declined substantially). Baldus' interrupted times series, regression analysis of relative responsibility laws led him to conclude that such laws have a "slight" deterrent effect. *Id.* at 201-02.

84. *See* Wyman v. James, 400 U.S. 309, 319 (1971) welfare department caseworker does not need search warrant to insist upon home visit with AFDC recipient; "one who dispenses purely private charity naturally has an interest in and expects to know how his charitable funds are utilized and put to work. The public, when it is the provider, rightly expects the same.") *See* Burt, *Forcing Protection on Children and Their Parents: The Impact of Wyman v. James*, 69 MICH. L. REV. 1259 (1971)

85.   *See* Liebman, *The Definition of Disability in Social Security and Supplemental Security Income: Drawing the Bounds of Social Welfare Estates*, 89 HARV. L. REV. 833 (1976). The AFDC program was not included in the merger. The decision was not surprising since AFDC recipients, no better off financially than those of other programs, were deemed less deserving. *Id.* at 865-66.

investigations have become the responsibility of payment analysts, instructed to take the word of applicants, rather than social workers trained to investigate fully and given a writ which runs to every aspect of a recipient's life;[86] critics of past and present welfare administration are beginning to formulate proposals for structural change which offer some hope that a truly humanitarian welfare system may eventually evolve.[87]

Despite some changes in the system, in the United States "welfare" has never been seen as an "insurance" program; unlike "Social Security," welfare recipients, "on the dole," are seen as less deserving because they have not earned the stipend.[88] The "needs" test, then, and the relative responsibility notion it engenders, serve multiple functions: by discouraging applications and demeaning even "qualified" applicants and their families, the policy saves welfare expenditures even as it reinforces the norm about welfare recipients.[89] We have exhibited a stubborn commitment

---

86. For a description of the routinization bureaucratization of welfare, *see* Simon, *Legality, Bureaucracy, and Class in the Welfare System,* 92 YALE L.J. 1198 (1983). Handler, *supra* note 70, suggests that, on balance, such changes have not significantly improved the welfare system for poor people.

87. *See, e.g.,* Handler, *supra* note 70, at 1280-86; Liebman, *supra* note 85, at 833.

88. *See, e.g.,* Baldus, *supra* note 19, at 220-21, *citing* Segalman, The Protestant Ethic and Social Welfare, 24 J. Social Issues, Jan. 1968, at 125, 128: "The dominant influence over welfare policy in the North has been the Protestant or middle class ethic, which sees the improvidence, idleness, and immorality of poor persons as the cause of their poverty." *See also* Handler, *supra* note 70, at 1271-72; Liebman, *supra* note 86, at 864-67.

89. Although some welfare administrators claim that reimbursement schemes help welfare recipients overcome their sense of inadequacy, Baldus, *supra* note 19, at 161, the National Welfare Rights Organization, the leading American Advocacy organization for welfare recipients during the 1960's, claimed that recovery adds to the stigma of welfare: "Welfare keeps us in a humiliated state of deprivation. To demand repayment compounds the humiliation and is a scandal." *Id.* See also Liebman, *supra* note 86, at 866: "Indeed, an important determinant of Social Security policy has been a widely held belief that recipients' feelings of entitlement and legitimacy depend on exclusion of the undeserving." *See also* note 91 infra. *See generally* Law, *Women, Work, Welfare, and the*

to distinguishing "earned" from "unearned" old age benefits - even
if a very large group of recipients of "earned" benefits have not in
fact earned them and the rest have been fooled into believing that
their premium payments are used only to pay for their own future
benefits.[90] But it is wise to try to diminish the psychological gap
between earned and unearned benefits? The "insurance myth"
may provide vital underpinning for continuing public support for the
taxes which pay for "Social Security." Is it also essential to insist
upon relative responsibility, as on other aspects of "needs"-related
welfare administration, as a continuing symbol of and as a way of
perpetuating the "undeservingness" of those who are "on the
dole?" Such questions cannot be avoided, in the end, if relative
responsibility issues are to be laid to rest once and for all.

III

American society has changed in a variety of ways since the
1960's and 1970's when egalitarian sentiments were politically
popular and legal advocacy for the poor (in the courts and the
legislatures) was helping to decrease "the great arbitrariness and
chaos of the welfare mess.[91] Support for welfare liberality has

---

Preservation of Patriarchy, 131 U. PA. L. REV. 1249 (1983).

90. *See* Cohen, *The Development of the Social Security Act of 1935:
Reflections Some Fifty Years Later*, 68 MINN. L. REV 27. 379 (1983). The authors
of the Social Security Act apparently began to use "insurance" and "contributions" language only after the Supreme Court upheld the Constitutionality of the
Act. "The emphasis on 'insurance' and 'contributions' terminology created a
sharp distinction in the public mind between 'welfare' and 'social security.' This
distinction was maintained until 1965." *Id.* at 398. Of course, there were many,
like Milton Friedman, who objected to the insurance terminology: "The very name
- old age and survivors insurance - is a blatant attempt to mislead the public into
identifying a compulsory tax and benefit system with private, voluntary, and
individual purchase of individually assured benefits." Cohen and Friedman, SOCIAL
SECURITY: UNIVERSAL OR SELECTIVE? 27 (1972).

91. Handler, *supra* note 70, at 1273. For some idea of the methods of legal
advocacy and how successful they sometimes were, *see* Note, *To Deem or Not
to Deem: Evaluating and Attributing Available Spousal Income to an Institutionalized Medicaid Applicant*, 67 VA. L. REV. 767, 775 n.47 (1981) (listing all federal

declined, even among liberals, as concern for the budget deficit has grown. It is clear, of course, that we will not have to worry about relative responsibility when our society's wealth has been spread among the population sufficiently so that all adult children have sufficient resources to support their parents as well as their own spouses and children - and if at that time all adult children recognize the moral obligation to support parents which is thought to be the societal consensus. Perhaps by then (simultaneously, perhaps?) the poor but "undeserving" aged will all have been incorporated into the supposed insurance scheme of OASDHI, completing the great expansion of coverage accomplished two decades ago[92] - and because insurance recipients' children need not repay their parents' monthly stipends, we won't have to debate the nature of the moral consensus. But, sad to say, those millennia appear to be more than a decade away at this writing. Until then, we will continue to struggle - with our aged poor and with our societal and personal ambivalence about their children's responsibility.

court cases brought to attack the validity of state Medicaid family responsibility provisions; twelve of thirteen suits successful prior to Supreme Court decision). *See also* Simon, *supra* note 87, at 1199: "For better or worse (and I don't intend to argue it has been only for worse) the welfare system has been transformed in the past two decades. Lawyers and legal ideas have played a central role in this transformation."

92. *See* OLD AGE SURVIVORS AND DISABILITY INSURANCE AMENDMENTS OF 1965, P.L. 89-97, 79 STAT. 286, July 30, 1965, 42 U.S.C. § 401 et seq. (1982).

LIVING ALONE IN OLD AGE:
The Needs and Rights of the Elderly

Valerie J. Grant[*]
New Zealand

What is it like to be old is a question which currently concerns a large number of people from a wide range of disciplines. Politicians, policy makers, economists, members of the legal and medical professions, psychologists, anthropologists and sociologists have all become interested in this topic. In the United States where social issues tend to take a sharper economic focus, there is already conflict between those who seek to improve the lot of the elderly (such as the Grey Panthers), and those who seek to ensure that such help is not given at the expense of other age groups (Americans for Generational Equity).

Workers v. Pensioners is the title of a recent publication which conveys the authors' attitudes to the coming crisis in funding. It comprises a searching look at basic statistics concerning the rise in both the number and proportion of old and very old people (the Age Wave), and what these figures mean for social and health economics. When studied in conjunction with falling birthrates, increasing longevity and earlier retirement, these statistics make for worrisome reading. Projections appear to show that fewer and fewer young to middle-aged adults will be faced with an impossible burden in trying to provide support for the elderly, and that as a consequence the very foundation of the welfare state will be crushed. The fundamental proposition upon which such states are based, namely that the current generation of workers pays to support the previous generation of workers, will no longer be viable.

What can be done to mitigate the impact of this growing

---

[*] Senior Tutor in Behavioral Science, Auckland School of Medicine, New Zealand; Chairperson of the New Zealand Board of Health's Standing Committee on the Health of the Elderly, 1985-87; Ph.D.

imbalance between generations? Hardly anyone would suggest increasing the birthrate. Some do suggest greater retirement flexibility, which would certainly be in the direction of retaining fundamental human rights in later life, but would probably not make a discernible difference to the problem. Either a 25 year old or a 65 year old holds the job; whoever it is, the other is either unemployed or retired and has to be supported. The third possibility is to look a little more closely at the nature of increased longevity, and at some of the assumptions made about it. That is the purpose of this chapter.

One of the difficulties of formulating policies for the care and support of people in old age is that policy makers are not usually themselves very old. Policies are formulated by those who have little or no knowledge of what it might be like to be over 80 years of age. People tend to assume that somehow the elderly are different, in spite of Dr. Alex Comfort's observation that one feels, as an old person, exactly as one does at any other age. Nor is homogeneity more a characteristic of the elderly than of any other age group. On the contrary, some authors have argued that individual differences range more widely in old age.

The well-documented rise in both the number and proportion of elderly people in the population in societies such as New Zealand's has led, via economic necessity, to urgent attempts to re-define what constitutes a fair and just society for all and what this implies with regard to the support of the elderly. In her paper *Perspectives on the Elderly in New Zealand*, Peggy Koopman-Boyden[1] outlines a range of attitudes and values which underlay the various government and other policies concerned with care and support of the elderly. These attitudes and values give rise to a number of overlapping perspectives, including the medical, institutional, community, dependency, empowerment and health promotion models. Members of the Royal Commission on Social Policy, for whom the report was written, regarded a balance or range of views as optimal in formulating policies, reiterating the importance of considering the attitudes of the elderly themselves.

---

1. P.G. Koopman-Boyden, Perspectives on the Elderly in New Zealand, Royal Commission on Social Policy, SOCIAL PERSPECTIVES, Vol. IV, New Zealand Government Publications (Wellington, 1988).

The right to work (perhaps more appropriately applied to the young old, i.e. those aged 60-75 years) and the right to active and meaningful participation in society are the rights favored by the New Zealand Royal Commission on Social Policy (that is, in addition to the basic human rights already well accepted in New Zealand).

What would the full acceptance of such a policy mean to the old, those aged at least 76, and more particularly those aged over 80 years? What would the right to active and meaningful participation in society actually mean to Mrs. Jones, aged 84 years, living alone, and struggling to maintain her independence in the face of physical, psychological, social and economic losses?

In New Zealand, most of the data gathered on the problems of aging has been quantitative in nature. The Aging Research Networks Directory (Australia and New Zealand) 1987 lists 18 major categories of research. These categories are assessment, biology of aging, community care, cross national and comparative studies, dementia, demography and migration, ethnic aged, education, family, feminist studies, geriatric medicine, hospital services and use, housing, retirement and social policy analysis.

While much of this research gives undoubted benefits, particularly in areas such as service planning and delivery, there remains a sense in which the findings give only a distant view of what it is like to be old. Even in the categories where more personal and individual issues might be legitimately included, such as family support, community care, retirement and education, there is very little attention given to individual viewpoints.

In a review article entitled *Social Bonds in Later Life*, Jerrome[2] discusses four major works. Considering first the American literature in this relatively focused area, Jerrome reports that "the 'silent majority' of elderly Americans who are independent and relatively autonomous are not featured, are not of interest and, if the literature is taken to reflect reality, hardly exist." A rapid scanning of titles of works on the elderly might give the impression that old age is inevitably a time of great difficulty, more so than any other period in the life span. It is a mute point however

---

2. D. Jerrome, SOCIAL BONDS IN LATER LIFE, AGING AND SOCIETY 497-503 (1986).

whether misrepresentation is better than no representation. According to Jerrome, research on the aging family and its social networks hardly exists at all in the literature of British gerontology.

Of all the social scientists working in gerontology, social anthropologists appear to have done the most to render the lives of elderly people comprehensible and interesting. More than ten years ago Hochschild's *The Unexpected Community* portrayed an old age sub-culture, describing the lives of elderly people living in apartments in the San Francisco Bay region. About the same time (1978), there was Myerhoff's *Number Our Days*, a moving account of both the rewards and the difficulties of living alone in old age. the elderly people whose lives were described in this book belonged to the Aliyah Center, the focal point of a Jewish community in Venice, California. More recently there is Clare Wenger's book, *The Supportive Network: Coping with Old Age*,[3] describing the everyday lives of elderly people living in rural North Wales. In Australia, Alice Day has described the lives of elderly people living in Melbourne in her book, *We Can Manage*.[4]

With the exception of the above works, however, and a few others like them, there appears to be a wide gap between what novelists, dramatists and poets are telling us about aging and what it is like, and what sociologists, geriatricians, statisticians and social psychologists are telling us.

As a result, there has been a call for a different kind of research. For example, in addition to the more easily ascertained facts
of aging, Wither and Hodges[5] note that we need research that "would contribute a more intimate understanding of the complex

3. G.C. Wenger, THE SUPPORTIVE NETWORK: COPING WITH OLD AGE, Allen & Unwin (London, 1984).

4. A.T. Day, *We Can Manage*, INSTITUTE OF FAMILY STUDIES MONOGRAPH NO. 5, Institute of Family Studies (Commonwealth of Australia: Melbourne, 1985).

5. A. Wither & I. Hodges, *Elderly People in View: A Bibliography of New Zealand Research 1972-85*, Health Services Research and Development Unit, Department of Health (Wellington, New Zealand, 1987).

reality elderly people experience."[6] Noting that New Zealand research to date has emphasized the use of structured question-naires, statistical surveys and clinical examinations, they advise that there is now a need "to complement and enrich these studies by including research methods which emphasize life history interviews, participant observation and other forms of intensive encounter with elderly people."[7] "In the past" they say, "the personal, subjective experiences of elderly people have made only a minimal showing in New Zealand research. Elderly people have not spoken in their own voices and often the researcher confines presentation of their ideas to tables and graphs, the human face becoming lost in the traditional stylistic requirements of a scientific report?"[8]

When looking over the breadth of research done with elderly people as subjects, especially the tables and graphs in which the human face has indeed become lost, one is left with the uneasy feeling that many of the elderly have been the subjects of various pieces of research simply by virtue of their powerlessness; an irony since so many researchers later report that the elderly should be given more power.

It is the norm for elderly people to live alone after the death of a spouse.[9] It is also clear that retaining as much control as possible over one's life, no matter what the setting, is seen by almost everyone as being of the highest priority.[10]

Our research was undertaken in the belief that elderly people themselves have both the right to make their needs known and the knowledge and expertise to do so. We wanted to find out if our ideas about what it is like to be old and living alone in the later part

---

6. *Id.* at 3.

7. *Id.*

8. *Id.* at 4.

9. A. Dale, M. Evandrou & S. Arber, *The Household Structure of the Elderly Population in Britain*, AGING AND SOCIETY 37 (1987).

10. E.J. Langer, THE PSYCHOLOGY OF CONTROL, Sage Publications (Beverly Hills, 1983).

of the twentieth century were in fact congruent with those who are actually doing it. Would a different perspective emerge if elderly people were given an open opportunity to express their views? Would some of our preconceptions about what is "good for" elderly people change if we listened carefully to what individuals actually say about their lives, their hopes and their fears?

In deciding which research methods to use, the over-riding consideration was the maintenance of the dignity and autonomy of the elderly people involved. In pursuit of this subject autonomy, several measures were taken. First, the method of inviting people to take part in the study was scrutinized carefully. We asked such questions as "What makes it difficult to say 'no' in these circumstances?" It had become apparent during previous studies that members of this age cohort feel that it is unmannerly to say no to any request to participate unless there is a clearly demonstrable reason why they should not, such as being out of town. So the method of asking was devised with care.

All subjects were asked about their willingness to take part by someone who was known to them personally and who was not connected in any way with the study. This was done by networking. When a subject had been interviewed he or she was asked if they knew anyone else who would be happy to do the interview. If they did, they were asked to make the first approach. They were able to say how they had found the experience of doing the interview themselves, and they were able to give a real opportunity to refuse by saying "Would that sort of thing appeal to you?" or "Shall I suggest your name as a possible person to interview?"

Another way of allowing the research to proceed with maximum independence for subjects was to invite elderly people themselves to be the interviewers. This proved to be a particularly felicitous idea. Three women, themselves in their seventies, were employed. Each brought with her a life time's experience in talking to people on topics requiring sensitivity and perceptiveness. All had been trained in reflective listening.

Third, the interviewers were asked to try to capture the spirit of what was being said. When it was suggested that they use tape recorders, they were emphatic in their unwillingness to do so, both from their own point of view, and from the expected adverse reaction of their subjects. These elderly interviewers said that people their age would not relax and speak freely if their voices were being recorded. The outcome of this decision was that interviewers wrote full notes during the interviews, notes that were available to the subject for perusal before the interviewer left if that was his or her wish. Interviewers added further details as soon as possible after leaving the subject's home.

The interviews were lengthy and quite taxing for both parties. Since being respectful and considerate were fundamental principles for all concerned, it was never assumed that simply because a person was elderly they would necessarily have a whole morning or afternoon to spare. And indeed, the interviewers had to wait two or three weeks sometimes before their elderly subjects could fit them in.

Finally, the selected interviewers had that added skill, the ability to show what Carl Rogers called "acceptance" or "unconditional positive regard."[11] They allowed the people to whom they were talking to speak their thoughts and feelings in an atmosphere of trust. Subjects were guaranteed anonymity, and, as we later saw, they did trust the interviewers with some very precious and personal information. Interviews were semi-structured and covered a wide range of topics. In addition, the elderly people were asked to say if any topic of importance to them had been left out. By listening to elderly people's own ideas, we hoped to gain further knowledge of both the advantages and the disadvantages of living alone. In addition, we were interested to know what makes for a satisfying old age, and whether anything further could be done by the community as a whole to ensure that elderly people were supported while they tackled the last of life's developmental tasks, namely that of looking back over life, coming to terms with what has happened and preparing to face its end.

The Subjects

The subjects were 40 "well" elderly people, each living alone in his or her own home. They all lived within a three kilometer radius of the Balmoral Post Office in Auckland city. Auckland, the

---

11. C.R. Rogers, CLIENT-CENTERED THERAPY, Houghton Mifflin (Boston, 1951).

largest city in New Zealand with a population of approximately 922,000 (just over one quarter of the total population of New Zealand), may be considered similar in many ways to other cities of comparable size in the western world. Population densities, however, are considerably lower since there is very little medium density, and no high density housing development. These 40 people form 1.3% of the total population aged 75 years and over in that area, and 2.6% of those 75 years old and older living alone. The high proportion of very elderly people (75 years old and older) living alone (47%) is comparable to other similar societies.[12]

For the purposes of this study, the definition of "well" was a pragmatic one. It meant, in effect, well enough to live alone without outside professional assistance. Many of the elderly people interviewed had some problems with their health, ranging from the comparatively minor to the quite serious, but none was sufficient to prevent their living alone independently.

Their ages ranged from 72 years to 94 years, the average age being 81. Almost all had already spent a number of years on their own, the average being 13 years. Nine of the subjects were male, this ratio again reflecting the proportion of elderly women living alone in the community. In New Zealand, again as in most similar countries, more than 94% of those people categorized as aged (over 65 years) live in the community and not in institutions.[13]

The subjects in this study lived in a variety of types of accommodations, representing the various options available in this country. Seventeen subjects (42.5%) continued to live in the family home. A further 11 subjects (27.5%) owned their own unit or flat. These would have been purchased from a developer or previous owner and be part of a group of three to ten units on a self-contained piece of land in a surrounding garden. Three subjects owned council units which are sold back to the local government authority on the death of the occupant, and three subjects rented state or council units. One person was in a state

12. Dale, *see supra* note 9; Wenger, *see supra* note 3.

13. Social Advisory Council, *The Extra Years: Some Implications for New Zealand Society of an Aging Population,* Office of the Minister of Social Welfare (Wellington, 1984).

rental house, and another was in a state house that she now owned. One person was in a rented bed-sitting room.

Since the emphasis in this study was on elderly people's views of their present situation, former occupations were not asked for in the original semi-structured questionnaire. It was assumed that a majority of the women in this age cohort would have been full-time mothers and housewives. It was true that the majority were; but there were more career women than expected. These were women who had either not married or had married later in life. Often in the course of the interviews, occupations, either of self or of spouse, were mentioned. These included dressmaker, book-keeper, shop assistant, forestry worker, shoe maker, nurse, tailor, carpenter, teacher, policeman, pharmacist and music teacher.

At one point in the interview, subjects were asked with whom they had lived immediately before they had started living alone. This information also helped to round out the picture of who these subjects were. As expected, the majority had been living with a spouse. Others had been living with a parent (four people), a son or daughter (three people), a sister (two people) a boarder (one person) or in an institution (one person).

Taking all the above information into consideration, the people interviewed can be considered to be representative of those living in an older part of suburban Auckland. In many respects, they can also be considered as representative of older New Zealanders as a whole. The fact that they live alone means that there are probably some differences between them and others who do not live alone. They may be more resilient and independent than contemporaries who live with others. On the other hand, they may rely more on the telephone and postal services to keep them in touch, and be more concerned about personal security than those who live with others. Their views cannot necessarily be taken as representative of older New Zealanders living in rural areas, nor can they be considered typical of our indigenous Maori people. Although Maori people currently comprise approximately 12% of the total population of New Zealand, reduced life expectancy in this group means that there is a far smaller proportion of Maori amongst the very old.[14] Older New Zealanders who belong to ethnic minority

---

14. Koopman-Boyden, *see supra* note 1.

groups from the Pacific Islands and South-East Asia are not represented here either.

The semi-structured questionnaire used in the interview was divided into four unequal parts. The first and last portions were brief, the first seeking the background details already described and the last comprising a visual analogue scale. The two middle sections of the questionnaire, which each consisted of several small sets of questions were on "health" and "the social environment" respectively. Questions were broad ranging and included several parts. The following is an example:

- Do you think some kind of exercise is an important part of keeping healthy for older people?
- Are you able to take any exercise?
- Would you be better off if you were able to?
- What sort of exercise do you recommend for elderly people?

In the section on "the social environment," there were questions on accommodation, pets, security, money and relationships with other people. Examples of these questions are:

- Do you like living here?
- If you could live wherever you liked, and with whoever you liked, where would that be? or
- What do you think is the ideal living arrangement for people in our situation?
- Is it more important to be near family or friends?

The material gathered from these questions was wide ranging, demonstrating a rich variety of attitudes and opinions. A number of common themes emerged, helping us build a picture of what it is like to be old and living alone at this time. More importantly, however, we found our elderly subjects' views were different, sometimes in subtle, and sometimes in not so subtle, ways to our own.

Health

Since keeping well appears to be a topic of great importance and wide interest among elderly people, this was tackled first, often even before the demographic data. It seemed to the elderly interviewers a legitimate and non-threatening way to begin the interview and set the style for the remainder of the questionnaire.

Another reason for asking this question at the beginning was its obvious face validity. These subjects by their very existence demonstrated a knowledge of how to live successfully into old age. Not only were they still alive when many of their contemporaries were not, but perhaps even more importantly, they were living entirely alone which in itself is evidence of independence.

Interviewers began with World Health Organizations standardized questions.[15] The first was "How do you feel about your health at present? Is it good, fairly good, fairly bad or bad?" The second was "If you compare your health with that of other people your age, is your own health better, about the same, worse or cannot say?"

Responses to these questions were very similar to those given by elderly people in other parts of the world, living in similar societies.[16] Almost all our respondents said their health was either good or fairly good (95%). More than two thirds of respondents said their health was better than other people the same age.

Before any more specific questions about health were asked, interviewers inquired what the subject felt were the most important things about keeping healthy for "people our age". As might be expected, there was a wide variety in both the number and content of replies, some people giving six or seven rules for healthy living and others suggesting only one.

The single most frequently mentioned category was food. Thirty-three subjects (82.5%) mentioned the importance of a healthy diet. Information about what exactly subjects considered to be a healthy diet was asked for in a subsequent question and views will be analyzed in that context. Although subjects had differing views on this topic, one woman's overall advice was,

---

15. G.G. Fillenbaum, *The Wellbeing of the Elderly: Approaches to Multidimensional Assessment*, WHO OFFSET PUBLICATION NO. 84, World Health Organization (Geneva, 1985).

16. *Active Health Report on Seniors: What We Think, What We Know, What We Do,* Minister of National Health and Welfare (Canada, 1989); G.O. Hagestad, *Able Elderly in the Family Context: Changes, Chances and Challenges*, 27 THE GERONTOLOGIST 4, 417-22 (1987).

132

"Remember your age and don't eat like a forty year old."

The next largest category concerned recommendations for mental health. Twenty-one subjects (52.5%) mentioned the value of keeping active and cheerful, staying interested in people and affairs and maintaining a good, positive outlook on life. Some gave more specific ideas on how to achieve these goals by recommending, for example, making an effort to keep contact with friends, keeping an open mind and being willing to learn. One said, "Don't dwell on little things."

The next most popular recommendation concerned physical exercise, mentioned by 18 subjects (45%). The most frequently offered advice was to keep mobile, especially by walking.

Other suggestions for healthy living included keeping to a routine (six people), going outdoors for fresh air and sunshine (six people) and getting sufficient rest and sleep (five people). Others mentioned the importance of having a craft or hobby (three people) and two the importance of a good doctor. One respondent summed up by saying, "Look after yourself as much as possible and just carry on."

The public perception of basic rules for healthy living appears to have changed very little over the years, at least in the type of culture referred to here, basically European in origin, and English-speaking. Today's young adults, when asked for their opinions in the future, may offer advice with more prohibitions in it (don't smoke, don't drink too much alcohol, guard against excessive exposure to sunlight), but the importance of good food, exercise and positive mental attitude are all likely to be basic to good health in their future too.

During the last few decades, population studies have indicated the importance of what are now termed behavioral factors in good health. Whereas in the past, from the political point of view, good medical care has been perhaps the major factor in policy decision-making, it now appears that ensuring adequate nutrition, encouraging physical activity, and discouraging excessive alcohol intake and tobacco smoking should receive an equal amount of attention from policy makers.

Other lifestyle factors which have already been described as important are loneliness, especially when combined with physical and intellectual inactivity[17] and motor vehicle accidents. The first was mentioned by some respondents, but the second not at all. It remains to be seen whether today's midlife and younger people will recognize these factors as important in maintaining good health in old age.

When subjects had offered their thoughts on keeping healthy generally, more specific information was sought on particular topics. Fortuitously, since so many respondents had already mentioned eating habits as being a most important part of staying healthy, more specific questions were first asked about food.

Our interviewers said "Some people think that diet is important" or "Diet seems to be important". "What do you think from your experience are the most important rules for healthy eating?"

The single most popular comment was about the importance of fresh vegetables (16 people, 40%), frequently followed by mention of fruit (9 people). Differences here may have been affected by the time of the year at which the survey was carried out, fruit being less available and more expensive during winter. Other specific foods mentioned as being both enjoyable and "good for you" were porridge, milk, fish and chicken. Twelve people mentioned the importance of having one main meal every day, consisting of meat or other protein as well as the vegetables.

The majority of comments however were more to do with the general rules for healthy eating. "Eat plain, healthy food" said eight people. "Have the meals regularly" said another seven. One subject said: "Have two good meals a day; don't get trapped into a little of this and a little of that."

A substantial minority did not wish to give any recommendations at all. Thirteen (32.5%) said they ate whatever they liked and enjoyed it. One man (86 years) said: "I was on a strict low fat diet, but I felt no better, so I might as well eat what I like."

Subjects were asked a number of other questions about healthy eating on issues such as whether or not they had noticed changes in methods of food preparation and cooking, changes in

---

17. A. Svanborg, G. Bergstrom & D. Mellstrom, EPIDEMIOLOGICAL STUDIES ON SOCIAL AND MEDICAL CONDITIONS OF THE ELDERLY, Regional Office for Europe, World Health Organization (Copenhagen, 1982).

personal views and habits so far as food was concerned, or changes in people's knowledge about healthy eating.

Overall, what appeared to the researchers as common-sense, middle-of-the-road views prevailed. There were some prohibitions, especially of "fancy foods" or "rubbish", these apparently referring to rich or fatty foods, including cakes or "takeaways" (fast foods). But overall subjects said they knew what was right for them and followed life-time habits based on a knowledge of good nutrition.

Exercise

There was a very high degree of consensus on this topic. Almost everybody agreed that some form of exercise is important, and 33 people said, "Walking is the best exercise for elderly people."

There was less consensus about how far one should walk to reap the beneficial effects. One subject walked literally "miles" several times per week. Another "walks to the letter box daily." As one subject said, "Walking according to ability is the thing."

Eleven subjects (27.5%) mentioned the importance of keeping active generally and noted that gardening and housework both require a degree of muscle exertion, for example stretching and bending, often using muscles not much used in walking.

Many additional activities were mentioned, ranging from sporting activities (e.g. bowls) to "eye exercises". Two people said they thought it was inappropriate to jog and one said, "Tennis and jogging only if *very* fit".

Smoking and Alcohol

These elderly people were no longer smokers, although almost half of them had been at earlier stages in their lives, especially during war-time. Only one admitted to having the occasional cigarette still, although the replies from three other subjects were equivocal.

Alcohol was much more acceptable. Thirty subjects (75%) said they had the "occasional drink" and many of these had drinks more frequently. Of those who did not, a number of reasons was given, including "it doesn't mix with my medication" and "it's meaningless alone." Two people said they were opposed to alcohol on principle. Of those that did drink, a wide range of favorites was mentioned, with sherry and wine topping the list.

Other Health Related Questions

Subjects were asked a number of other questions directly related to establishing health status and the use of health-related services. Some were again the standardized World Health Organization questions, used so that comparisons with other countries could be made accurately. In reply to the question "Do you suffer from any chronic illness or condition which makes it difficult for you to get about or do your work?" nine subjects gave an unqualified "no" and a further 19 subjects said "no, not really." Thus 70% of the people interviewed said they were hardly constricted at all by health problems. The other 30% mentioned disorders or difficulties that hindered them to a greater or lesser extent, but none seriously enough to warrant outside professional help beyond consultation.

The only response in the entire survey in which there was 100% unanimity was to the question "Can you get medical help whenever you need it?" All the subjects said "yes" and everyone had a reliable general practitioner. Half of the subjects went on to say, uninvited, how very helpful and kindly they found their general practitioners. In addition, some consulted with other members of the health professions (such as the chiropodist or pharmacist) but very few consulted with unorthodox practitioners.

Interviewers went with subjects to the medicine cupboard to see for themselves what medicines were in store and which were being taken on a regular basis. There was the expected range of anti-hypertensive, diuretic and anti-inflammatory drugs. Six subjects (15%) took no drugs of any kind.

Subjects were asked specifically about sleep problems. The question were "Do you ever have problems sleeping?" and "Do you take tablets to help you sleep?" Contrary to expectations, 29 subjects (72.5%) said they had no problems and never had any medication of any kind to help them sleep. Being awake at night was not considered to be a problem. One subject said "I do not expect to sleep all night." People mentioned a range of activities undertaken during the early hours of the morning, including reading, making cups of tea, and listening to and taking part in the radio talkback sessions.

Commentary on Health Findings

Improvements in health in any group of people are doubtless the result of both individual and group or government action. Maintenance of good health into old age could be attributed to a number of factors including good health promotion programs, sensible one-to-one advice from professionals and the wisdom to act upon it by individuals.

Elderly people hear and evaluate the same health promotion messages that beam out to all of us. In fact, there is some evidence to suggest that they do this more conscientiously than other sections of the community. Not only do they pay more attention to media presentations, but because they often have more time for and interest in such programs, they think more about the messages and where appropriate, apply them to themselves. For example, in New Zealand this summer there have been many messages about the necessity to protect the skin from too much exposure to the direct rays of the sun. Elderly people have appeared to be among the most conscientious in taking sensible precautions.

There does not appear, however, to be any reason why health promotion programs should be aimed specifically at the elderly, unless the message is one that concerns them alone. For example, advice on the prevention of accidents in the home might include a warning about the dangers for elderly people of having things stored in high cupboards. Since falls are one of the commonest reasons for admission to hospitals in this age group,[18] it could be argued that preventative measures should be implemented.

An example of a government initiated program which was more specifically targeted to the elderly was that which sought to reduce the use of night-time sedatives. In this case it was probably true

---

18. A.J. Campbell, M.J. Borrie & G.F. Spears, *Risk Factors for Falls in a Community Based Prospective Study for People 70 Years and Over*, 44 JOURNAL OF GERONTOLOGY 112 (1989).

that elderly people in New Zealand, more than any other age-group tended to be the over-users[19]. Re-education appears to have been accomplished through general practitioners. It is they who were first alerted to the excessive prescribing of sedative drugs. They then took it upon themselves to point out to elderly people that it was normal to have periods of wakefulness during the night, and to suggest creative ways of dealing with this. They also assisted long time users in modifying their habits by forewarning them of the side effects they would suffer temporarily when decreasing dosages.

Apart from a few age-specific topics such as this, however, one could argue that an elderly person who has kept him or herself fit and healthy for 80 years has earned the right to make all the decisions about his or her lifestyle. This right would be promoted on the grounds that such a person has already demonstrated a good working knowledge of what to do to stay healthy. One might go further and argue that if (as seems likely) almost every country will need to begin rationing medical technology and if that technology is rationed for people over the age of 80, then the least society could do in return is to be much more liberal about what constitutes acceptable behavior on the part of these same elderly people. Smoking, drinking, eating too many or unhealthy foods, or sitting in the sun would not then be the focus of disapproval in the same way as they currently are for the rest of us.

In New Zealand, where hospitalization and pharmaceutical drugs are largely free, there are already some expensive medicines and diagnostic procedures which are no longer available to those over the age of 60 years. As private insurance companies have long ago made plain, care of the elderly chronically ill is not economical. Others have pointed out that as much as 80% of the health budget is spent on those in the last twelve months of life. Few would argue that these months are not an important and legitimate extension of life for a young person. But what real difference does it make whether one dies at 85 years or 86 years? Clearly there are very complex ethical issues concerning equity in

---

19. J. Reinken, M. Sparrow & A.J. Campbell, *The Giving and Taking of Psychotropic Drugs in New Zealand*, 95 NEW ZEALAND MEDICAL JOURNAL 489-92 (1982).

the allocation of health resources, and much of the debate is already centered on the rights and needs of the elderly.

Would it be possible to take too much time and care looking after oneself? Surely one has earned the right to do a little risk-taking with one's health by the age of 80? Some would say there is something rather admirable about the death-defying recklessness of the 80 year old smoker, sunbather, sports-person or traveler.

Whether or not the idea of risk-taking elderly people presents an attractive picture to the average, reader however, is irrelevant to the central point. The questions is, has an elderly person earned the legitimate right to adopt the kind of lifestyle, healthy or not, that he or she would prefer? One could argue that recklessness in a parent is unfair to the child, or that recklessness in a child would ruin a potentially fruitful life, but recklessness in an elderly person? Why not?

The Physical Environment

When asked about the environment in which they lived, 90% of the subjects said they were very satisfied with their living arrangements. Most people said things like "I just love it here" or "This place is perfect for my needs" or "I don't want to move ever again." These comments were made whether people were living in the same family home they had lived in for 40 or 50 years, or in a flat, a cottage or a unit. Each had his or her own reasons for wanting to stay there. An 85 year old woman said:

> "These council cottages are marvelous. You buy them then sell them back to the Council again so your family has no worries. There's a nice crowd here. We do anything for each other. I never want to move; I'd like to slip off here, in my bed, tucked up and in my sleep."

A speaker, (82 years) for the alternative viewpoint, that of staying on in the family home, said, "I'd hate to have to move. I *couldn't* move from here. I think of all the people who've sat round this table - the talking and laughing. I sleep in the same double bed - one side one week, one side the other - then change the sheets every two weeks . . . ."

A woman (94 years) who shifted into a flat said: "I paid $500 extra to have the front flat. I see everybody. I don't want to go to a home (old people's residence) *ever*. I hope I can stay here till I die - and I'm ready any time. Lots of people pop in."

Although these people's views represented by far the majority, not everyone was satisfied. Four respondents were either doubtful about or unhappy with their living arrangements. Two were considering whether or not they should move, and both had their names down on waiting lists for residential villages. For these two subjects there was doubt about whether they could continue the upkeep on house and garden, yet they felt deeply unhappy about the idea of having to shift out of a long held family home.

A lady of 88 years, who maintained her house and garden almost unaided said: "I've lived here 62 years - all my married life. I can't bear to leave it as long as I can manage."

These responses, both the satisfactions and the dissatisfactions, as well as the reasons given for them, correspond closely to those given by Ramian[20] in a study of the housing needs of the elderly in Denmark. The results of these investigations clearly indicated that continuity, independence and family and neighborhood considerations were the most important.

In another study which considered only 70-96 year old women living alone, Grant & O'Connor[21] found that there was considerable pressure to maintain the house and garden to a standard that had been set when the husband was still alive. When asked to be more specific about this pressure, some of the elderly women subjects said they felt guilty about occupying a three bedroom family home on their own when younger people with families had inadequate accommodation. The researchers had the impression that, for these elderly women, their ability to maintain the house and garden - either by paying for help or by struggling on alone - was a measure of their right to stay there. "But they do find the continual work of running a house tiring, and we think they may use this energy at the expense of other things such as joining a

---

20. K. Ramian, *The Needs for Housing of the Elderly*, DANISH MEDICAL BULLETIN 119-21 (1982).

21. V.J. Grant & K.C. O'Connor, *The Informal Social Support Network Among Well Elderly Women*, Unpublished Paper for the Medical Research Council (Auckland, New Zealand, 1988).

local community group."[22]

It was also noted that it was rare that physical help (such as housework, house or ground maintenance) was given by members of the family, even although family members were in daily telephone contact and assumed the major supportive role in caring for these elderly people.

As mentioned in the introduction to this report, subjects' accommodation arrangements covered a wide range of possibilities. Overall, this seems to be one of the advantages of living in a stable and comparatively well off society such as this one. Individuals for the most part have a range of choices about where they can live, and with whom. People can choose to live in the kind of environment that suits them best. The real difficulties arise when it comes to making a decision about whether or not to stay on in a stand-alone house and garden, with all its inherent maintenance problems on the one hand, and its strong emotional associations on the other, or whether to move to a smaller dwelling where privacy or independence may be compromised, but maintenance and upkeep problems are largely taken care of.

A society which agrees in principle that elderly people should have the same right as any other member of society to choose where and with whom they should live will probably discourage any pressure to influence the decisions of its elderly citizens to move from long held family homes. On the other hand, unless alternative accommodations are available to people in every district, choices will be limited in the opposite direction. Economic factors may also assume some importance when it comes to exchanging an older but larger home for a smaller, newer one.

Feeling Safe

Another aspect of living alone in the community is that of feeling secure from harm in one's own environment. From time to time there is a frightening story in the news media illustrating the vulnerability of elderly people living alone. We asked our subjects "Do you feel safe, living alone as you do?" Thirty-one subjects (77.5%) said "yes," but qualified this remark by saying "I've

---

22. *Id.*

learned to live with it," or, "You just have to get on with it." There appeared to be a kind of resignation with a not-altogether-satisfactory situation.

Their fears were not unfounded. Six subjects (15%) had been burgled or had had some other scary incident in the last couple of years. Two had had two day-time burglaries each. One had had a break-in, but nothing had been stolen. One had had a drunk male caller late at night. To add to the fearfulness, two further subjects had had neighbors burgled in the recent past. One subject told the interviewer, "There've been three burglaries in our street this week."

Nine subjects said "no," they did not feel safe, and of these six had been burgled. One said: "I was so upset after the burglary, I considered shifting (moving)." Another said, "I get frightened of noises in the night."

Two subjects said how much they still missed their husbands when it came to feeling safe. And one mentioned that she was much less composed when her neighbors were away.

Subjects tackled the problem of security in a number of ways. Apart from security doors, safety chains and burglar alarms, subjects most frequently mentioned the role of neighbors. Eleven subjects said they felt safe because they knew their neighbors would be with them instantly if there were trouble. A woman of 80 said: "Since my day-time burglary, I'm apprehensive when I come in during the day. I don't worry at night so much - I've got good locks on the doors. The community policeman says nothing will stop a determined burglar though."

Only seven subjects (17.5%) said they did not worry at all and took no special precautions. One of these said, "Too much talk creates anxiety."

Elderly people, like everyone else have the right to protection from harm, both to themselves and their property. And in this country, elderly people are probably exposed to fewer unpleasant or frightening situations than their counterparts in some other countries. Nevertheless, from time to time a very unpleasant assault on an elderly person is reported in the media, and this adds to the stress for all. It could be argued that everything possible should be done to ensure security, and that after that it is perhaps less stressful if not too much emphasis is put on the problem.

Money

One of the most surprising findings of this, or indeed of any of the studies we have done on elderly people, was the response to the questions about money. The original question was worded very carefully thus, "I suppose we'd all like more money than we've got? If you had a bit more, what would you do with it?"

An amazing 32 subjects (80%) said, "No, thank-you, I don't want any more money." Thirteen subjects (32.5%) said, "If I had more than I've got, I'd just give it to my grandchildren (or children, or favorite charitable organization)." A typical response was: "I manage quite good on the pension. I budget - always have done and my daughters do the same. Well, I don't know what I would do with any more at my age - share it with the grandchildren I suppose."

This type of response was not confined to people who may have had plenty of money. The quotation above is from a woman who pays a small rent for a council flat - and to qualify for such a flat a person must have no assets. Of the five people paying rent, three said they did not want any more money.

Of those that would like some more money (eight subjects), their wants were as follows: help with the rent (two subjects), help with the electricity bill, home maintenance, a new stove, curtains, a new T.V., a larger unit (this from a person in a bed-sitting room), and an allowance for toll calls to family members in America (all one subject each).

The general theme of subjects' responses in this area was that what they had was adequate for their needs. In New Zealand, there is a Guaranteed Retirement Income (formerly National Superannuation) which everyone receives, which is not means tested, which is indexed to inflation and is generous by world standards.

Where an elderly person owns a mortgage free property or lives in a low rent cottage or unit, this income proves adequate for most needs. Many elderly people have in addition to the Guaranteed Retirement Income private superannuation or work pensions. The income from these provides the extra needed to run a car or to employ people to help with the maintenance of house and grounds.

The extent to which these subjects represent others in this age group assumes new importance when considering our subjects' responses to the questions about money. We judged that almost a quarter had no income other than the government one. They could have been reluctant to admit financial hardship. On the other hand, our interviewers were expecting to have to read between the lines, or reinterpret brave statements about "managing." Instead, they heard forthright replies and no apparent ambivalence.

If a large proportion of elderly people say they do not want any more money and that what they have is adequate for their needs, it may be of interest to look at how people under the age of 80 would spend additional money. A good indication of what people in other age groups would do with extra money might be gained by a study of the things that are offered as prizes in the ubiquitous commercial product competitions. In New Zealand, overseas travel with accommodation costs and spending money added, and expensive new cars, probably together form the most popular prizes in the top of the range competitions. After this come specialty holidays within New Zealand (such as a week skiing in Queenstown) and state of the art technology in the form of personal computers, video-recorders and movie cameras.

People in their 60's and 70's (the young old) often have the time, energy, health and technical skill to make good use of many of the above prizes. For those over the age of 80 however, these and other "luxury" items tend to have less appeal. This, coupled with the adequate government income, may explain in part the elderly subjects' lack of interest in having more money.

At best however it is a partial explanation. Developmental psychologists have shown how each stage in the lifespan brings with it a number of developmental tasks. According to Erikson's widely known and accepted theory of human development,[23] the last stage in the life cycle requires that the individual reintegrate, in an age-appropriate way, all the earlier psychosocial themes. In addition, each individual endeavors to resolve the last of the life tasks, which Erikson describes as existential integrity, or integra-

---

23. E.H. Erikson, J.M. Erikson & H.Q. Kivnick, VITAL INVOLVEMENT IN OLD AGE, W.W. Norton (New York, 1986).

144

tion of the self.[24] It is possible that this integrating process, so different from the generativity which precedes it, requires a different attitude to life as a whole. In the search for wisdom, the acquisition of material goods is no longer the marker of success that it may have been in earlier years.

Social Contacts

Subjects were asked several questions about the extent to which they were able to get out and about. The purpose of these questions was not only to gain an idea of mobility, but also to establish the existence of some basis for contacts with others.

Subjects were asked "Do you get out and about much?"; "How far are you able to go?" and "Do you experience difficulties that mean you can't go as far as you'd like?" We wanted to know if these elderly people found it difficult to do their own shopping, visit friends and relatives, or take part in other social events which required leaving the house.

Thirty-three subjects (82.5%) said that they go out everyday or nearly every day. They added that they get out and about "a lot" or "as much as I want to."

Seven subjects mentioned difficulties in getting out and about as much as they would like. Five of these gave reasons associated with failing health or eyesight. Five subjects also mentioned the number of friends now unable through disability or death to offer rides or accompany them as much as they had done in the past. A woman of 88 years said:

> "It's nice to get taken (to church and to her club), but there are not many of us oldies left now. I've lost a lot of my friends from around here. I get very lonely. Yes, I would like more outings, but I can't go alone and I can't be dependent on other people all the time."

In contrast to this woman, others were totally independent when it came to mobility. A man of 82 years of age said:

> "I go out nearly every day - often into town. You make contacts that way - see someone you know - sometimes people who need help. I met

---

24. *Id.*

a Vietnamese family on the bus. They spoke little English and needed help."

Fifteen subjects (37.5%) were still able to drive their own cars. The people who did so valued the additional independence this gave them, but were careful to add that there were some conditions under which they were not prepared to drive. Most were not comfortable with motorway driving. One said "not in the country," for fear of breaking down a long way from home. Others said "not at night" and "not in the rain," mainly because they said they did not see well enough in these conditions. Two said that difficulties in parking might soon lead them to begin using public transport for trips into town.

The next largest and most independent group (14 subjects - 35%) used public transport all the time. An additional eight subjects mentioned using public transport for long distance and international travel. Three more said they went on outings in the minibuses with their clubs.

Those who were late comers to public transport, having recently had to give up driving themselves, had the most difficulty in adjusting to the demands of traveling by bus. One subject said: "It's hard getting on; worse getting off."

Eleven subjects said they were largely dependent on family and friends to drive them were they wanted to go. Only four subjects made use of taxis and then only very occasionally.

Because of low densities, people living in Auckland are probably more dependent on private transport than citizens in other parts of the world. Low population densities also mean that there are fewer mobile services and street vendors. In New Zealand, the loss of the corner store has been both more recent and more dramatic than in some other countries. A small number of elderly people live near enough to walk to the supermarket, bank, church or post office. Some live near a bus route and make the transition from private to public transport, albeit with difficulty. For the rest however, elderly people living alone in the suburbs become totally dependent on others for transport once they lose the ability to drive.

Being dependent on others for something as basic as access to food can change an elderly person's perception of him or herself dramatically. As a consequence of something as comparatively minor as inadequate long distance vision, a person's entire self image can be changed over night. Instead of being the person who helps others and is totally independent, one is now the person who has to be helped and is dependent on others. It is this which accounts for the anguish which often accompanies the loss of the driver's license, particularly when the driver is the second person in the partnership to lose a license or when the driver is an elderly person living alone.

There can be little doubt that some elderly people need more and better transport options than they currently have. If one were living in an ideal world, some inexpensive call-up taxi service could well help solve the problems. Such a service however, would be out of the question in the current economic climate in this country.

The extent to which elderly people might claim to have a right to such transport is another interesting question. Many gerontologists, economists and politicians now agree that elderly people should have the right to remain independently in the community as long as they wish. And most countries of similar culture now see it as sociologically and psychologically beneficial that they should do so. Should governments, therefore, be involved in, or responsible for, a workable, convenient transport facility for their elderly citizens? Whatever the answer to this question, the need remains, and as Barker and Bury comment, "We look for the development of enabling rather than helping structures."[25]

The Telephone

It became clear from our subjects' responses that a very important way of maintaining an active and meaningful role in society is by means of the telephone. The questions we asked were, "Do you have a telephone?" and "Is it a nuisance?"

They were framed in this seemingly odd way because, in the past, we have noticed that unless questions about the telephone are very carefully worded, they can cause considerable distress. For example, some elderly people find it painful to be asked how

---

25. J. Barker & M. Bury, MOBILITY AND THE ELDERLY: A COMMUNITY CHALLENGE, AN AGING POPULATION, V. Carver & P. Liddiard (eds.), Open University (Sevenoaks, Kent, 1978).

often people phone them because they receive many fewer calls than they would like. So in this case, we tried very hard to protect people from this embarrassment and perhaps, in so doing, we leaned a little too far the other way. In suggesting that the telephone could possibly be a nuisance, we may have pushed replies into being more assertive in the opposite direction. Nevertheless, our results show that the telephone is a matter of great importance to elderly people living alone in New Zealand.

Only one person did not have a telephone. The rest (97.5%) did. Not only did they have telephones but they were emphatic about the necessity for having one. Thirteen subjects said "I couldn't be without it," or words to that effect. Five subjects said it was "most essential" or "vital." One person even said she "couldn't **live** without it." The overall opinion, strongly held, was that no elderly person should be without a phone. In this there may be a difference between New Zealand and other similar countries. One explanation for the difference would be New Zealand's lower population density. Most of these elderly people lived in stand-alone units or homes, surrounded by gardens. Neighbors were not simply upstairs, or on the other side of the wall. There is more need to be able to alert others by means of the telephone in times of emergency, where simply banging on the floor or calling down the stairs is not an option. Six subjects said they "feel safe because of the telephone."

Eleven subjects also pointed out that "it keeps you in touch with the outside world." It was in expanding on this point that several people added further practical information. In discussing the important role that the telephone has in their lives, some mentioned the difficulty of reaching the phone before it stopped ringing, and the disappointment and frustration this could bring. In order to prevent this situation arising, many said they have "lots of jack-points." Several people had arranged for the phone to ring outside so they could hear it in the workshop or garden. One subject had the ring amplified to overcome her hard-of-hearing problem.

Not only does the telephone appear to serve as the basis of security for those living alone, it also appears to serve as a means of keeping in touch with the outside world. In addition, it clearly has an important role in helping to maintain basic social support in communities where even a close neighbor can be too far away to walk, especially after dark.

"I love it like a friend," said one lady. "It was awful when it was out of order," said another. One subject, a man of 74 years said, "Yes, we and other friends make many calls to each other - we would be ruined if the powers that be brought in a law that made us pay for each call."

Unlike most countries of the world, where each telephone call must be paid for, domestic users in New Zealand pay a flat rate rental and all local calls are free. This is a matter of great importance to elderly people and any attempt to bring in charges for local calls, especially timed charges, would meet with fierce resistance by elderly people's representative groups. It was clear from our subjects' emphatic responses that the telephone and its free availability were matters of even greater importance than we had thought. In listening carefully to the reasons given it became clearer why it had such importance.

One of the most consistent findings in the research on the problems of maintaining elderly people in the community is that of the availability of social support networks.[26] If elderly people are to remain in the community, living alone and independently for as long as possible, it must be possible for them to have quick access to the human contacts which we all depend on for the maintenance and stability of mental health. These elderly people were also aware of this need and some were sensitive and courageous enough to say so. A man, 84 years said: "I noticed old friends tended to ring at dinner time - at the close of day, and I wondered if this is a time of loneliness. I tend to get a bit depressed as daylight fades - and I'm conscious of the shortening days too."

Other elderly subjects, in speaking of some of the more personal matters they did not wish recorded, mentioned how important it was to be able to pick up the phone and make immediate contact with a family member or friend whenever they needed to.

At the end of the conversation about telephones, some people raised the subject of the disadvantages of having one. Three people mentioned scary or threatening phone calls. They found

---

26. Wenger, *see supra* note 3.

these very hard to cope with. Two people mentioned the expense of long distance phone calls, saying that they found it harder to keep in touch with sons or daughters in far away places when every moment had to be paid for.

Two people said, "The only problem is when it doesn't ring," re-iterating what some of our subjects in earlier studies had said, that if no one rings all day, elderly people sometimes feel that is the reason it was not such a good day.

In summary, for these New Zealand subjects, the telephone represents a vital part of their everyday lives. They value the fact that it provides a fast and convenient link with the outside world, for reasons of safety, social contact and social support. It appears to be one of the key components in maintaining autonomy, in that with a telephone, elderly people may remain in their own homes and continue to have independence at the same time as being secure and feeling safe and in touch.

Important Relationships

Finally in this section on social contacts with others we asked about interpersonal relationships. In an effort to avoid hurtfulness and to assume nothing, we asked, "Are relationships with other people important to you?" and if so, "Could you say who are the most important people in your life now?" All but one respondent said that relationships were important, and most named family members as the most important people in their lives. As other researchers have found, we noted that daughters play the predominant role.

In this study, by far the largest group of specific people mentioned were daughters. Twelve people (30%) mentioned a daughter or daughters as being the most important people in their lives. Only one person had a daughter but did not mention her first, and this person was male. Otherwise, daughters appeared to be special to all who had them. One subject said, "I do miss my daughter. I always have to make the first move with my daughter-in-law."

Taken altogether, family members formed the largest group of "people important in my life now." Twenty-five respondents (62.5%) mentioned family first. This group includes those who said, "my family is the most important" without specifying any one member in particular. Of special interest was the fact that even though families were mentioned first, they were followed very closely by friends, especially friends of many years. The general view of those who put their families first was:

> "My sons and their families are the very most important to me. But my longstanding friends are also very important - trouble is so many of them are dead now. They were the ones that gave me emotional support."

Eight subjects, who either had no relatives, or whose relatives lived in other countries, said that their friends were the most important to them. Said one lady, whose husband, sister and son had all pre-deceased her, "I have several wonderful friends. The grandchildren are very lovely, but they are too far away."

Of those who said families were most important, almost all mentioned friends as a very close second. The most frequent additional comment, however, was that whereas contemporaries used to provide good support, they could no longer be counted on in this age group. One person said, "I'm losing all my friends. They're dying. One died last week."

It was clear from the remarks made by a number of people, that many considered friends to have a special place in their lives that younger family members could not fill. A woman of 87 years spoke of her family, saying, "They are all lovely (many daughters, grandchildren and great-grandchildren). I can't imagine life without them." Her lounge was full of photos that bore witness to her comments. She said they were always in touch with one another and that she went to stay with one or the other at weekends. In spite of all this she said, "I am lonely," and spoke wistfully of many former friends, all of whom had died.

A few of our respondents had neither family nor friends. One person who had "never had a family you could count on" and whose friends had pre-deceased her said, "Nobody is terribly important to me now."

In contrast to this, another person who had very few contacts left said, "Relationships are very important . . . I don't let myself get down . . . I can go to the shops and the butcher says 'Hi!, how are you?' and I come back and make myself a cup of tea and feel better."

Several respondents mentioned how important their good neighbors were to them. They valued them for the security they gave as well as friendship and help in times of difficulty. Frequently the most helpful neighbors were themselves elderly.

For the most part elderly people living alone appear to work hard at maintaining links with their families, one another and the wider community. It seems appropriate to label such activity as work, given the efforts that must be made, and the determination and sensitivity with which such contracts are sustained. As Rathbone and McCuen[27] have pointed out, the pressures upon elderly people that push them in the direction of isolation are both pervasive and powerful. Psychological, social, economic and environmental factors may combine to engulf an elderly person living alone. A lot of skill goes into mitigating their effects.

Since Zena Blau's pioneering work, social relationships in old age have been regarded as very important. It was Blau[28] who first described the role of contemporaries in old age and the sustenance that such friendships provide. Successful aging appears to include a willingness and an ability to undertake a kind of on-going life review, as though integrating all one's past experiences into a rounded, meaningful whole. Such work is often facilitated by being able to describe and compare one's earlier experiences and impressions with those who lived through similar historical, political and social events. Not only do one's contemporaries share the overall perspective, but they are not critical of individual interpretations of events as younger family members may be.

Contemporaries may affirm each other's views of what it used to be like to live under specific conditions, such as wartime or depression. The interchange can verify and authenticate the memories of each in a way that would be scarcely possible for different generations. Blau's observations about the value of reminiscence and the importance of contemporaries in old age have

27. E. Rathbone-McCuan & J. Hashimi, ISOLATED ELDERS, Aspen Publications (Roackville, Maryland, 1982).

28. Z.S. Blau, OLD AGE IN A CHANGING SOCIETY, New Viewpoints (New York, 1973).

since been confirmed in many other research settings.

Family members probably provide feedback of a different kind, re-living the same memories from a different perspective, and saying with hindsight, what various family events meant for them, both at the time, and as adults later.

Ways in Which Elderly People Support Others in the Community

When so much emphasis is put on what may be done to help the elderly, we were determined to follow Clare Wenger's lead and to ensure there was an opportunity given to mention the help that elderly people themselves give others. We hesitated to ask outright for a number of reasons. First, our subjects were the old old, whose energy one might think would be totally used up in maintaining their own independence. Second, these elderly people are members of a cohort that find it difficult to acknowledge the good they do, for fear of sounding conceited. And third, there is little acknowledgement of expressive support as opposed to instrumental support given, even when these two are both appreciated when the elderly person is the receiver.[29]

To help circumvent the difficulty people have in describing their own helpfulness, the first question in this section of the interview was whether the elderly people knew any other people in their age group who were helpful to others. We later asked if any of their relatives, friends or neighbors looked to them for support. As expected there was a certain reluctance to talk at any length about the contributions made by subjects themselves. Even so we were surprised at the extent to which these very elderly people contribute to the community in which they live.

We compiled an extensive list of all the things that people aged about 80 years (friends and acquaintances of our subjects) are doing to help others. The first, perhaps most obvious group of things is that to do with the skills these elderly people have acquired over their life times.

Elderly people cook for those in need, taking food to neighbors and friends who are ill or otherwise incapacitated. They also take

---

29. Wenger, *see supra* note 3.

gifts of fresh vegetables or flowers that they themselves have nurtured in home gardens. They also give gifts of craft work, often being responsible, for example, for the extended family's wardrobe of handknits. The older men were often able to provide carpentry, plumbing or electrical skills to the advantage of neighbors, family and friends. One of our subjects was still assisting elderly clients with their tax returns.

For those still able to drive a car, the range of possibilities was further increased. As already mentioned, lack of transport may become a serious problem for people in old age. Foreseeing this, it appears that it is the elderly themselves who are supporting those who can no longer drive. They are the ones who provide the transport when elderly friends and neighbors need to go to a specialist doctor on the other side of town. They are the ones who take elderly friends to see contemporaries who are ill or too frail to get out and about. They take groups of people to visit others in rest homes. One of our respondents even took others to continue his prison visiting.

Sustaining those who are temporarily unable to cope is another area of contribution. Even the very old people in our survey were able to help in a number of important ways when elderly neighbors fell ill. In addition to sitting with them and helping in the preparation of food, these good neighbors collect milk, newspaper and mail for those unable to do it, attend to the laundry, provide emotional support and sometimes even help care for the children.

In the wider neighborhood, it is often the oldest members of the group who appear to form its core, possibly because they are there during the day when other people are at work or at school. In this setting, elderly neighbors bring in the washing, keep an eye on property and pets and generally act as a clearing house for messages, fielding unexpected callers and/or helping with work phone numbers in an emergency. Sometimes it is the fact that an elderly neighbor has noticed that the blinds are still down when they would normally be up that alerts the community to inquire if all is well.

Letter writing can also be a way of contributing to the community as a whole. Not only is it a means of keeping in touch with more distant friends, it is also a means of offering comfort and support at difficult times. Often it is an elderly person's letter which brings most comfort when a family is bereaved. In addition to these personal letters, the more public letters to the newspaper provide a means by which even the very old can and do stay politically influential. When, for example, pressure needs to be put on the local council or government agency to improve conditions in the neighborhood, it is often elderly letter writers who make a measurable impact.

The most frequently mentioned and perhaps the single most important of supportive acts available to even the very frail elderly is to telephone a person in time of need. More than a third of our subjects mentioned this. In this way elderly people express their sympathy and give emotional support, particularly to one another. Such contacts are probably also important in that the knowledge gained, when not confidential, can be passed on to others who can then give other kinds of help.

Several people in our survey mentioned that they had elderly friends "who would do anything for anybody." A woman of 78 years said, "Most of my friends my own age are very caring of other people's welfare. When friends, relatives or neighbors are sick, they try to help practically with meals, washing and emotional support."

When prompted by the interviewer, who already had some idea of this person's contributions, a woman of 86 years said:

> "Oh, yes. I'm the message girl around here. I collect letters and milk for D . . . . Yes, and distribute the local paper to everyone (14 flats). The grandchildren love to stay in the holidays . . . . Of course I call on any neighbors who are sick. I was visiting a sick neighbor and had to call the ambulance, but he died before it arrived . . . . Well, if it's wet or windy I bring D's washing in . . . ."

An 82 year old woman said, "A day when there isn't anything I can do for anyone seems a wasted day." This lady also said, "I try to keep a watch out for the under-dog. Don't know if I'm any good though. There is this matter of *wanting* to help and *being* able to."

This same lady drives for meals-on-wheels, transports frail elderly people to the Day Center and visits elderly people in rest homes.

Only two people in our survey felt unable to support others in any way. They felt they needed every bit of their resources to enable them to stay independent. One said "I keep myself to myself."

One person, who was herself helpful, pointed out the difficulties that she felt some elderly people had in sustaining others. She had regular contact with a lady who complained a lot.

> "I feel I can only cope with her once a fortnight. Another friend and I try to jolly her along. But too much of her pulls me down in spirits. I feel I can't afford the good spirits to visit too many sad cases. I just have to be a bit economical. There's no one at home to off-load to."

Since the 1950s there have been innumerable studies documenting attitudes towards old age in general, and towards elderly people in particular. Researchers have found that negative attitudes towards aging commence very early in life and are remarkably consistent. Elderly people have themselves been shown to hold negative stereotypes about themselves and their contemporaries. This negative stereotype includes the use of words such as "useless," "inadequate" and "dependent" in descriptions of elderly people as a group.

The studies reported here would seem to give the lie to any real basis for such stereotypes. The people we interviewed are representative of all but a very few of the older groups of people in our society. Altogether they represent more than 80% of elderly people over the age of 80 years living in New Zealand at the present time.

The negative and false stereotype may continue to exist for a number of reasons. One may be because so much of what is reported about elderly people in the media is problem-centered and largely concerns the 6% of that age group who live in institutions of one kind or another. It is arguable whether even the elderly people living in institutions deserve to be labeled as "useless," or "inadequate" given the active role so many of them play in supporting others. But to label the active, independent elderly in the suburbs thus is only to express gross ignorance.

As mentioned earlier, there is little evidence to support any increased homogeneity in old age, except that very old people may share a knowledge of how to maintain healthy attitudes. Among the young old there may even be less homogeneity than there is at younger ages. Yet the negative stereotype remains strong. Of all the needs and rights that elderly people might legitimately claim, surely the right to be free of negative stereotyping would be one of the strongest. In this, societies like ours still have a long way to go.

Life as a Whole

At the conclusion of our lengthy interviews, subjects were invited to sum up their feelings about their lives so far. This is not at all the sort of question that can be asked of people except, we think, in the context of a comprehensive and wide-ranging discussion about all the other things that also matter. In every instance however, our elderly interviewers were able to bring the visit to a close in an appropriate manner by inviting the person they were interviewing to say something about their lives as a whole.

When planning the interview, we thought that one of the best ways of doing this would be to provide a visual analogue scale. This consists of a line of known length being presented to the subject. Each end of the line represents an extreme view. In this case, the ends of the line were labeled "very satisfied with life as a whole" and "not at all satisfied with life as a whole." Subjects were asked to make a mark across the line at a point which they thought would represent their feelings about this question. Later the line was measured and a score given according to where the line was marked. This method of measuring an emotional attribute or feeling is used quite frequently in research in psychology and has been validated in a number of different contexts. We thought it would prove simple and interesting for our subjects.

In this we were quite wrong. Instead of spontaneously giving their first reaction and marking the line within a few seconds, some subjects took a long time to consider their feelings on this matter. One subject pondered for 45 minutes before feeling able to make her mark. Some might argue that this lack of spontaneity invalidated the responses. On the other hand, when one is asked to evaluate one's life, maybe thoughtfulness as well as feelings should play a part.

Ten subjects (25%) marked the line at the extreme positive end and a further ten subjects marked it so close to the end that their scores were recorded as 90% or 95% satisfied with life as a whole. Three subjects scored 40%, 45% and 55% respectively at the other extreme. All the remaining subjects were 65% satisfied or more.

Subjects were also asked, "Are there any ways in which you would have liked your life to be different?" In response to this question almost all subjects expressed regrets about some aspects of their lives.

The regrets were mainly for things not done, or for things not done at the right time. A number of people spoke of marriage and children. "Funny, I've been thinking about that lately," said one lady of 82 years. "I can't say I *would* have re-married . . . ."

One subject regretted having had no children. Another wished she had had more children. Another said, "Perhaps I would have been happier if I'd married earlier." Still another said, "I wish I'd developed some cultural skills. . . . I would like to have achieved excellence in some sphere. . . ." A 79 year old woman said, "Wish I'd learned to drive a car" and a 91 year old man said, "Should have written poetry."

In all, eight subjects (20%) wished they had had further education or training; a further two wished they had made more use of their skills.

In speaking about their lives, these elderly people were almost invariably thoughtful, and spoke in a way that indicated this was not the first time they had thought about these things. Many valued the opportunity to speak about them on this occasion. It was good that so many of the elderly subjects told the interviewers that they had enjoyed the interview, a response that confirmed the skills and empathic attitudes of those who carried out the research.

A greater value however, lies in the fact that everyone who has yet to become old may learn from these elderly people. It was demonstrated over and over again what a privilege it is to talk to a thoughtful elderly person. Because people at this particular stage of life are frequently engaged in life review, and in thinking about what is now of importance to them, those who are fortunate enough to hear them are given a new measure by which to make some of their own life decisions.

Not only are they given a new perspective on their own lives, they are also often given a glimpse of what it might be like to be old which is very far from the old age stereotype. A woman of 85 years said, "I have joyful feelings of well-being and vigour and forget my age."

Summary

As interest grows in the question, "What is it like to be old?," elderly people more and more become the focus of research. This chapter is based on studies of the elderly which had as their primary goal the creation of an opportunity for elderly people to give their own views. The autonomy of the participants was paramount.

This autonomy was in part guaranteed by asking elderly people to be the interviewers. They talked to 40 people, average age 81 years, all living independently and alone in a low to middle-class Auckland suburb. These elderly people showed, by their very existence as well as by their answers to questions, that they know what to do to keep healthy. Their ideas on nutrition, exercise, sleep, smoking and alcohol and other health-related matters all bore witness to their knowledge and good sense. They all had access to good health care and knew when and what to ask of their general practitioners.

Many thoughtful comments were offered on the characteristics of both the physical and social environments that facilitate good aging. It appears that so long as primary needs for food, warmth and social contacts are well met, having a lot of money is no longer important to these very elderly people. What is important is being able to maintain an active and meaningful participation in society to the extent that one wishes and is able. Most often this means being able to sustain relationships with both families and contemporaries in mutually supportive ways.

In fulfillment of these needs, more attention might be given to those aspects of the environment that make a difference, especially good telecommunications and transportation. Having a choice of accommodation would mean not feeling pressured by either the family or society to give up long held family homes before the time was right, that decision being the elderly person's own.

If more resources were to be put into making life in the community easier for elderly people by providing good transportation, free telephones and a range of choices in accommodation and if medical procedures that make an obvious difference to quality of life, such as cataract operations and the replacement of arthritic hips, were freely available at the time of need, then it could be argued that fewer resources should go into maintaining the lives of hopelessly ill people over the age of 80. Further, one could argue, people who are healthy and independent at 80 have earned the right to take risks with their own health. They have earned the right to live as they wish. They have earned the right to die as they wish, without technological intervention from the medical profession.

Elderly people also have the right to be regarded as normal active members of the community unhindered by old age stereotypes. It should be acknowledged that far from being a burden on the community, elderly people are sustaining members of all age groups, including their own. The elderly people we listened to, who spoke with such dignity, sense and good humor about all aspects of their lives, command our respect, invite our continued attention, and deserve our admiration.

THE ELDERLY IN GREECE
DEMOGRAPHIC AGING AND LIVING CONDITIONS

Dr. Ira Emke (Poulopoulos) *
Greece

Introduction

A series of surveys conducted in Greece during the 15 year period, 1972-1987 revealed some interesting and significant demographic information about Greece's elderly population. According to the surveys, Greece faces a future comprised of a much higher percentage of older, well-educated, healthy citizens than is present in the Greek population today. This trend poses a significant challenge to Greek society - which must find a way both to support and to fully utilize this valuable human resource.

The surveys conducted during the period 1972-1987 made it possible for us to examine the profile of the elderly in Greece. As a group, elderly persons are very diverse. They cannot be analyzed as a single, homogenous age category. Sex and differences in age, marital status and living area must be considered. The Greek elderly population is predominantly female and getting older. The majority report that they suffer from different health ailments.

They are not isolated from family and society as a group. The role of family and kin is important in their life. Apart from their strong family ties, they maintain contact with neighbors and friends. Nevertheless, elderly people living in rural areas experience feelings of loneliness more than any other in their age group from among 11 countries.

Significant differences in pension levels exist and poverty is a problem for the elderly. Labor force participation has fallen since the 1970's but in reality the number of the elderly in the labor force is much higher than that declared in the statistics. This is

---

* Responsible for the Demographic Section of the Institute for the Study of the Greek Economy in Athens, Greece; Member of Board of Greek Society for Demographic Studies; Diploma of Law and Economics, Diploma 2nd Cycle, Ph.D.

problem for the elderly. Labor force participation has fallen since the 1970's but in reality the number of the elderly in the labor force is much higher than that declared in the statistics. This is because an unknown number are employed in the underground economy. In rural areas, the majority still work in agricultural activities. One out of four persons aged 60 and older is illiterate, with very few having graduated from a university. Generally speaking, the elderly own their homes, but the housing facilities are poorer than for other age groups. Housing conditions in rural areas are poorer than those in urban areas. Relaxing at home, watching television or listening to the radio are the activities which bring the greatest enjoyment, but differences exist between the two sexes.

Between 1985 and the year 2020 the number of elderly 65 and over will increase by 58.1%.[1] The basic challenge that the demographic statistics pose is how society will be prepared to deal with the increasing numbers of healthier, better educated and probably more active elderly. The prolonged survival of many severely disabled and sick people who advance into old age is also a new phenomenon which our society will have to address.

Steps which must be taken include: (a) preventive health measures to insure that the elderly remain healthy and active to an advanced age, (b) distribution of information on how to improve health and enhance the quality of life, (c) development of health programs at a community level, (d) support for the personnel working in health and social services programs for the elderly, (e) home help for the lonely elderly who cannot take care of their housing needs, (f) homes for chronically disabled adults in all of the country's prefectures, and (g) help for women in their 50's looking after their elderly parents who are in their 80's or 90's. This age group requires particular attention as many find themselves extremely isolated and lonely.

The aged in Greece are not an isolated social group. They are a useful and valuable human resource. Improving the lives of the population as a whole, including the aged, is essentially a question of redistributing social resources.

---

1. G. Tziafetas and J. Tzougas, *Projections of the Population of Greece EDHM*, EUROPEAN DEMOGRAPHIC COMMUNITY, THE PLACE OF GREECE, ATHENS 65-67 (1988, in Greek). These projections were made based on fertility levels in 1985.

The Surveys

In the period 1951-1986, two developments which demographers were not expecting changed the age structure of the Greek population. The first was a decrease in the number of children. From 1951 to 1986 the number of children younger than 15 years fell from 2,200,451 to 2,041,192 (by 13.8%). The second development was a rapid increase in the number of elderly people. During the same period, adults aged 65 and older increased from 514,099 to 1,342,440 (by 261%).[2]

The proportion of the Greek population aged 65 and over has been rapidly increasing as a share of the total population from 6.8% in 1951 to 8.2% in 1961 and 13.5% in 1986. (Table I) It is expected to continue its steady rise at least until the year 2050.[3]

Women comprise a large majority of older persons, while in the younger age groups (up to 30-34 years) there is a larger proportion of males. The ratio of men to women (males per 100 females) with respect to age shows a generally progressive decline throughout the age cycle, from an excess of boys among young children (107 boys for 100 girls in the group aged up to 4 years) to a large deficit of men in very old age. In 1986 there were only 80 males for every 100 females 65 years and older in Greece. At 75 years and over there were only 73 males for every 100 females, and at 85 years and older only 63.[4]

There are several explanations for this fact: (a) declining death rates have benefitted women more than men, (b) more men than women died in World War II and the subsequent Civil war in Greece, and (c) emigration from Greece is a predominantly male

---

2. STATISTICAL YEARBOOK OF GREECE 1974, NSSG Athens 27 (1975). I MONTHLY STATISTICAL BULLETIN; National Statistical Service of Greece 9 (Jan. 1989).

3. G. Tziafetas & J. Tzougas, *see supra* note 1, at 65-67.

4. MONTHLY STATISTICAL BULLETIN, *see supra* note 2.

164

phenomenon.[5]

Aging of the older population. The proportion of adults 75 and over is increasing. In 1951 it was 2.1% of the total population, and in 1986 it was 5.7%. As a percentage of the population 65 and over the respective figures were 31.9% and 42.2%.[6]

Marital status and marriage. Personal statistics vary among adults aged 60 and older. Most men are married and live with their wives. Women are much more likely to be widowed and more likely to be living alone. Population distribution according to marital status shifts considerably with increasing age (60 and over, Table 2). The primary factor for the differences between the sexes is the much higher mortality of older married men compared to older married women. The ages between husbands and wives differ, and there is a higher remarriage rate for widowers.

Geographic distribution. During the period 1971-1981, the proportion of elderly people in rural, agricultural regions increased from 7.3% to 19.3%, and from 6 to 10% in urban areas.[7] In 1981, thirty-eight of the 52 departments of Greece presented an Aging Index greater than the national average.[8]

Health of the Elderly
in the Urban areas

Urban areas in Greece, especially in Athens and Thessaloniki, are characterized by air pollution, noise, incessant traffic, long distances between destinations and a lack of parks or sheltered areas. Among other problems, crowded conditions exist in

5. Ira Emke-Poulopoulos, *Le vieillissement demographique en Grece. Causes et Consequences,* ECONOMICA 183-220 (Paris 1982); Ira Emke-Poulopoulos, *Problems of Emigration and Return Migration,* IMEO-EDHM 62-78 (Athens 1986, in Greek).

6. STATISTICAL YEARBOOK OF GREECE 1974, *see supra* note 2, at 27. MONTHLY STATISTICAL BULLETIN, *see supra* note 2, at 9.

7. N.S.S.G., RESULTS OF THE CENSUS 1971, 1981.

8. Ira Emke-Poulopoulos, *Demographic aging in Greece and its consequences* (1951-1981), EDHM, DEMOGRAPHIC CRISIS IN GREECE 125 (Athens 1985).

apartment buildings and there is a shortage of household help. In such an environment, the adjustments required of the urban elderly upon retirement are difficult, especially for those whose pension is small compared with past earnings. All these factors have an adverse influence on their health.[9]

Health status. In the survey conducted in Athens in 1974,[10] a majority of urban men and women reported that they were not in good health. Many more women (63.5%), however, than men (49%) viewed their health as bad. Forty percent of men and only 23% of women said that their health was good or very good. Sixty-eight percent of men and 82.5% of females reported that they were suffering from one or more ailments.

Education and income levels among the respondents influenced their perception of reported health conditions. Among health perceptions of respondents in Philothei (a luxury suburb), persons of a higher socio-economic status were by far more positive than those in all other areas of the sample. A variety of ailments were mentioned. Among the health problems mentioned most often were circulatory ailments (involving heart trouble and high blood pressure), followed by arthritis and rheumatism, respiratory problems and complications with the digestive system. Thirteen point three percent of the respondents needed to see a doctor, but could not pay for his services. The physical mobility of the elderly, measured by the proportion of those who were confined to the house varies markedly by sex (11.2% for female compared to 3.6% for males). The majority (72%) was getting out on a daily basis or several times per week.

According to the survey conducted in 1982-83[11] four out of ten urban respondents said they were in good health. Ailments frequently mentioned included heart trouble (26.1%), rheumatism (16.9%), problems of the digestive system (6.7%), respiratory

9. J. Zarras, *Greece*, INTERNATIONAL HANDBOOK ON AGING 167 (E. Palmore, ed., (Westport, Connecticut 1980.

10. E. Pitsiou, p. 157-170.

11. A. Amira, J. Triantafyllou-Hollis, THE ELDERLY IN RURAL GREECE, 1979/80 - 1985/6 (in Greek) (hereinafter THE ELDERLY IN RURAL GREECE).

ailments (4.9%) and diseases of the thyroid (4.5%). Three out of four persons reported having no health problems.

Utilization of health care services. The survey conducted by the CAPH of the Community Zografou showed that 55.5% of the respondents had not seen a physician in the 12 months prior to the survey, and 44.5% had made at least one visit. Among them one third made just one visit, another third saw a physician 2-4 times and the remaining third made 5 visits or more. The majority had no x-ray (66.5%) and more than half of the respondents (54.9%) did not undergo microbiological tests. One third of the respondents had an electrocardiogram.[12]

Health of the Elderly
in the Rural Areas

In some rural village areas the only available health service is the rural dispensary. Poor health in these regions creates acute and sometimes unsolvable problems.

Health status. According to the WHO Survey, 42% of men and 55% of women aged 60-64 and 83% and 81%, respectively, of the elderly aged 85-89 reported that they were not in good health. Nevertheless, only 15% of men and 18% of women aged 60-64 declared that their health was bad or very bad. The respective percentages in the age group 85-89 are 48% and 55%.[13]

In the survey conducted in seven villages of Epirus, Northern Greece, half of the rural respondents considered that it is easy to find a doctor. Visits to a dentist are difficult and few see one, even though 40% have problems with chewing and 62% wear dentures. Sixty-four percent said they were in poor health, while

---

12. J. TRIANTAFYLLOU-HOLLIS, A. AMIRA, E. GEORGIADOU, HEALTH AND HEALTH CARE UTILIZATION 44-45 (KAPH Zografou 1986) (hereinafter HEALTH AND HEALTH CARE UTILIZATION.

13. Heikkinen et al. 41 (1983).

50.8% suffer from ailments which restrict their daily activities.[14]

Utilization of health care services. The longitudinal survey[15] showed that 36.1% of the rural elderly had a doctor visit them during the previous 12 months compared to 31.4% in 1980. The survey also reveals that there is a definite trend among those in the older age groups to have more home visits. Thirty point eight percent had an x-ray examination in 1980 and 33.3% in 1986 had 1-4. Approximately two-thirds of the sample had no X-RAY examination during the past year. Microbiological tests were being conducted on 41.7% of the respondents in 1986, significantly higher than the 29.9% undergoing similar tests in 1980. Concerning dental care, only 5.2% visited the dentist for their teeth and 8.3% for their dentures. Rural women were less likely than rural men to have x-rays, tests, or visits to the dentist. More than one out of three persons (35.9%) had 1-4 visits to hospital outpatient departments, polyclinics or specialists.

Health Care of All Elderly

Hospital care. The elderly show a far higher incidence of hospital use than the rest of the population. The average length of a hospital stay of persons 60 and over per thousand inhabitants (191.4) substantially exceeds that for the population as a whole (98.0).[16] According to another study, 23.4% of the respondents were hospitalized during the 12 months before the survey.[17]

Nursing home care. A particularly acute problem concerns the question of caring for elderly persons who are bedridden or semi-

---

14. Th. Kazantzis, R. Gattai-Kazanzti, *Survey on the population 60 and over of seven mountainous villages of the Region Filiata Epirus* (Mimeo) - (In Greek).

15. J. Holis-Triantafyllou, L. Mestheneos, A. Amira, HEALTH AND USE OF SERVICES BY THE ELDERLY IN RURAL GREECE, COMPARATIVE ANALYSIS 1980-86 (Athens 1988) (hereinafter HEALTH AND USE OF SERVICES).

16. National Statistical Service of Greece (NSSG), *The Elderly in Greece, National Report*, GREEK NATIONAL COMMITTEE FOR THE WORLD ASSEMBLY ON AGING 15 (Athens 1982, in Greek) (hereinafter NATIONAL REPORT).

17. HEALTH AND HEALTH CARE UTILIZATION, *see supra* note 12, at 42-44.

invalid and for whom there is no hope of recovery. The problem
represents a grievous burden for their families and for Greek health
care services.

There is a lack of centers equipped to provide home care -
medical treatment and social services - as well as nurses special-
ized in the care of old people. It is difficult to find household help
and almost impossible for low income elderly to pay for it.[18]

Less than 1% of elderly people in Greece live in nursing homes,
compared to up to 8% in other countries.[19] The Greek Ministry
of Health and Welfare has estimated that there were 6,000 elderly
Greeks in nursing homes in 1989.[20]

Family Structure and Family Support

A few decades ago, the patriarchal family constituted the
characteristic mode of Greek social organization. Today the
nuclear family is the rule.

In the Urban Areas

In urban areas, situations where both parents and their married
children find it necessary or preferable to live under separate roofs
are increasing.[21]

According to the Athens survey,[22] 86% of the respondents
reported they had at least one surviving child and 77% said they
had at least one brother or sister living. Roughly one third of all
children (33%) lived in the same household with their parents.
Only 2% of brothers and sisters still living were in the same

---

18. Zarras, *see supra* note 9, at 174.

19. NATIONAL REPORT, *see supra* note 16, at 22.

20. Figures communicated by the Division for the Elderly, Ministry of Health
and Welfare.

21. J. Zarras, *see supra* note 9, at 165.

22. E. Pitsiou, *see supra* note 10, at 97-101.

household with a respondent. Twenty-three percent of all children lived in the same neighborhood or community as their parents, while only 7% of the respondents' brothers or sisters did so. Eighteen percent of all children and 50% of all living brothers or sisters lived outside of the immediate vicinity of the respondents, in another town in Greece or in another country.

Proximity is an important factor in the frequency of contact between children and their parents and between the older persons to determine the extent to which older people feel lonely when they live alone or when children and other relatives do not live nearby. The elderly had contact with a child (48%) and sibling (5%) on a daily basis. On a weekly basis the percentage was 13% and 7%, respectively, monthly (9% and 18%), several times a year (8% and 24%) and less often (7% and 24% respectively).

According to the 1982-83 survey,[23] 21.4% of women lived alone, while only 6.7% of men did. Nevertheless, the percentage of men over 78 years old living alone was higher (44.9%) among all elderly men living alone than the respective percentage of women (29.7%).

A large proportion of women (37.5%) reported that they were receiving financial help from their children, while very few male respondents (3.4%) said that their children were helping to support them.[24] Sixty-nine point three percent said that they were quite capable of managing their own affairs while 30.7% replied they needed some help. Women at low and middle income levels were more dependent than men.

The majority of men (60.8%) and women (68.3%) were helping their children and grandchildren by giving them money at regular intervals, either monthly or less frequently.[25]

In the Rural Areas

The patriarchal family continues to be of some importance in

23. THE ELDERLY IN RURAL GREECE, *see supra* note 11, at 40-41.

24. E. Pitsiou, *see supra* note 10, at 87.

25. E. Pitsiou, *see supra* note 10, at 94.

rural areas, and there are still cases where grown children continue living with the parents, even after marriage. It has been stressed that in the villages, even old men without relatives feel less lonely than they would if they lived in an urban area. Their long life of honest, hard work has earned them respect. A congenial atmosphere exists in the coffee house, where they enjoy the daily companionship of their fellow villagers.[26]

The departure of young people from rural areas is a reality in Greece. They leave their homes in the village to start a new life in urban areas or to go abroad. Consequently, in some rural areas of Greece the elderly are the only inhabitants left in the village, with no desire to join their children in the city. As a result, the relationships change between the old villagers and their children in the urban centers. The bonds between them remain, with the younger people continuing to respect their elders and to accept them in certain roles. The frequency of the children's visits home depends on how far away they have moved from their village.[27]

The longitudinal study,[28] showed that in 1986 only 14.1% of the subjects lived alone, with the majority living with at least one other person. There are large differences between males and females, with women more likely to be living alone or in an extended family (6.8% and 20.5% respectively).

Nevertheless, in the rural areas the percentage of respondents in Greece who felt lonely is very high (24% to 51% in 1986 according to sex and age group),[29] and as the WHO survey[30] has indicated, men living in rural Greece in 1980 showed the highest figures for the elderly from 11 countries. These high percentages need further research in order to distinguish between

---

26. J. Zarras, *see supra* note 9, at 165-166.

27. A. Teperoglou, *Open Care for the Elderly - Greece*, OPEN CARE FOR THE ELDERLY IN SEVEN EUROPEAN COUNTRIES 81-93 (A. Amann, ed., Oxford, 1980).

28. THE ELDERLY IN GREECE, *see supra* note 11.

29. THE ELDERLY IN RURAL GREECE, *see supra* note 11.

30. E. Heikkinen, *see supra* note 13, at 109.

feelings of loneliness and actual isolation.[31]

Income of the Elderly

Determining the retirement income of the elderly is, to a large extent, dependent on labor market activity. Pensions are not uniform. There are great disparities not only among different elderly groups but also among new retirees and those who started receiving a pension some years ago. In 1985 the average yearly pension ranged between 66,567 and 545,327 drs.[32] Poverty is common among the elderly. In 1974, it was estimated that 25% of all ages and 46.9% of the elderly aged 75 and older lived in impoverished conditions.[33]

Noncash benefits refer to those goods or services obtained without any expenditure or at a rate below their market value. These include benefits provided by the State or municipalities, such as health services and medicine, by employers or labor unions, or by private business. Noncash benefits to the elderly aged 65-74 represent 9% of their expenditures, and for those aged 75 and older they amount to 19%, which is similar to the United States where it has been estimated that noncash benefits add about 10% to the incomes of elderly persons.[34]

It is useful to compare the income of elderly families with the income of younger families. Families with members aged 60 and over had incomes considerably lower than families in general (5197 drs and 7682 drs, respectively). In addition, a great income gap exists between families maintained by elderly men and families maintained by elderly women.[35]

---

31. THE ELDERLY IN GREECE, see supra note 11.

32. NSSG, STATISTICAL YEARBOOK OF GREECE 1965 107-11 (1986).

33. J. Yfantopoulos, POVERTY AND HEALTH, to be published.

34. NSSG, HOUSEHOLD EXPENDITURE SURVEY 1981/82 161-162; M. Moon, THE MEASUREMENT OF ECONOMIC WELFARE: IT'S APPLICATION TO THE AGED POOR (Academic Press 1977).

35. K. Kanellopoulos, 52-53 (1986).

In the Urban Areas

A survey conducted in 1984 in Athens,[36] showed that the average income of Greek retirees has been estimated to be lower than the average individual income (in 1984, 633,000 and 744,000 drs, respectively). It also determined that pensions constituted the only source of income for 84% of the respondents.

According to the Athens survey,[37] a fairly large proportion of women (40.4%) along with a smaller percentage of men (29.3%) considered their incomes insufficient to live on. The majority of men felt that it was just enough to get by, while the majority of women stated that it was more than enough comfortably to meet all their needs.

According to the survey conducted in 1982-83,[38] the single most important source of income for the elderly was Social Security benefits (86.7% both sexes, 86.2% men, 87.1% women) although a small minority who were still working continued to earn a salary (5.5% both sexes, 8.6% men, 3.2% women). Very few (4.1% both sexes, 4.6% men and 5.1% women) earn income through interest on property, dividends or rents. Home ownership is common among the elderly.

In the Rural Areas

Social Security benefits for elderly people in the rural areas were instituted in 1961. Women, however, have been eligible to receive their own benefits only since 1983. In 1989, the monthly social security payment averaged 10,000 a month. (1 kilo of meat costs 1,000 drs.) It has been argued that "the pension, though small, has raised the morale of a whole category of persons who previously had to look to their families for even their minor expenses. The measure has also strengthened the position of the elderly not only within the family but within the community as a

---

36. Karagiorgas et al., 152 (1988).

37. Pitsiou, *supra* note 10, at 80-94.

38. THE ELDERLY IN RURAL GREECE, *supra* note 11, at 27.

whole."[39]

The survey, conducted in seven villages of Epirus, where 85% of the respondents are retirees, found that 83% considered their pension to be their principal source of income.[40]

According to the longitudinal survey,[41] the pension is the primary source of income for the elderly, with only a small percentage (4.5%) still receiving income from a job and a similar percentage (4.8%) who depend primarily on their families for financial support. The vast majority of the subjects receive the Agricultural Workers Pension (OGA), which amounted to 7,000 drs per month at the time of the interview. Since 40,000 drs a month is considered to be just above the poverty line, it is inevitable that those not admitting to financial help from other sources must be getting additional income or help in kind - food, clothing, etc. - from family members. Of course, in agricultural areas people continue to cultivate their land and raise animals without consider-ing these activities either work or a source of income. Physically dependent subjects require assistance to tend chickens and goats or to cultivate small plots of land.

Elderly Participation
in The Labor Force in Greece

During the decade 1971-1981, the proportion of elderly men in the labor force registered sharp declines (i.e. working or looking for work). The participation in the labor force of males over 65 dropped from 44% in 1971 to 25% in 1981.[42] In contrast, the proportion of older women in the labor force has remained relatively constant, with a notable increase of women aged 55-64

---

39. Zarras, *supra* note 9, at 166.

40. Kazantzis, *supra* note 14.

41. HEALTH AND USE OF SERVICES, *supra* note 15.

42. NSSG, NATIONAL REPORT, *supra* note 16, at 23.

working.[43]

According to the 1987 Manpower Survey, only 122,4000 adults aged 65 and older were economically active, representing 9.1% of the workforce (13.9% men and 5.3% women).[44] In actual fact, the number of working elderly is higher than the figure declared in the statistics, because an unknown number is employed in the underground economy. Both retired elderly who are working and the employers who hire them do not declare their activities for tax reasons. Part-time work among the elderly is very common. Unemployed older workers encounter difficulties in finding a job because of age discrimination in hiring.[45]

A combination of factors accounts for the steady decline of older men in the labor force. These include: (1) the increase in voluntary retirement associated with the more widespread eligibility of workers under social security and other pension plans; (2) the increase in disability-related retirement; (3) pressure exerted by employers to get older workers to retire; and (4) withdrawal of older workers from the labor force who become discouraged by age discrimination in hiring.[46]

In the Urban Areas

According to the Athens survey,[47] a large proportion of male respondents (28%) replied that they thought they might have been better off if they had continued working. Only 8.5% of women expressed the same opinion. Fifty-five percent of male and 43%

---

43. NSSG, STATISTICAL YEARBOOK OF GREECE 1985, 33, 55-57.

44. NSSG, NATIONAL REPORT, *supra* note 16, at 23.

45. Ira Emke-Poulopoulos, *Vieillissement demographique et la vie des personnes agees en Grece*, COLLOQUE FRANCO-HELLENIQUE DE DEMOGRAPHIE, 18-21 Mai, 1987 (in press).

46. US Department of Commerce, Bureau of the Census, DEMOGRAPHIC AND SOCIO-ECONOMIC ASPECTS OF AGING IN THE UNITED STATES, Special Studies Series 23, 101 (Washington 1984).

47. E. Pitsiou, *supra* note 10, at 80-81.

of female respondents who wanted to work said that they missed the interest and satisfaction they derived from their job. The majority (61% and 82%, respectively) did not think that if they had continued working they might have been better off.

In the Rural Areas

According to the WHO survey,[48] more rural men than women were engaged in full-time or part-time employment, with the number showing a marked decrease with age. In the age group 60-64 the percentage of those working was as high as 75% for men and 39% for women. The respective percentages in the age group 85-89 were 12% and 6%.

In 1986 only 4.5% of the villagers surveyed were still in paid employment.[49]

The survey in seven mountain villages[50] showed that 77% of the respondents are working in agricultural activities.

Another survey[51] showed that the majority of subjects stopped work for reasons of age (79.5%), but a significant number also stopped for reasons of ill health (15.5%). More men fall into the former category, with more women in the latter. Among those still working, most were men in the younger age group and were employed outside the home, whereas women reported doing housework.

The Manpower Survey conducted in 1987[52] showed that 90,500 people aged 65 and older worked in agriculture (87.4% of the working population for this age group).

---

48. Heikkinen, *supra* note 13, at 93, 108.

49. HEALTH AND USE OF SERVICES, supra note 15.

50. Kazantzis, *supra* note 14.

51. HEALTH AND USE OF SERVICES, supra note 15.

52. NSSG, NATIONAL REPORT, *supra* note 16, at 64-72.

Literacy and Educational
Attainment of the Elderly

The level of education attained by older people is much lower than that of the younger generation. Figures from the 1981 Census[53] show that in Greece 445,000 elderly aged 60 years and older were illiterate, more than one quarter (27%) of the population for this age group, while among the age group 25-29 the figure was only 1.3%. The percentage of the population aged 60 and older that had graduated from university was 3.4% as compared to 14.6% of young people aged 25-29.

Although there has been a relatively large drop in the illiteracy rate among the elderly since 1961, a large number still could not read and write in 1981.

Levels of literacy and education among the elderly population vary according to age and sex. Illiteracy is higher among women, with three out of four (72.6%) being illiterate. This category represented more than half (53.3%) of the total number of illiterates in Greece. Illiteracy is higher in rural areas of the country.

According to the 1982-83 survey,[54] in the Centers of Open Care for the Elderly, the educational level of the sample was lower than that of the overall population. Illiteracy rates were higher and only 1% of the respondents had a University Diploma (instead of 3.4% of the total population aged 65 and over). In the survey of the Community Ymittos[55] in the Athens area, 47.7% of the elderly women have only a few years of schooling. Great differences exist between men and women; men who finished primary and secondary education represented 65.9% of the total sample, while women represented only 46.4%.

---

53. STATISTICAL YEARBOOK OF GREECE 109 (1984).

54. THE ELDERLY IN GREECE, *supra* note 11, 34-35.

55. A. Teperoglou, SURVEY ABOUT THE ELDERLY, COMMUNITY YMITTOS, SOCIODEMOGRAPHIC CHARACTERISTICS.

Housing Conditions Of The Elderly

In the Urban Areas

In the large urban centers, particularly in Athens and Salonica, there is a pressing need for housing for the elderly. Moreover, those living on a small income or pension face considerable difficulties when they live in rented accommodations. A veritable impasse awaits those who live in dilapidated dwellings that are scheduled to be torn down to make room for modern apartment buildings. They often find themselves in the tragic situation of having no place to go.[56]

Home Ownership. Home ownership was common among the urban elderly. According to the Athens survey, over half of the sample (52.7%) said they owned their home, with a larger proportion of men than women responding in the affirmative (65.6% and 45% respectively). Twenty-two percent of men and 28.5% of women said they paid rent and 11.3% of men and 25.9% of women said they lived in their children's home or in the home of a relative.[57]

According to the 1982-83 survey,[58] two out of three men (64.3%) and more than half of women owned their home, and both sexes paid rent in the same proportions (13%).

Living Conditions. Living conditions are considerably poorer for the elderly than for the younger adults, and great differences exist in the living conditions of older persons.

According to the Athens survey,[59] the majority of households were equipped with a kitchen (97.8%) and an inside flush toilet (95.4%). More than one third of the respondents reported that they did not have a private bathroom (38.4%) or adequate heating in the winter (35.5%).

---

56. J. Zarras, *supra* note 9, at 191.

57. E. Pitsiou, *supra* note 10, at 52.

58. THE ELDERLY IN GREECE, *supra* note 11, at 46-48.

59. Pitsiou, *supra* note 10, at 56.

178

The survey conducted in 1974,[60] showed that urban families with members aged 60 and older have an electric (95.9%) or gas (99.6%) stove, but few have an inside WC (17%) or bathroom (35%) and telephone (37.5%).

In the Rural Areas

Dwellings in the countryside are larger than those in urban areas, and they have more open space (gardens, yards). Larger homes present the possibility of the elderly being able to live with their children, but when they live alone the house is usually bigger than they need.

Housing conditions in rural areas are poorer than in the cities. The aforementioned survey[61] indicated that only three out of four elderly families with members 60 and over had a kitchen, and only 17.5% had an inside flush toilet. Less than half (46.7%) had running water. A bathroom is considered a luxury (only 8% have one). Only 10.7% of the elderly have a telephone, although a telephone is obviously important for the elderly who often need to get help for health problems and other difficulties.

According to the WHO survey,[62] the percentage of people with a bathroom or shower ranged from 16% to 33% according to the sex and age group. Those who had a telephone at their disposal ranged from 9% for women 85-89 years old to 30% for men aged 60-64 years.

Among the seven villages surveyed,[63] respondents tended to own their homes. The dwellings have three rooms and a kitchen with limited facilities. The survey also found that most of the day's activities were done out of the house.

---

60. K. Kanellopoulos, THE ELDERLY IN GREECE 48, (KEPE, Athens, 1984, in Greek).

61. *Id.* at 48.

62. Heikkinen, *supra* note 13, at 63-66.

63. Kazantzis, *supra* note 14.

Housing conditions are described in the longitudinal survey[64] as follows: 16.5% of the subjects did not have a room for their own personal use. Women (19.7%) were more likely than men (12.1%) not to have a room of their own; and, 64.4% of the households have no bathroom compared with 79.7% in 1980 (males 56.8%, females 62.4%). The percentage of homes with hot running water was 39.3% in 1986, compared to 17.1% in 1980. But 96.1% of the subjects had a cold water tap, either in or outside the house. In this category, however, 16% only had running water outside, with 3.9% having no piped water at all. Fifty-one point two percent of the respondents only have an outside lavatory, which poses a particular problem for elderly persons with mobility or orientation difficulties. Three point nine percent of subjects reported no lavatory at all, either inside or outside the house. Seventy-one point nine percent of the subjects reported having their own cooking stove, but no clear distinction was made concerning whether it was gas, electricity, wood or oil burning.   Only 23% reported having an automatic washing machine, although 89.8% of respondents (75.8% in 1980) possessed a refrigerator, with more men (91.5%) owning one than women (88.4%).

A telephone,[65] an amenity which is considered almost essential, especially for the isolated elderly, is present in only 30.1% of households. This represents a significant increase over 1980, when the comparative figure was 18.7%. Nevertheless, in Greek society one communal telephone located in the local cafeteria (kafeneion) or a shop often adequately serves the needs of the community.

There were still 16% of women and 7.4% of men who had neither a radio nor a television.[66]

The majority of subjects (86.4%) live in a single story house and on the ground floor, with only 7.8% not living on the ground floor. Thirteen point six percent of subjects live in houses with

---

64. HEALTH AND USE OF SERVICES, *supra* note 15.

65. HEALTH AND USE OF SERVICES, *supra* note 15.

66. HEALTH AND USE OF SERVICES, *supra* note 15.

more than one floor. It follows that the question relating to the presence and use of an elevator was virtually irrelevant for the subjects of this survey. Moreover, two-thirds of the respondents have relatively easy access to the road, as long as they have no severe mobility problems. In many cases, however, the distance was assessed as 'one hour or more' by foot to the road, giving some idea of the extreme isolation in which many elderly villagers live.[67]

Eighty-eight point one percent of the subjects lived within one-half kilometer of the nearest food shop. Nevertheless, for 6.8% of the subjects there was a significant problem obtaining food, while for 21.9% obtaining it was difficult.[68]

Social Relations And Recreational Activities of the Elderly

In the Urban Areas

Old men in the large cities consistently see their role and authority dwindling. They do not understand the changing patterns of family and social life in the city. They move unnoticed among crowds of strangers. While they do not encounter any obvious expressions of hostility or even unkindness, they find that the public respect formerly shown by the young towards the elderly is gradually disappearing.[69]

In the Athens survey, the majority of the respondents had strong family ties and a large number indicated that they had weekly contacts with friends and neighbors (40% and 61% respectively).[70] Membership in voluntary organizations was not common among the aged included in this study. But more men (21.5%) than women (6.5%) reported that they were members of

---

67. HEALTH AND USE OF SERVICES, *supra* note 15.

68. HEALTH AND USE OF SERVICES, *supra* note 15.

69. J. Zarras, *supra* note 9, at 167.

70. E. Pitsiou, *supra* note 10, at 130.

organizations.[71]

The activities which gave men the most enjoyment, according to the same survey,[72] included their jobs, working around the house, repairing things and taking care of the garden (33.5%). Another considerable proportion (24.1%) said they liked to relax around the house, listening to the radio or watching television, reading or writing. A third group of respondents (20.4%) liked to take walks, or go to the local coffee house or church. Heading the list of activities which women reported enjoying were staying around the house, resting or listening to the radio or watching television (44.1%). Household work was second (25%), while doing nothing was last (13.8%).

At the time of this survey, the Centers of Open Care for the Elderly (Local Government Sponsored Community Centers for the Elderly known by the Greek initials as KAPH) did not exist. The first centers were established in 1979, and by 1989, 250 were functioning throughout Greece. The number of inscribed members totaled 250,000, but only 125,000 (50%) actually participated.

In the Rural Areas

The longitudinal survey[73] showed that only 4.3% (6.4% in 1980) of the sample reported membership in a club or organization. There was a marked difference between men (9.2%) and women (0.3%) in this respect. Only one subject attended a KAPH Center, but this is due to the fact that very few villages are served by such a center.

The services most desired by the rural elderly include (1) medical advice; (2) health check-ups; (3) companionship services; (4) telephone; and (5) old peoples' homes and clubs. It is tempting to make a connection between elderly persons' needs for medical advice and health check-ups and their dissatisfaction with available medical care. One might then conclude that these two points are

---

71. E. Pitsiou, *supra* note 10, at 143.

72. E. Pitsiou, *supra* note 10, at 141.

73. HEALTH AND USE OF SERVICES, *supra* note 15.

potential areas for service improvement. However, skepticism seems warranted as people's responses are limited by their experience and knowledge.

Ninety point four percent of the respondents said that they have good friends, and the majority 81.5% (78.4% in 1980) reported very close supportive relationships with neighbors. A further 15.1% (18.1% in 1980) said they had good relationships with neighbors but little or no exchange of contact.[74]

---

74. HEALTH AND USE OF SERVICES, *supra* note 15.

Table 1

Year	Population	0-14 (Y)	15-64 (A)	65+ (E)	Index of Aging*	Support Ratio Total**	Support Ratio Elderly***
1951	7,632,801	28.8	64.4	6.8	23.4	55.2	10.5
1961	8,388,553	26.7	65.1	8.2	30.6	53.7	12.6
1971	8,768,640	24.9	64.0	11.1	44.8	56.3	17.4
1981	9,739,589	23.7	63.6	12.7	53.7	57.3	20.0
1986	9,963,604	20.5	66.0	13.5	65.7	51.4	20.41

* The number of persons aged 65 and over per 100 persons aged 0-14.
** The number of persons aged 65 and over and 0-14 per 100 persons aged 15-64.
*** The number of persons 65 and over per 100 persons aged 15-64.

Table 2

Marital Status of Older Population by Sex and Age
Greece 1981
(Numbers in Thousands)

Men					
Age Group	Single	Married	Widowed	Divorced	Total
60-64	8.0	173.7	5.5	1.7	188.9
65-69	8.0	177.9	1.5	1.6	199.0
70-74	6.3	137.8	15.7	1.1	160.9
75 and over	6.8	139.6	41.9	1.0	189.3

Women					
60-64	13.6	147.2	56.4	3.7	220.0
65-69	12.3	134.0	80.3	3.0	229.6
70-74	9.8	91.3	92.3	2.3	195.7
75 and over	10.4	74.9	176.7	1.5	263.5

Source: National Statistical Service of Greece
Statistical Yearbook of Greece 1985, Athens 1986, p. 31.

LEGAL ISSUES IN SURGICAL CARE
OF ELDERLY PERSONS[*]

Margaret A. Somerville[**]
Canada

Surgical care of elderly persons focuses on many of the difficult legal and ethical dilemmas that have arisen in modern medicine. Relatively safe surgery is a modern phenomenon, and the large numbers of aged persons in our communities is a recent development. This combination of factors, which identifies a rapidly emerging area of critical issues at the intersection of medicine, ethics and law, gives rise to the problem of determining guidelines. Such guidelines must envision the provision of high-level medical care for a large number of aged persons.

It is suggested that it is more important to be aware of the medicine-ethics-law issues that are raised in any given situation, than to think that we necessarily have found the right answers. In a sense, awareness is the right answer. Moreover, we need to realize and acknowledge that general goodwill and personal integrity are not sufficient for dealing with these medical-ethical-legal problems; disciplined thinking and decision-making procedures are also required.

This means that we need to develop a decision-making structure which, among other functions, will accommodate decision-making regarding health care at macro and micro levels. Macro level decision-making is largely the concern of institutions and governments, and any controversy is likely to center on failure to provide medical care and the issues involved in allocation of medical

---

* This article was previously published in 8.2 CANADIAN JOURNAL ON AGING 128 (1989). © 1989 by Margaret A. Somerville.

** Gale Professor of Law; Professor on the faculty of medicine; Director of McGill Centre for Medicine, Ethics and Law; A.M., F.R.S.C., A.u.A.(pharrn.), LL.B., D.C.L.

resources, especially those that are scarce. In contrast, decision-making at a micro level relates directly to individual persons and usually involves rights in medical care. An example is the decision-making involved in resolving the conflict between a patient who refuses treatment and a physician who wishes to impose this. Both levels of decision-making are relevant to a discussion of legal issues in the surgical care of elderly persons, but only the latter will be addressed in this article, because the former is discussed elsewhere.[1]

However, it needs to be kept in mind that issues raised by macro level decision-making regarding health care are an integral element of micro level decision-making. Macro level health care decision-making considerations may be present, pertinent and important, although not necessarily identified at the micro level, because often such considerations function only at an unconscious level in the decision-making process concerning an individual patient. For example, it is pointless to consider whether or not there is an obligation to offer surgical treatment to a given elderly person if the treatment is not available.

The areas chosen for discussion are: informed consent; dying elderly patients; pain relief treatment; and medical research. But first, a very brief introduction will be given to the legal concept of medical malpractice, which is relevant to all of the other areas discussed.

Medical Malpractice

Much has been written about medical malpractice. The general legal concepts governing it are fairly well known. These can be summarized as follows: First, in treating the patient the surgeon must live up to the standard of care of a reasonably competent surgeon (or sub-specialty surgeon, as appropriate) in the same circumstances. Second, this standard will almost always be set at the level indicated by expert medical evidence, although courts

---

1. M.A. Somerville, *Should the Grandparents Die?: Allocation of Medical Resources with an Aging Population*, 14 LAW, MEDICINE & HEALTH CARE 158 (1968).

have a discretion to reject such evidence and themselves set the standard. The legal standard comprises a range of conduct, not a single "right" act. This concept can be best envisioned by imagining a range of conduct on the part of the surgeon, one end-point of which comprises the worst treatment that could be given and the other end-point the best treatment. It is only conduct that falls below a certain point on this continuum that constitutes medical negligence or malpractice. This point is determined when the conduct becomes such that no reasonably competent surgeon would have done likewise in the same circumstances. Third, not all errors constitute negligence; only those that no reasonably competent surgeon in the same circumstances could have made, do so.

Informed Consent

The literature on informed consent is voluminous[2] and the doctrine is still being developed. Recently, it has been realized that the functions of this doctrine are broader than simply promoting respect for the patient as an autonomous person, important as this aim is, as an end in itself. In addition, the process of obtaining informed consent can help to reduce patients' suffering, by giving them a feeling of having more control over what happens to them. Further, this process can promote trust in the surgeon which can have a healing effect - the surgeon as "true placebo" - because it enables patients to activate their own self-healing mechanisms.[3]

It is also important to realize that although the doctrine is referred to as that of informed consent, it equally requires that refusals of treatment be informed; that the required information be disclosed to the patient; that the patient be competent; and that the patient's decision to refuse treatment be voluntary. Moreover, informed consent is a process and not an event; this means that

---

2. For references to some of this literature, *see* M.A. Somerville, *Consent to Medical Care*, PROTECTION OF LIFE SERIES, Law Reform Commission of Canada (Ottawa, 1979).

3. J. Katz, THE SILENT WORLD OF DOCTOR AND PATIENT 191, The Free Press (New York, 1984).

the requirements of the doctrine must be continuously fulfilled throughout the treatment relationship. The same is true for informed refusal, but it is much less likely that further events, requiring further action in order to re-validate a refusal, will occur in situations in which patients have refused treatment. Refusal of treatment is not the same as termination of the surgeon-patient relationship, although the two events may occur simultaneously and be effectuated by the same act on the patient's part. When the surgeon-patient relationship continues after a refusal of treatment, the surgeon has all the obligations that normally flow from that relationship. Care needs to be taken to remain aware of this, because there can be a danger of malpractice by abandonment in situations where a patient refuses treatment that the surgeon regards as necessary.

The requirements of the doctrine of informed consent cannot always be applied in a uniform manner in relation to all patients. This is well-recognized with respect to children and mentally ill persons, but it may also be true, in some regards, with respect to aged persons. Such a statement calls for a warning. The "prima facie" presumption from which one works in determining the legal requirements with regard to consent in a given case must be that the requirements of the "basic" doctrine of informed consent - that is, the form of this doctrine applying with respect to a free-living, competent adult person - are applicable unless some modification of these requirements constitutes a substantial benefit to the patient and this benefit clearly outweighs any harm involved in the modification. In such a case, the surgeon would have the burden of proving that the usual requirements ought to have been modified in the way that they were; that is, the surgeon must show that the usual requirements need not and, even, ought not to have been applied.[4]

What is regarded as constituting a harm, avoidance of which makes it permissible to modify the requirements of the doctrine of informed consent, is neither unlimited nor entirely open to personal definition on the part of the surgeon. For example, the possibility that a competent, aged patient will refuse surgery that the surgeon

---

4. See M.A. Somerville, *Variations on the Theme of Informed Consent: Therapeutic Privilege*, 12 LAW MEDICINE AND HEALTH CARE 4 (1984).

considers necessary, if told of its risks and potential benefits and those of alternative treatments, including the option of no treatment, does not constitute such harm. It is the patient's right to make such a decision and the purpose of the doctrine of informed consent is to ensure that this right can be exercised.

Informed Consent

1. Information

Disclosure of information is one of the fundamental requirements of the doctrine of informed consent. In general, a patient must be given that information concerning possible treatments and their effects which would be material to the reasonable patient in the same circumstances.[5] It is worth noting, first, that under this approach the reference point for setting the standard of care required with respect to the scope of disclosure of information, is the reasonable patient. It is not, as in some jurisdictions, the reasonable physician in the same circumstances and the information that he or she would disclose. (The "reasonable physician" is the legal standard most commonly used to assess whether or not there has been negligence in relation to "medical acts", such as surgery.) Second, the patient can vary the content of this legal standard for disclosure of information, either by asking questions, when it can be extended or by giving an informed waiver of the right to be informed, when it will be restricted.[6] Third, this standard will be varied in situations in which the doctrine of "therapeutic privilege" or that of necessity applies.[7]

Even in a situation where the standard for disclosure applies in its normal, unmodified form, the content of the necessary information could differ between patients needing, for example, the same

---

5. *See e.g.*, Reibl v. Hughes 114 D.L.R. (3d) 1 (S.C.C.) (1980).

6. *See*, M.A. Somerville, *Structuring the Issues in Informed Consent* 26 McGILL L.J. 741 (1981).

7. *See* M.A. Somerville, *Variations on the Theme of Informed Consent: Therapeutic Privilege*, 12 LAW MEDICINE AND HEALTH CARE 4 (1984).

surgery. The circumstances of different patients are unlikely to be exactly the same and these affect the scope of disclosure. Moreover, because age could be taken into account as a relevant circumstance, the content and scope of disclosure of information could vary as between a young and an old person undergoing the same surgical procedure. Apart from other factors, the risks and chances of benefit will be likely to vary between two such persons. It could also be that information which would be material to a younger person might not be material to an elderly person - for instance, information that the person might not be able to return to work if certain risks eventuated.[8]

It is becoming clear that some degree of sophistication and nuance is required with respect to the form that the risk disclosure takes and, again, that what is appropriate in this regard can vary between old and young persons. For instance, although the facts disclosed are identical, people decide differently when the disclosure on which a decision is based differs. Compare being informed that there is an eighty percent risk of failure with a disclosure focusing on the twenty percent chance of success which is also present. Patients tend to make different decisions depending on whether the focus of the disclosure is on the risk of failure or the chances of success.[9]

Old persons asked to choose between options with varying risks and potential benefits, where the worth of the possible benefit is proportional to the degree of risk, are more likely than younger persons to choose a no-risk option if one is available. But, if there is no such option, they are no more likely than younger persons to choose lower risk options.[10] Old persons are also more likely to agree to take risks if they believe that other members of their group

---

8. See Reibl v. Hughes, supra note 5.

9. Tversky and Kahneman, The Framing of Decisions and the Psychology of Choice, 4 SCIENCE 211, 453 (1981).

10. R.M. Tarzan, Cautiousness, Risk and Informed Consent in Clinical Geriatrics, 30 CLINICAL RESEARCH 345 (1982).

are agreeing to take like risks.[11] But, the option to make no choice is selected by elderly persons more often than younger ones. This can act as a protection against serving as a research subject, but raises difficulties in clinical situations. It may be a decision not to have treatment (which should be respected as such) or it may be a symptom of depression in a situation where the old person has, in effect, made no decision.[12]

It is especially important to be aware of these considerations in obtaining consent to research involving surgery because particular care must be taken in this context to avoid manipulative behavior that might induce consent. But such considerations also have application at a level as simple as surgeons making statements to their patients that almost all patients, who suffer from the same condition as the one for which the patient is considering surgery, decide to have a certain operation and, for instance, that anyone who did not, must be senile or mad. The fact that the surgeon's statement (that most patients choose surgery) is true does not mean that it cannot be coercive. The statement will be considered coercive by the law and, as a consequence, have the effect of invalidating consent if it is regarded as improperly and unduly influencing the patient. Whether or not the statement is regarded as improper and an undue influence will depend upon assessment of the total context in which consent was obtained. This is to raise the issue of voluntariness which is discussed below. The point which I wish to make here in relation to disclosure of information is that it is not only non-disclosure of information which can cause a problem in obtaining an ethically and legally valid informed consent; certain disclosures can also be a source of difficulty. This needs to be kept in mind, and surgeons need to develop a certain degree of sensitivity in this regard.

Finally, for surgeons to fulfill their legal obligations with respect to disclosure of information, it is sufficient that patients "apparently understand" the content of the required disclosure. That is, it is

---

11. *Id.* It would be interesting to compare this phenomenon with that of adolescent peer group conformity and with the reactions of a group of middle-aged persons with respect to conformity or non-conformity with their peers.

12. *Id.* at 351.

192

sufficient if the reasonable surgeon in the same circumstances would have thought that the patient understood whether or not the patient did, in fact, subjectively understand. This question of the patient's understanding of the information disclosed is also linked to competence. which will be discussed shortly.

2. Voluntariness

The second fundamental requirement of the doctrine of informed consent is that a patient's consent be voluntarily given, that is, be free of duress, undue influence or coercion. The presence of such factors invalidate a purported consent entirely, with the result that the surgeon could be held liable in battery, an intentional tort, which can carry more extensive awards of damages than negligence.[13]

Again, in this regard, it needs to be considered whether old persons vary from younger persons in their potential for being susceptible to duress, coercion or undue influence. Conduct which might not constitute coercion of a younger person could amount to coercion of an old person who felt frail, weak, dependent and helpless. Old persons can be more susceptible to lesser influences if they are frightened of losing necessary physical or emotional support by offending their caretakers, whether health care professionals or family members, by not agreeing to the course of conduct recommended by such persons. The issues involved in determining what does or does not amount to coercion and how best to avoid it can be very delicate and each case needs to be addressed on an individual basis. For instance, an old person may feel more able to state his or her real wishes when a family member is also present. Another old person may feel entirely the contrary. Each old person and the circumstances of each case must be assessed individually in these respects.

Another form of coercion of special relevance to aged persons, because, as a group, they are more likely to find themselves in institutions than younger persons, is the phenomenon known as institutionalization. The theory behind this concept is that patients often modify their conduct because of pressures - subtle or overt -

---

13. Somerville, *supra* note 6.

from other patients and from the system established within an institution, including the component of that system which is comprised of the institution's staff. It is possible that conduct modified for such reasons could be considered to have been coerced.

The lack of voluntariness present in the types of situation described above could be referred to collectively as "extrinsic" coercion. "Intrinsic" coercion is also possible. In one sense, we are all intrinsically coerced by our conditioning and even our genetic make-up. Further, some forms of mental illness which do not affect cognitive competence (and, therefore, the person is regarded as competent by the law) could be regarded as a form of intrinsic coercion with the result that consent given by persons suffering from such an illness could be invalidated for a lack of voluntariness, when it could not be invalidated for a lack of competence. However, a more common form of this intrinsic type of coercion, particularly among aged persons who are often on multiple drug regimes, is the effect of drugs on the voluntariness of consent. It is easy to find examples of courts holding that, because a person signed a consent form after being given medication, the consent form does not provide evidence that consent was given at that time.[14]

The reasoning in such cases can take several forms, at least one of which focuses on a lack of voluntariness. It can be held that the drugs affected the patient's will in such a way that conduct on the part of a person who is usually in some position of power or authority with respect to the patient - often the patient's physician - amounted to coercion or undue influence with respect to the patient's consent. The consent, therefore, is invalidated. It is important to note that the conduct concerned might not have been coercive in normal circumstances, that is, if the patient had not been affected by drugs. The presence of this form of coercion or undue influence is frequently shown by proving that, on the balance of probabilities, the patient would not have made the same decision, if he or she had not been affected by the medication. Alternatively, it may be held that the drugs affected the patient's

---

14. *See, for example*, Kelly v. Hazlett, 15 O.R. (2d) 290 (Ont. C.A.), p. 318 (1976).

competence, and consent is invalidated on this basis. The concept of competence will be discussed shortly.

A third line of reasoning that can apply to invalidate consent given by a patient affected by drugs operates through the information requirement of the doctrine of informed consent, rather than the voluntariness one. This is that the medication caused the patient to be unable to understand the required disclosure of information and that this lack of understanding was apparent to the physician, or would have been apparent to the reasonable physician in the same circumstances.[15] The effects of holding that one or other of the above circumstances are present vary: in the first two instances, the patient's consent will be negated; and in the third, it will be regarded as defective. In these cases, the issue then becomes, did the patient give informed consent at some previous time? If he or she did not, the surgeon has operated either without consent in the first two instances, or with defective consent in the third case. Battery will lie where there is no consent and the surgeon will be liable whether or not damage (in the legal sense of the law) is caused. In the third instance, because negligence is the only cause of action available, the surgeon will only be liable if there is legally cognizable damage. In all cases, imposition of liability will give rise to an obligation to pay compensatory damages.

Two other important issues, which merit discussion, are the legal nature of consent forms and the legal doctrine of causation in relation to failure to obtain informed consent.

To sign a consent form is not necessarily to give informed consent. The signed consent form is simply some evidence that such a consent was given. However, a written consent may be required by law. For instance, in the province of Quebec, consent to surgery or general anesthesia must be in writing.[16] Legislation making the signing of a consent form mandatory provides yet another example of the need for a high degree of sensitivity to possible difficulties that can be encountered in obtaining informed

---

15. *See*, Reibl v. Hughes, *supra* note 5, at 10-11.

16. ORDER IN COUNCIL 3322-72 (November 8, 1972), passed pursuant to the Health Services and Social Services Act, R.S.Q., c. S-5, Quebec Legislature.

consent from aged persons. Provided that consent forms are not being used simply as a form of token compliance with the requirements of the doctrine of informed consent, they are, in general, regarded as having a purpose of underlining the seriousness and importance, for both patients and for health care professionals, of obtaining patients' informed consent to treatment. That is, they are meant to and do, when used properly, have a protective function. However, some old persons who were asked to sign a consent form later became concerned at having done this. They could remember that they had signed something of importance, but not what it was, and were most anxious that they had agreed to something which they ought to have refused.[17] That is, the requirement of written consent was not a source of protection, but of anxiety and suffering for these old persons.

A brief explanation of the legal test of causation applied in "negligent-failure-to-obtain-informed consent" cases is also warranted here. Causation addresses the issue of when a surgeon's failure to obtain informed consent - for example, because of a failure to give a patient all of the information to which he or she is entitled - be held to have caused the damage (usually the crystallization of some risk of the treatment) of which the patient complains? Surgeons will be held to have caused damage through a failure to obtain a patient's informed consent, when (1) but for the conduct on the surgeon's part which constitutes this failure, the reasonable patient in the same circumstances as the particular patient would, on the balance of probabilities, have made a different decision; (2) this different decision would have enabled the patient to avoid the damage; and (3) this error in decision-making by the patient was a reasonably foreseeable result of the surgeon's breach of the standard of care.[18]

---

17. *See*, M.P. Lawton, *Psychological Vulnerability of Elderly Subjects*, in PROTECTION OF ELDERLY RESEARCH SUBJECTS, 6 SUMMARY OF THE NATIONAL INSTITUTE ON AGING CONFERENCE (July 18-19, 1977) 12 DHEW Publication No. (NIH) 79-1801.

18. Somerville, *supra* note 6.

196

3. Competence

The third major requirement of the doctrine of informed consent is that the patient be competent. There are two forms of competence - legal and factual competence. Legal competence requires, in general, that the person be an adult and has not been declared incompetent by a court with jurisdiction to do so. In practice, factual competence is more important than legal competence in relation to informed consent. This requires that the patient must be able to understand the nature, consequences and risks of consenting to or refusing all treatment. That is, the legal definition of factual competence focuses on a capacity for cognitive functioning; if a patient can apparently understand the information required to be disclosed, he or she is competent to give an informed consent to or refusal of treatment.

Recent developments in the theory of competence include, first, the abandonment of an approach based solely on global competence or incompetence and the introduction of the notion of possible partial competence and partial incompetence.[19] That is, a person may be competent for the purposes of consenting to or refusing treatment, but be incompetent in some or (although unlikely) even in all other respects. Secondly, and related to the development of a concept of partial competence, is the introduction of a "functional assessment of competence" approach. That is, competence is tested by determining whether or not the person can carry out the functions necessary to undertake the task (for instance, to give informed consent) in relation to which competence is being assessed.

Another recent development with respect to competence has been consideration of whether or not a concept of emotional competence should also be included within the legal definition of competence. This would apply where a person was cognitively competent - that is, in relation to competence to give informed consent, apparently understood the required disclosure of information - but his or her emotional reaction to that knowledge was so far outside a range of reactions that could be regarded as normal, that the person could be described as emotionally incompetent.

---

19. *See, for example*, DEPENDENT ADULTS ACT R.S.A. 1980, c. D-32 (Alberta).

There are risks of abuse in admitting such a concept into the law and, if it were decided to do so, procedural safeguard mechanisms should be employed. These could include, for example, that a refusal of consent by a cognitively competent person could only be overridden with the approval of a court, except in emergency situations in which a defence of necessity would apply.[20]

It also needs to be emphasized that surgeons should be just as wary of relying on the agreement of incompetent persons to undergo surgery, as on such persons' refusals of treatment. This may not always be the approach taken. Certainly, most matters involving allegations of incompetence on a patient's part, brought before a court, concern patients' refusal of medical treatment. While it would be rare[21] that a surgeon would be going to court alleging that a patient gave an incompetent consent (the surgeon would simply withhold the treatment if the treatment were elective; or seek the authorization of the legal representative of an incompetent person; or rely on the defense of necessity in an emergency), it is not unlikely that a patient would make such an allegation in a suit for failure to obtain informed consent. The issue of whether a patient's consent was competent could also arise outside such a context, for instance, in criminal or professional disciplinary proceedings in which it was relevant to know whether or not a patient competently consented to treatment.

In the same vein, it is worth noting that the more a patient's decision deviates from that which the physician thinks is appropriate and would make if he or she were in the same circumstances, and the more serious the outcome of the patient's decision, the more likely it is that the patient will be designated incompetent.[22]

---

20. For an in-depth discussion of the concept referred to here, *see* M.A. Somerville, *Refusal of Medical Treatment in 'Captive' Circumstances*, 63 CAN. BAR REV. 59 (1985).

21. Such a case could arise where the surgeon wanted to test the validity of the consent of a doubtfully competent person to a non-therapeutic intervention, for example, non-therapeutic contraceptive sterilization, when the law only allows this to be undertaken on competent persons with their informed consent.

22. L.H. Roth, A. Meisl, C.W. Lidz, *Tests of Competence to Consent to Treatment, 134* AMERICAN J. OF PSYCHIATRY 279 (1977).

198

In short, the concept of competence can be used as a patient control mechanism. It is more subtle and less obvious in its operation as such a mechanism than more overt mechanisms, such as commitment or interdiction (a formal declaration by a court that a person is legally incompetent) or involuntary hospitalization. It should be noted here that while the two former mechanisms depend on finding that the person is incompetent or subject to periods of incompetence, the latter does not. In order to confine a person pursuant to an order for involuntary hospitalization a finding is required that the person is dangerous to himself or herself or others, or in danger of imminent and serious physical harm, unless so confined.[23] That is, such persons are not necessarily incompetent. There is often confusion in this respect, especially regarding whether or not refusal of treatment by involuntarily hospitalized patients must be respected. The short answer is that the refusals cannot be overridden on the basis of any presumed incompetence and, in the case of competent persons, would have to be respected unless some other justification for not doing so - for instance, there was legislation authorizing such overriding - were available.

It is also relevant to consider irrational decisions by patients or those based on irrational or non-rational (unconscious) factors. Again, it is highly probable that only those decisions with which surgeons disagree will be challenged on such bases. Provided patients are competent, they have the right to have their decisions respected even if they are irrational, unless some other justification for overriding them exists (for instance, the doctrine of necessity might apply in some such cases), but such justifications do not include simply that the decision is irrational. It is recognized that it can be extremely difficult for surgeons to live with a patient's decision when they regard the patient's decision as irrational and serious in outcome, and in some cases the best solution might be to transfer the patient to another surgeon. In such circumstances, great care needs to be taken to ensure that the patient is not abandoned. Abandonment occurs if the surgeon-patient relation-

---

23. See, M.A. Somerville, *Changes in Mental Health Legislation as Indicators of Changing Values and Policies*, in M. Roth and R. Bluglass, Psychiatry, HUMAN RIGHTS AND THE LAW 156, Cambridge University Press (Cambridge 1985).

ship is terminated in a way that no reasonably competent surgeon would adopt and termination causes damage to the patient. Further, in some cases where there is no other appropriate surgeon to whom the patient can be transferred, termination of the surgeon-patient relationship, including by transfer, may not be acceptable legally.

In cases of disagreement between surgeons and patients as to the appropriate form of treatment, surgeons may need to take care not to adopt a "package approach". In effect, this means that the surgeon gives the patient an ultimatum - he or she can either accept the "treatment package" that the surgeon offers or have no treatment at all from that surgeon.[24] This can be a form of arrogance, professional imperialism and manipulation on the surgeon's part. Legally, it could be held to amount to coercion to consent to the "package" and, consequently, invalidate consent. In addition, surgeons should recognize that respecting a patient's refusal of treatment, or of part of the treatment, can prove therapeutic. This would occur if it causes the surgeon and patient to explore their differences through conversation, share their uncertainties and build mutual trust. Such exploration can result in activation of the "true placebo" effect mentioned before[25] - the surgeon as a placebo enabling patients to release their own self-healing capacities - which can be compared with "false placebo" effects (those which are mediated through deception).[26]

The overriding of a competent patient's refusal of surgery raises difficult medical, ethical and legal issues. The courts have been faced with a variety of such cases. They can range from a woman's refusal of a caesarian section when such a refusal endangers the life of her unborn child; to an elderly person's refusal of an amputation in a situation where this refusal means almost certain death; to a prisoner's refusal of surgery to remove life-threatening pieces of wire lodged in his esophagus when he had

---

24. *See*, Somerville, *supra* note 19.

25. *See*, Somerville, *supra* note 19, at 130.

26. Katz, *supra* note 3, at 190-95.

200

swallowed them in a suicide attempt.[27] Factors, which may or may not be treated as relevant by a court in such cases, include whether the refusal of treatment endangers the life of another person, for instance, that of the pregnant woman endangers her child; whether the condition requiring surgery was deliberately self-induced; whether the person is or is not incarcerated; and, even, whether the person does or does not have dependents. It would seem that surgeons have no power to override such refusal without the authorization of a court. While the precise basis of any jurisdiction on the part of a court to give such an authorization is unclear, the reality is that a surgeon would be protected from the imposition of legal liability by such an authorization and it is highly unlikely that the judge who gave it would be sued.[28]

When a patient is incompetent to consent to or to refuse surgery, someone else must make the decision on behalf of the patient. Traditionally, this situation has been referred to as one involving "proxy consent", but it is proposed that a preferable term is "third party authorization". This makes it clear that the parameters of what one may consent to with respect to someone else are not necessarily the same as those which govern what one may consent to with respect to oneself.

An incompetent patient's legal representative is the appropriate person to authorize any surgery on the patient. If a patient is subject to a declaration of legal incompetence, the court will have appointed a legal representative. This, however, is likely to be the exceptional situation. When this is not the case, in most common law jurisdictions the next-of-kin is treated as the legal representative of an incompetent person, although this may not be soundly based legally, except with respect to parents in relation to their minor children. There is usually no or little legal risk involved in this practice, however, provided the surgery is intended to be therapeutic, is necessary, and is not a research intervention. This is especially true when there is consensus among all family members and members of the health care team that the surgery should be undertaken. The same is also likely to be true with

27. Somerville, *supra* note 19.

28. Somerville, *supra* note 19.

respect to withholding surgery, although there is a stronger possibility that an "outside" person could consider that surgery was wrongfully withheld, rather than wrongfully undertaken, and seek to intervene because of this.

It is important to be particularly sensitive to the issues raised in carrying out surgery on incompetent persons. First, such persons must not be denied necessary surgery simply because they are incompetent.[29] Second, they must not be subjected to unnecessary surgery. Although this is probably more unlikely in the case of incompetent aged persons than with younger incompetent persons (especially young incompetent women who may be subjected to hysterectomies for reasons of family or institutional convenience), it could occur. In particular, care needs to be taken, in cases which are borderline as to whether or not surgery is indicated for an old person, that there is no conflict of interest involved, such as that a young surgeon in training is seeking opportunities to practice difficult surgical techniques and this influences the decision to carry out surgery. Third, just because a person is incompetent with respect to informed consent, does not mean that the person has no feelings concerning what happens to him or her. The approach taken should be to work from a presumption that the incompetent patient's feelings should be taken into account and respected to the greatest possible degree and that any overriding of such feelings must be able to be justified by the surgeon. Consequently, in situations of equal doubt as to whether or not amputation surgery, for example, should be undertaken on an incompetent old person, that person's strong feelings about not having his or her bodily integrity interfered with should govern.

Dying Elderly Persons

A matter often of particular importance to elderly persons is for them to have control over the medical treatment that they will or will not be given should they become incompetent, especially if they are dying. There has been doubt in the law whether the wishes of a person, expressed while competent, as to the medical

29. *See, e.g.*, Re Superintendent of Family and Child Services and Dawson, et. al. W.W.R. 618 (B.C.S.C.) (1983).

202

treatment to be given or withheld should he or she become incompetent, govern such treatment decisions. To deal with such doubts, "living will" and "durable power of attorney" legislation has been passed in some jurisdictions. In some jurisdictions, legislation of the former type, which governs the rights of incompetent terminally ill persons to have their "advance directives" regarding treatment respected, is incorporated into statutes of a broader nature that deal with rights to refuse medical treatment, in general.[30]

The "living will" consists of a document signed by the patient directing his or her physician and family as to the treatment that should be given or withheld should the patient be terminally ill and incompetent to make a decision at the time. A "durable power of attorney" enables a patient to appoint a substitute decision-maker of his or her choice, who will make decisions regarding medical treatment of the patient, should the patient become incompetent. Such an approach is less invasive of the rights of incompetent persons who have been competent, than simply having a certain person, for instance, the next-of-kin, automatically designated as the person's legal representative. The patient, while competent, can choose someone whom they trust, who is likely to know the patient's wishes, and who can be given directions by the patient in the durable power of attorney document or otherwise, as to the content of the decisions that the patient wants to be implemented in certain circumstances. Such a mechanism not only reduces any future suffering of the patient caused by inappropriate decisions which are contrary to what the patient would have decided if he or she had been competent to do so, but also it reduces any present suffering arising from anxiety caused by anticipation that such a situation could occur and that nothing can be done to prevent it. The latter is a frequent and real source of suffering for many aged persons.

Surgeons sometimes have difficulty in accepting patients' refusals of treatment, in some cases because they have been trained only in interventionist approaches and have great difficulty standing by and not acting, even when this is the most appropriate

30. Legal Advisors Committee, Concern for Dying, *The Right to Refuse Treatment: A Model Act*, 73(8) AM. J. OF PUBLIC HEALTH 918 (1983).

course of conduct. In comparison, it would probably be rare that most surgeons would feel uncomfortable complying with a patient's decision to undergo surgery. Part of the solution to this problem will be to change the authoritarian model transmitted in some medical education, that is, the role model that indicates, subtly or otherwise, that surgeons may impose their decisions on patients when they consider this to be in the patients' "best interests."

Thought also needs to be given to educating surgeons in such a way that they will come to view helping a dying patient by their presence, and with care and concern, as a worthwhile, appropriate and successful use of their skills. Although such forms of medical intervention are not surgery, it might be that surgeons are the only persons able to provide patients with the care of this kind that they need, and, sometimes, need desperately. This will occur when the surgeon has been in a treatment relationship with a patient who is now dying, and further surgery is regarded as medically inappropriate or refused by the patient, but the patient needs the surgeon-patient relationship to continue. Surgeons should be careful not to consider that their treatment role is terminated in such circumstances and psychologically, or even physically, abandon the patient. Failure on the part of surgeons to continue to communicate with terminally ill patients, or failure to make themselves available to discuss with patients their condition, prognosis and feelings can create in patients a feeling of psychological abandonment and a state of intense "pre-mortem" loneliness, which, as Katz says, is "more fearsome to patients than death itself."[31]

Pain Relief Treatment

Provision of adequate pain relief treatment is an issue of relevance to all patients undergoing surgery, including aged persons, and often of special relevance to terminally-ill persons. It is dehumanizing and cruel to leave persons in pain and persons fear not only the pain, but also the dehumanization and the cruelty this involves. To experience such fear constitutes additional suffering for a person who is already suffering pain.

---

31. Katz, *supra* note 3, at 223.

204

It can be argued that there is a legal obligation to provide adequate relief treatment, breach of which amounts to medical malpractice, that is, professional negligence.[32] There should be no fear of incurring legal liability in giving necessary pain relief treatment to dying persons, even where this could shorten their lives.[33] This is not to advocate euthanasia (intentional killing in order to relieve suffering), which can be distinguished from the situation in which possibly life-shortening pain relief treatment is made available. In the latter case, the primary aim in giving the treatment is to relieve pain and the means used are necessary to achieve this end. It is an unwanted secondary effect that this treatment may, or even will, shorten life. Such a "double effect" justification can be criticized as a facade or semantic cover-up and sometimes it can be used as this. This would certainly be true if the real situation were one in which pain relief treatment was given in order to shorten life. Then it is not distinguishable from euthanasia in which life is shortened in order to relieve suffering and, sometimes, pain.

However, because allowing a particular justification means that abuses are possible, is not necessarily a reason to abandon that justification. It should not be abandoned if, as it is suggested is the case here, it is needed and appropriate. Some "slippery slopes" either cannot or should not be avoided; however, as in skiing, negotiating these always calls for judgment and control. In some senses, to accept a justification that allows life-shortening pain relief treatment to be given, but does not permit euthanasia, is to strike a middle course in balancing the values of sanctity of life and quality of life. Respect for the principle of sanctity of life is upheld to the greatest degree possible, consistent with not abandoning persons to a state of unbearable pain. To provide non-terminally ill persons with pain relief treatment that might shorten life raises many more difficulties, although it would probably be a rare situation in which it would be necessary. Such treatment might be made available, for instance, where the risk of the patient commit-

---

32. M.A. Somerville, *Pain and Suffering at Interfaces of Medicine and Law* XXXVI U. OF TORONTO L. J. 286 (1986).

33. *Id.*

ting suicide if treatment were not given, was far greater than any risk to life presented by the pain relief treatment.[34]

The most important factors for surgeons to keep in mind in relation to the provision of adequate pain relief treatment are, first, the harmful effects that their own attitudes can have on both patients and other health care professionals. For instance, attitudes may be held that the patient is simply a "complainer", or is exaggerating the pain, or might become a drug addict. Secondly, surgeons may not, in comparison with nursing staff, have a sufficient opportunity to perceive the patient's pain. Further, it needs to be kept in mind that establishing a system in which patients feel frightened that they will not be provided with adequate pain relief treatment can augment the intensity of the pain suffered by those patients. Correlatively, introducing measures such as allowing patients to administer their own pain relief treatment as required, within certain limits, can reduce both the level of pain experienced and the doses of pain relief medication required by the patient.

Medical Research

The issue of medical research has been raised at various points throughout this article. Old persons may need special consideration and protection in this regard because they may be particularly vulnerable to being coerced to participate as research subjects, or they could be seen as a target population. The latter can be true when they form a readily available group such as when they are institutionalized. Further, institutionalized aged persons may be seen as especially desirable as research subjects, because they constitute an easily manipulated and, in some aspects, homogeneous population -for instance, with respect to diet. Old persons may also be used as research subjects because, were damage to result, any liability to compensate would be of a lesser amount than if a young person were injured. This is true because there may be no loss of income from employment; damages for future loss would be assessed for a shorter period of time; and old persons are less likely to have dependent children, who could also

---

34. *Id.*

recover damages for any loss which they suffered as a result of the person on whom they depended being injured.

Carrying out medical research on dying, elderly persons is a particularly sensitive issue. This should not be prohibited; to do so would be to deny elderly persons the same opportunities as other persons have for altruism and feelings of contributing to others, and, perhaps, of using their illness for some positive end. However, care needs to be taken. In particular, only competent persons who have given a fully informed and voluntary consent may participate in non-therapeutic research. It is also necessary to ensure, in carrying out certain procedures, that research is not disguised as therapy, whether intentionally or through lack of sufficient awareness of one's own motives as a health care professional. Such confusion is particularly likely to occur when research is combined with therapy in situations where the intervention either is doubtfully therapeutic for the particular patient, but is scientifically and ethically valid research, or is non-therapeutic research carried out in a therapeutic setting.

This is to raise the distinction between therapeutic and non-therapeutic research; the use of this distinction has advantages and disadvantages.[35] The danger in labeling an intervention as therapeutic research is that insufficient care will be taken to safeguard the research subject's rights. This is because the characterization of the intervention as therapeutic and, therefore, intended to benefit the person, will reduce awareness of what is needed in view of the fact that it is also research. But, a disadvantage of abandoning the characterization of some research as therapeutic is that this may not reflect reality. Some interventions may then be labeled "pure" therapy when it has research elements and, likewise, this reduces the level of protection of research subjects.

It also needs to be considered whether elderly persons should serve as research subjects for surgical procedures involving high level medical technology, such as organ transplantation, although

---

35. M.A. Somerville, *Clarifying the Concepts of Research Ethics: A Second Filtration*, 2 CLINICAL RESEARCH 29, 101-105 (1981); M.A. Somerville, *Therapeutic and Non-therapeutic Medical Procedures - What Are the Distinctions?* 2 HEALTH LAW IN CANADA 85 (1981).

in almost all cases they have a therapeutic aim.[36] In particular, it needs to be queried whether it is acceptable to classify a dying person as being too old to receive a human heart transplant, for example, but then to offer this person transplantation of an artificial heart. The issues are not easy. Is it more acceptable not to offer any treatment, when this will mean certain death, than a highly experimental treatment such as transplantation of an artificial heart? When there are inadequate numbers of organs to supply all who need them or, even if shortage of organs is not a problem, there are inadequate resources to fund all the transplants which are required, is it acceptable to use a cut-off age beyond which transplantation will not be carried out, although there is no sound medical basis to justify such discrimination? Discrimination on the basis of age, which has widespread legal and ethical ramifications, will not be discussed here. It is interesting to note in this regard, however, that the "Report of the Massachusetts Task Force on Organ Transplantation" recommended that there should not be discrimination on the basis of age in providing transplantation treatment.[37] But, even when such approaches are adopted, care is still needed to ensure that decisions not to offer treatment, in reality taken on the basis of a prohibited ground (such as age discrimination), are not disguised as having been taken on some acceptable basis such as medical unsuitability.

Conclusion

The considerable dialogue that has taken place in regard to medical-ethical-legal issues in the last fifteen years, somewhat paradoxically, has placed us in a situation in which it might be said that we are just at the beginning of a long exploration of rights "to" and "in" medical care in general. This exploration will take the

---

36. An example of a situation in which such an aim would not be present is where kidneys from aborted fetuses are transplanted into the arms of research subjects in order to test the functioning and continued growth of the kidneys and whether or not they are rejected by the host research subject.

37. *The Report of the Massachusetts Task Force on Organ Transplantation*, reported in part in 13 LAW MEDICINE AND HEALTH CARE 8 (1985).

form of in depth examination of very specific matters. There is no doubt that the subject matter of this article, the rights of elderly persons "in" surgical care, will form an important part of this debate. Undertaking surgery has a certain dramatic impact which is not easily concealed or avoided and it can crystallize issues and act as a focus for the generation and expression of deep feelings.

Because of the greater visibility and identification of old persons needing surgery than of those needing some other forms of medical care, it could well be that this will provide one of the important arenas in which issues related to medical care of elderly persons will be addressed and solutions sought. As always, the guiding principles must be first, to do no harm; second, to try to do some good; and, above all, to try to act humanely and with respect for others. We need to do this not only for the sake of others who are affected by our decisions, but also for our own sakes, both now - because we must live with our decisions - and in the future - because if we are fortunate, we, too, will become elderly persons and we may need surgical care.

EUTHANASIA IN THE NETHERLANDS:
CURRENT COURT DECISIONS
AND LEGISLATION

J.L.M. Elders [*]
J. Wöretshofer [**]
Netherlands

In the Netherlands, euthanasia takes place in somewhere between 5,000 and 40,000 cases every year.[1] Until 1990, approximately 25 cases of euthanasia, or cases related to euthanasia, were tried by the criminal courts. A case of euthanasia generally receives publicity (and the public prosecutor is only informed about the case) if the physician states on the patient's death certificate that the patient did not die from natural causes or if the physician voluntarily surrenders to the authorities. Before a euthanasia charge is brought, however, the public prosecutor can decide to drop the charge. The authority of the prosecutor to make this decision is found in the Dutch principle of discretionary powers based on the opportunity doctrine.

---

[*] Deputy Member of the Court of Appeal; former Professor of civil law at the University of Limburg, Maastricht, Netherlands; Editor of EUTHANASIE, RECHT EN PRAKTIJK, 1985;

[**] Master of Law, Groningen, 1983; currently preparing a thesis about euthanasia and other life-shortening actions of physicians.

1. The various estimates differ. Until 1990 it is estimated that in the Netherlands between 5,000 and 10,000 euthanasia-cases occurred. Extrapolation from a poll in the spring of 1990 gave a number between 10,000 and 40,000. The high number was argued against by the most important organization of physicians in the Netherlands: the KNMG (Koninklijk Nederlandsche maatschappij ter bevordering van de geneeskunst). *See* VOLKSKRANT, February 22, 1990.

Current Court Decisions

1. Statutory Provisions

The most important articles in the Dutch Penal Code (DPC)[2] concerning euthanasia are Articles 293 and 294 DPC. Both articles are part of Title XIV of the Second Book of the DPC. The Title reads: "Crimes against life." In Art. 293 DPC homicide upon request is subject to prosecution. Homicide upon request is a less serious offense than manslaughter and murder.[3] Murder is the most serious offense against life. The important part of Art. 293 DPC is that the actor must have acted intentionally and with premeditation. Manslaughter requires intentionally killing and homicide upon request is intentionally killing. The Criminal Law of the Netherlands does not make allowances for motives. The essential difference between murder and manslaughter on the one hand and homicide upon request on the other is the express request for the act. The following sections deal with such homicide:

Art. 293 DPC

"A person who takes the life of another person at the other person's express and serious request, is punishable by a term of imprisonment of not more than twelve years or a fine" of up to Dfl. 100,000.00.

Article 294 DPC is generally given the heading of "aiding suicide."

---

2. Wetboek van Strafrecht, Sr.

3. See H. J. Smidt, *Geschiedenis van het Wetboek van Strafrecht*, Volledige Verzameling van regeeringsontwerpen, gewisselde stukken, gevoerde beraadslagingen, enz., DEEL II, Haarlem 1981, (23 druk), p. 463. The district court of Breda, Nederlands Juristenblad (NJB) 1984, 503, found a physician guilty of death on request, although he was charged primarily with murder. Subsidiary charges of manslaughter and even more subsidiary charges of death on request were also brought. The evidence was found sufficient to convict him of murder.

Art. 294 DPC

> "A person who intentionally incites another to
> commit suicide, or who aids such a person or
> provides him with the necessary means, is
> punishable by a term of imprisonment of not
> more than three years or to a fine of up to Dfl.
> 25,000, - where death ensuses".

Art. 294 DPC is a delictum sui generis.[4] The act by itself (suicide) is not punishable, however aiding suicide is, but only if the attempt succeeds. By making aiding suicide, but not suicide itself, punishable, Art. 294 DPC differs from the usual rules regarding complicity. Another exception is that attempted suicide is not punishable. The legislature of 1886, the time from which the DPC dates, had practical reasons for that. If an attempt to commit suicide was not successful, the right to prosecute lapsed. The legislators did not want to regard the failure in the act of suicide as a criminal offense, neither for the suicidal person, or his accomplice, because the legislature regarded an unsuccessful attempt in a certain way as extraordinary. Furthermore, they feared that a prosecution (of the suicidal person or the participant) might lead to another attempt.[5]

The Dutch nowadays generally speak of "self-killing" instead of "self-murder." From this one can see a changed attitude about killing oneself: the purpose is to avoid the negative connotation of the word "murder" in this respect.

2. Definitions of Euthanasia

According to the most commonly employed definition of euthanasia, euthanasia is an "intended act (or omission) intended to shorten life carried out by a person other than the person

---

4. See H. J. Smidt, II, *supra* note 3, at 465.

5. See H. J. Smidt, II, *supra* note 3, at 466.

concerned upon the request of the latter."[6]   Without additional
information this definition is only a reformulation of art. 293 DPC,
without changing the meaning of the article.   Each homicide upon
request would, therefore, be considered euthanasia.   The definition
is too wide.   Some years ago there was also another definition
more frequently used, which nowadays is used only incidentally.
The Dutch Society for deliberate euthanasia (Nederlandse Verenin-
ging voor Vrijwillige Euthanasie = NVVE) defined euthanasia as "an
intentionally life-shortening act carried out on another person in the
latter's interest."   In this definition, "upon his request" is substituted by "in his interest."   "In his interest" is both narrower and wider
than "upon his request."   Narrower, because a third person has to
act in the interest of the person concerned and wider, since a
request is not required.   "In his interest" may also apply to patients
who cannot or can no longer express their will, e.g., newborns,
comatose patients and seriously mentally retarded persons.   As the
killing of seriously disabled persons recently has been playing a
more prominent role in the discussion about euthanasia, some
would stress the expression "in his interest."   In our view - and in
accordance with general opinion - there should be a clear difference
between homicide upon request and killing someone without his
request.   Therefore, we define euthanasia as "a life-shortening act
carried out by a person other than the one concerned, upon the
latter's request and in his interest."

The word "upon his request" is frequently replaced by the
adverb "voluntarily."   But "voluntarily" might also be read to
connote an assumed wish.   Therefore, we prefer the words "upon
request."   However, our definition of euthanasia is - like the others
- only a first attempt to define the concept.   For practical purposes
- in law in particular - the definition must be more precisely
constrained.   We shall return to this point.

In its report published in the autumn of 1985, the Dutch
Government   Commission   for   Euthanasia   (Staatscommissie
Euthanasie) defined euthanasia as "an intentionally life-shortening
act by a person other than the one involved upon request of the

---

6. See H.J.J. Leenen, *Rechten van mensen in de gezondheidszorg*, ALPHEN
AAN DE RIJN 213 (1978).

latter".[7]   The Commission did not want to incorporate other elements into the definition. Otherwise a normative element would be inserted in the definition of euthanasia.

For a clear discussion another difference is important. Frequently a distinction is made in the euthanasia debate between punishable and non-punishable euthanasia. Homicide upon request, as described in Art. 293 DPC, is taken to be the punishable form. Homicide upon request, which is not covered by Art. 293 DPC, is the justified act, the non-punishable euthanasia.   To prevent confusion we shall speak of euthanasia hereafter only when the justified act is meant. Otherwise, we shall speak of homicide upon request. Euthanasia does not include aided suicide.

That the earlier mentioned "inciting someone to suicide" does not meet the terms of euthanasia is obvious, so that we need not discuss it further. But it is not true of the other two kinds of aiding suicide: helping a person to commit suicide or provide him with the necessary means for suicide. It is questionable whether who finally performs the fatal act is important in euthanasia.[8]

Some persons deny that there are differences between euthanasia and aiding suicide. They regard both acts as forms of euthanasia. The meaning of the legislation of 1886 does recognize a difference, however, as can be seen by the great difference in the maximum penalty of Art. 293 as opposed to Art. 294 of the Dutch Criminal Code. The justification of this difference is that in euthanasia, from the very moment the patient has expressed his will, he is only an object, so that a change of mind may be difficult.

The patient who takes the deathly medications himself keeps the decision about his life in his own hands and carries the full responsibility for his own action.

One could also ask if a person may authorize someone else, physician or not, to end his life, by renouncing his right to live. Another school may see euthanasia as a medical act, expressly restricted to a physician. According to them, the physician is the

---

7. *Rapport of the Staatscommissie Euthanasie*, Deel I 26 ('s-Gravenhage 1985). The staatscommissie Euthanasie was installed by the government.

8. *See* Sutorius, *Vrijwillige Euthanasie of de Gewetensfunctie van een rechtspolitiek conflict*, Nederlands Juristenblad (NJB) 56 (1984).

one who decides - but of course only upon request of the patient - if euthanasia should be committed for medical reasons.

We prefer to make no distinction between euthanasia and aiding suicide other than inciting suicide. In both cases the purpose is to help someone to achieve mercy killing.[9] Naturally, in both cases the necessary conditions must be fulfilled.

3. Euthanasia and Pseudo-Euthanasia

In the first years of the debate about euthanasia in the Netherlands, which started around 1970, a difference was made between several kinds of euthanasia. Differences were noted between active and passive euthanasia and between direct and indirect euthanasia.

Euthanasia is active if death is induced by an act, a doing. If death of the person is a consequence of remaining passive, of following the person's request to do nothing, then it is called passive euthanasia. In the relationship between physician and patient the refusal of (further) treatment by the patient would be regarded as passive euthanasia (with the death being caused by non-treatment). When the physician does not act due to the expressed will of the patient, then the patient dies from a cause of death within himself. In recent years, gradually, the opinion has gained ground that non-treatment upon request should not be seen as a kind of euthanasia. A physician who acts contrary to the will of the patient can eventually even be found guilty of malpractice.

Active euthanasia requires the active participation or help of a third person in the carrying out of the fatal act. The person who gets killed is not dying from a cause of death within himself, but from a external cause. This could happen in two ways. First, a third person could want to reduce a patient's suffering, but the remedy which might help has as an unwanted side-affect - a reducing of the life of the patient. So the "helping person" has deliberately shortened the life of the patient. If the third person is a physician and if he has no other means to reduce the suffering without this side-effect and if the patient clearly accepts this kind of treatment, then the acting of the physician is justified. This act

9. See H. J. J. Leenen, *Euthanasie en hulp bij zelfdoding*, NJB 103 (1982).

was called active, indirect euthanasia. It is indirect because the intention was directed to reducing the suffering and the death of the patient was "only" seen as a side-effect. Shortening the life of a patient in this manner is no longer regarded as a kind of euthanasia so long as the physician has no other means of helping the patient. In other words, the act must be proportional and subsidiary.

Nowadays it is also generally accepted that a physician is not obliged to continue treatment in cases in which - from a medical point of view - the treatment would be regarded as superfluous. A treatment is superfluous if it does not have any medical purpose and only lengthens or even increases the patient's suffering. As the judgment of the effect of a treatment is a purely medical one, the physician has no obligation to fulfill the request of a patient for treatment when he, the physician, regards the treatment as superfluous. Should the physician in such a case not comply with the request of the patient, he could be found guilty of malpractice.

We can thus distinguish between euthanasia and what nowadays is called "pseudo-euthanasia". These pseudo kinds are when death of the patient follows:

* non-treatment of a patient upon his request or with his permission,

* life-shortening treatment of suffering upon request of the patient and with permission,

* non treatment when treatment has to be regarded as superfluous.

The government wants to restrict euthanasia as it is now practiced. But even the government has excluded these three pseudo kinds of euthanasia from its definition of euthanasia. We shall discuss the government's draft statement on euthanasia later.

Excepting the pseudo kinds of euthanasia, only active killing upon request can be regarded as euthanasia. As such, euthanasia is a delictum commissionis.

4. Conditions for Euthanasia

Advocates of euthanasia consider euthanasia a form of

medical aid. Not every request for euthanasia by a patient is, therefore, sufficient to justify it and not every act helping the ending of life can be seen as aid. The protection of human life, the respect for human life, which is based on Articles 293 and 294 DPC, has to take a primary place in law. For some, this respect always excludes euthanasia. In their opinion, human life has an intrinsic value, independent of the state of the human being. Others demand room for exceptions. According to them, there are emergency cases which allow for an exception to the general rule. Or, said another way, under certain conditions reverence of human life includes the possibility of death in a dignified manner. There are necessary conditions respecting the patient. If one of these conditions is not fulfilled, then the act surely cannot be called euthanasia, but must be seen as a criminal act. However, even if in a given case these conditions are fulfilled, there arises the next question: can one call the actions aid? Aid always has to be meticulously applied, but in the case of euthanasia there should be special emphasis on meticulous aid.

The conditions relating to the patient's situation and the requirements of care due in medical aid are elaborated in court decisions and literature, but they are not always explicit. In this article we will clarify them. The first two decisions formulating conditions and requirements for justified euthanasia set the law of euthanasia. Later verdicts only supplied nuances.[10]

The Conditions Relating to the Patient's Situation

In the court decisions we find the following conditions which are required to be satisfied by the patient:

> * a well considered decision - voluntarily made and expressed,

---

10. The first two verdicts are the verdict of the district court Leeuwarden, February 21, 1973, NJ 1973, 183 and the verdict of the district court Rotterdam, December 1, 1981, NJ 1982, 63. Of great importance are further the verdicts of the district courts of Groningen, March 1, 1984, NJ 1984, 450 and Alkmaar, May 10, 1983, NJ 1983, 407, because these verdicts led to verdicts by the Dutch Supreme Court. NEDERLANDSE JURISPRUDENTIE (NJ) is a weekly magazine filled with important court decisions.

        *   persistent and unbearable suffering, and

        *   a hopeless situation.

The district court of Leeuwarden in its verdict of February 21, 1973,[11] did not demand that the patient had to be terminally ill. But the demand that the patient be terminally ill has been inserted into the government's proposal.

Requirements Imposed in Respect of the Degree of Care Provided

The only person who is entitled to administer euthanasia is a physician. The decision for euthanasia must be made by more than one person. Experts who are involved shall give an independent opinion on the patient's condition.

Because euthanasia is regarded as not punishable only if it is performed by, or at least under supervision of, a physician in the context of medical treatment, we restrict our further discussion to euthanasia performed by physicians. Of course, it is possible there may be situations in which members of the family or friends feel obliged to accede to a person's request to die. In court decisions, such cases are never excused. The courts deny relief to the defendants holding that they could and should have chosen another way. In other words, the defendants should have consulted a physician.

Illustrative of this type of case is the verdict of the district court Almelo of September 26, 1989.[12] A spouse suffered from dystrophy and had reached the terminal stage of this illness, which meant complete paralysis. The spouse several times requested that her husband and a mutual female friend end her life. The husband and the friend ultimately agreed. The patient stopped eating and told several other friends about her wishes. By accident, the family doctor (with whom the relationship obviously was not that good) heard about the plans. He did not want to

---

11. *Id.*

12. Almelo, NJ (1989).

engage in euthanasia so the husband and the friend ended the life
of the woman by giving her lethal tablets. The court rejected their
plea that there were no alternatives because the family doctor did
not want to cooperate. The court decided:

* that the family doctor could still have come to a
  responsible decision,

* that it could not be said that there were no ways to
  contact other physicians and finally:

* "It could have been that any conscientious working
  physician under the circumstances according to
  present views would refuse cooperation. In that case
  the family doctor had not cut off other ways."

It can be seen that euthanasia may only be administered by
a physician. But it is not sufficient that it is administered by a
physician. The patient's situation must also be hopeless. Whether
a patient's situation is hopeless is partly a medical and partly a
subjective judgment. A situation which a physician regards
precarious becomes hopeless or as it is sometimes called unbearable, only if the patient says so. If the condition is truly hopeless
from a purely medical perspective then treatment would be
considered superfluous. When a physician finally concludes that
the situation is superfluous, it is a medical judgment which the
patient, family members and friends have to accept. It then falls
within the class of the above mentioned "pseudo-euthanasia."

Euthanasia and the Position of the Physician

Under the existing law, euthanasia by a physician may be
exonerated in two ways. First, the physician can plead that he
acted contrary to the law expressed in Articles 293 or 294 DPC,
but that his act was justified. Second, the physician can plead not
guilty because of a lawful excuse.

Grounds for Personal Excuse

There are two possible grounds of personal excuse for
euthanasia: force majeure (psychological compulsion) and the

absence of culpability.[13] A plea of force majeure by a physician has little chance, because in doing his job a physician is regarded as capable of withstanding the psychological pressure arising from such situations.[14] A plea of the absence of culpability might be more successful. A personal excuse does not offer a general answer. If the exemption of the physician is a result of a plea of the absence of culpability, then the problem of euthanasia gets individualized. The situation of the patient is no longer the main concern, but the focus is on the physician. This second form of excuse is a common form of excuse.

Accepting a lawful excuse results in a finding that euthanasia was justified, whereas a successful plea of personal excuse results in the physician being found not guilty. Therefore, the judge must always first discuss a plea of lawful excuse, if one has been made and if he rejects it, he can then respond to a plea of personal excuse.

Lawful Excuse

Under current legislation three kinds of lawful excuse are important. Two of them are non-statutory, they originate from jurisprudence: the absence of substantive unlawfulness and the medical justification. The third lawful excuse is statutory: necessity. Art. 40 DPC states that one is not punishable for a crime caused by emergency. It is quite difficult to translate Art. 40 DPC, because Dutch jurisprudence derived if from two excluding grounds; one is lawful excuse: the just mentioned necessity. The other one is force majeure, a ground which generally exempts from punishment. We shall discuss here the lawful excuse of necessity. But first we shall discuss the other two lawful excuses which are important for euthanasia. We start with the absence of substantive unlawfulness.

---

13. AVAS refers to AFWEZIGHEID VAN ALLE SCHULD.

14. The Dutch Criminal Law uses the German word "Garantenstellung" for these special demands on someone in his profession.

Absence of Substantive Unlawfulness

At the beginning of the thirties a veterinarian had cows moved from a meadow to a stable. As the veterinarian knew there were at that moment some cows in the stable with hoof and mouth disease. Art. 82 of the "Veewet" of those days forbad bringing cattle intentionally into a state of harm. The veterinarian did not deny the charge. He declared, "I did so because, from a veterinary point of view, it is better that cows stay dry and get infected with hoof and mouth disease, than that they give milk, in which case the disease spreads to the udders and causes other diseases. Dry standing cows can better get through hoof and mouth disease." This case led to two decisions by the Supreme Court (Hoge Raad), which are known as the "Huizer veearts" cases.

In the second "Huizer veearts" arrest, in 1933[15], the Supreme Court recognized the fact that there can be situations, in which an act fits the words of a statue but should not be judged unlawful, because the statute is not really applicable. In other words, the action should not be seen as a criminal offense, although the words of the statute apply. We call that lawful excuse the absence of substantive unlawfulness. In this expression, "substantive" ("materieel" in Dutch) is used as the opposite of "formal." "Formal" unlawfulness is actions which fit the words of the statute.

The best argument for euthanasia is the absence of substantive unlawfulness. Such euthanasia does not fit the classification, of Articles 293 and 294 DPC. The second "Huizer veearts" case is often cited for this principle. A second reason for referring to it will be given further on. Because the absence of substantive unlawfulness is not express grounds for exculpation, the Supreme Court in the "Huizer veearts" cases gave two cumulative criteria for a successful plea of this lawful excuse:

* both the act and the text of the law shall have the same purpose;

---

15. HR Feb. 20, 1933, NJ 1933, 918, m.nt. Taverne.

*   the fact that this act is against written law must be
    clearly seen as an "error" made by the legislator when
    drafting the text.

In euthanasia there are two different sorts of interests concerned. On the one hand, there is the respect for human life in general which constitutes the basis of the Articles 293 and 294 DPC. On the other hand, there is the interest of the individual requesting euthanasia. If these interests are opposite, then a plea of the absence of substantive unlawfulness cannot be successful.

In 1984, for the first time, a euthanasia case came before the Supreme Court, namely the "Alkmaar case."[16] Here the physician's lawyer defended the interests of the suffering by referring to two, as he put it, "norms." The first was the right to self-determination as far as ending one's own life is concerned. The second was the norm to aid a person in utter distress, the maintenance of his dignity and the alleviation or ending of his unbearable suffering. With the second "norm" he really expressed another view of the respect for human life in a specific case (as opposed to the general meaning of Articles 293 and 294 DPC). The lawyers argued that the interest in human life can be expressed as making it possible that a human being can die in a dignified way.

The court of appeal Amsterdam rejected the lawyer's arguments noting that these "norms" cannot be found in the law. Therefore, they can only lead to non-observance of a statutory provision if public opinion regarding euthanasia has become so clear that it is actually possible to speak of two separate norms.

The court of appeal thus acknowledged that a social norm under certain circumstances can be of more importance then the "norm" which stems from a statutory provision. In that case, the statutory provision shall not be applied when one acts in accordance with the social norm. But the court of appeal added that while a trend in favor of euthanasia under certain conditions could be perceived in society, the court still thought it premature to speak of its having general acceptance.

---

16. HR Nov. 27, 1984, NJ 1985, 106 m.nt. Th.W. van Veen.

Rejecting the appeal the court of appeal[17] used the words "quite apart from the question whether a judge has such discretionary power," namely to choose between a statutory provision and a norm which contradicts the statutory one. The Supreme Court upheld the court of appeal. The same words were used by the Supreme Court in its second case on euthanasia.[18]

Even if a very large majority of society would be in favor of euthanasia, it would be hard for a judge to find the absence of substantive unlawfulness. The courts were right to formulate the question, because Art. 11 Wet AB denies a judge the right to consider the inner value of a statute. If the law no longer expresses the opinion of a large portion of society, then it is the task of the legislature, if they find it necessary, to change the law. This, with the exception of applying a law of a higher kind, such as international conventions, is the appropriate process.

The Medical Justification

In a case of euthanasia the district court of Groningen described medical justification as follows:

> "This medical justification means that acting or neglecting to act, whereby - according to the statutory provision - a criminal offense has taken place, is however not punishable, if this behavior is necessary from the point of medical necessity, or if it is very desirable from the point of medical assistance, if and in as far as the behavior consists of a medical act or the neglecting of one, whereby all care and practice demanded by the medical science has been respected."[19]

The former professor and former member of the Supreme

---

17. Hof Amsterdam Nov. 17, 1983, NJ 1984, 43.

18. HR Oct. 21, 1986, NJ 1987, 607, m.nt. G.E. Mulder.

19. Rb. Groningen, 1 maart 1984, NJ 1984, 450.

Court, Enschede,[20] in the Netherlands, was in favor of impunity for a physician who was engaged in euthanasia out of medical justification. According to Enschede, a physician does in fact perform several acts which may lead to death, and euthanasia is only one of them. The fact that, under certain conditions, physicians are entitled to administer euthanasia need not be expressed in the DPC itself. For his point of view, Enschede refers to the history of the DPC and also to the "Huizer veearts" cases.

As to the history of the legislation, while discussing the statutory provision about a new penal code and more specifically about the law on abortion in the parliament in 1880, it was suggested that an exception clause be drafted for abortions carried out by physicians in cases of danger to the life of the female or the fetus.[21] The Minister of Justice at that time, Modderman, pleaded against a written exception clause. He thought it superfluous and said:

> "Generally a physician's acting is completely justified, if he acts in compliance with the rules of his profession (lege artis). . . . It seems better to omit written exception clauses for physicians in such cases on the assumption that the written law will only be interpreted by lawyers, who, even without such a statutory provision, acknowledge the principle: not punishable is the physician who is acting lege artis . . . . There is no indication whatsoever that in the Netherlands the legislature with its always imperfect general expressions (statutory provisions) should intervene, either to protect the physicians against the lawyers, or the society against the physicians . . . . According to the proposed exception, a physician who resorts to abortion in the beginning of pregnancy, would be punishable although foreseeing with certainty that the mother would not be able to give birth to a living

---

20. Ch. J. Enschede, *Euthanasie rechtswetenschappelijk beschouwd*, in Euthanasie - recht, ethiek en medische praktijk, Beschouwingen over een gezamenlijke vergadering ban de Rechtskundige Afdeling van het Thijmgenootschap en de Calvinistische Juristen Vereniging op vrijdag 1 maart 1985 te Amsterdam, Amsterdam 1985; Ch. J. Enschede, *Wetgeving door nalaten en euthanasie*, NJB 241-44 1(985); Ch. J. Enschede, *Euthanasie en overlijdensverklaring*, NJB 797-802 (1985). *See also* G.E. Langemeijer, Ch.J. Enschede, and Th. W. van Veen, *Euthanasie heeft geen wetgeving noding*, NRC HANDELSBLAD, Jan. 14, 1986.

21. H. J. Smidt, II, *see supra* note 3, at 468.

child and would completely unnecessarily slowly pine away. After all, the life of the female would not be in danger at that moment. However, culpability cannot be defended in such a case. The legislature cannot decide what is to be undertaken in such circumstances and therefore it should leave it to the physician to decide."[22]

We have quoted quite a long part of the answer of Modderman, as in our view he - at least for a great part - expressed the attitude with which the legislature in the late 1880's tried to make a new penal code.

Neither chamber of parliament contradicted this statement by Modderman. Neither the article on abortion nor the one on mistreatment was extended by an exemption clause for physicians.

The first question is whether euthanasia can be seen as part of medical treatment. If medical treatment is defined as "the acting of a physician to relieve or end the physical and/or psychological suffering of persons in distress," then euthanasia might be considered part of it. In that case euthanasia would be the final opportunity for a physician to render aid.

The broad definition of health which underlies the definition is in accordance with the one formulated by the WHO in 1948. But quite a few physicians and other citizens do not want it used for euthanasia. For this view they cite the Hippocratic oath which says that a physician is not allowed to give deadly medicines. The task of the physician is not to end human life, but to keep it going. In their view, the broad definition of health by the WHO in 1948 had only a restricted meaning. This was a reaction to acts by physicians in the Third Reich in Germany.

Adherents of euthanasia distinguish between what is sometimes called the old medical ethics and the new medical ethics. In the old medical ethics, a human being must be treated as long as it is technically possible. In the new medical ethics, a human being may only be treated as long as the treatment is reasonable. For them, the new medical ethics became necessary because of the advanced medical technology which can lead to unnecessary human suffering.

But even if euthanasia is not regarded as medical treatment

---

22. H. J. Smidt, II, *see supra* note 3, at 469-470.

it still could be seen as a medical act. The second question is: Can medical justification lead to an exception of a statutory provision?

According to the quote from Minister Modderman, this seems to be the case. But the Minister said that "in general physicians are completely protected . . . . We think that with the words "in general" he wanted to express that exceptions are usually possible. As far as the legislature has expressed his view (even if there is no statutory exception for physicians, the absence of express medical justification is overruled by the will of the legislature.

While discussing Art. 293 DPC (homicide upon request) in the second chamber of the parliament, the Minister said:

> "Consent cannot discharge a person from criminal liability for homicide but it will give the facts a completely different cast. The law does not any longer punish the assault on an certain individual's life but punishes the violation of respect of human life in general instead, regardless of the offender's motives. The act remains a criminal offense against human life. The assault against the life of a certain person vanishes."[23]

In the deliberations of the Dutch Penal Code, the medical justification was discussed. The discussion centered on instances in which it was obvious to everyone, not merely to members of the medical profession, that a physician's intervention was justified. Euthanasia, however, is controversial even among the physicians. In the discussions of Articles 293 and 294 DPC, the special position of the physician was not mentioned. It seems to us highly unlikely that the legislature regarded the assignment of an exceptional position to physicians as self evident and, therefore, did not discuss it, while they mentioned such a position in cases of abortion and malpractice. Therefore, our view is that the legislature did not intend to create an exception for physicians practicing homicide upon request or aiding suicide.

According to the meaning of the Supreme Court on the (second) "Huizer veearts" case, medical justification will only justify non-observance of a statutory provision if the legislature has left room for this while drafting it or has evidently failed to do so

---

23. H.J. Smidt, II, see supra note 3, at 464. *Compare* for Art. 294.

by mistake. Additionally, the act must be the same purpose as the one which constitues the essence of the article.

Enschede in particular refers to the first "Huizer veearts" case and not the second. The first, indeed, supports his view better than the second one. We think, however, the second "Huizer veearts" case to be of greater importance because the Supreme Court provided the necessary distinction in that case. We agree with Klijn[24] that in the "Huizer veearts" case the facts were not punishable - not on the grounds of a veterinarian's justification - but because the acts were not held to be unlawful because the legislature had not explicitly meant to make them unlawful and because they clearly made a mistake in formulating the text of the statute.

The case of the district court Groningen, which provided the above quoted definition of a medical justification, was appealed to the court of appeal of Leeuwarden. In 1984, this court rejected the plea of medical justification.[25] The Supreme Court affirmed.[26] In its view, medical justification of homicide cannot be based on positive (unwritten) law. Neither the history of the legislation nor a change in society's view would admit any other interpretation.

The Supreme Court did not adopt the view of the defense lawyer, that euthanasia performed by a physician was accepted by a great majority of society. First, it was not convinced that a majority judged euthanasia by a physician positively. Even if majority approval was established the court queried whether a judge would be free to establish an exemption from punishment which had not been recognized by the legislature. However, it did not resolve this question.

Necessity

In case law, two sorts of grounds precluding punishment

---

24. W. C. M. Klign, *Euthanasie en de Hoge Raad*, NJB 245-54. (1985).

25. Hof Leeuwarden, Oct. 11, 1984, NJ 1985, 241.

26. HR Oct. 21, 1986, NJ 1987, 607 m.nt. G.E. Mulder.

were derived from the open formulation of Article 40 DPC:[27] the aforementioned force majeure (psychological compulsion) and necessity. Force majeure is a ground precluding punishment and necessity is a lawful excuse. We can demonstrate the meaning of necessity in the context of euthanasia. A physician pursues what in his opinion is a justified aim. The aim is to release a patient from his suffering. The physician is not overpowered by the situation - as is the case with force majeure - but he chooses "rationally" between his conflicting duties and does what he thinks is necessary. His intention is to pursue a higher purpose through euthanasia than the one the legislature adopted in Articles 293 and 294 DPC. The interest of the patient (his situation of suffering coupled with his request for euthanasia) is contradictory to the protected interest in articls 293 and 294 DPC (respect for human life in general). To succeed with a defense of necessity, it must be established, objectively, that the aim pursued is more important than the one protected by the law (principle of proportionality). Furthermore, the physician must demonstrate that he did not have an opportunity to achieve his aim in a less drastic way, e.g., by administering pain-killers (principle of alternatives).

So far, appeals based on necessity are the most successful ones in euthanasia cases. The Supreme Court, in the Alkmaar case, opened the door to this justifying ground for the first time in a case involving euthanasia.[28]

The Supreme Court accepted the physician's appeal in that case on the grounds of emergency as an aspect of necessity, because the physician had carefully weighed the conflicting duties and interests, "in particular, observing the standard of medical ethics and with the knowledge he presumably possessed by virtue of his profession as a physician. The physician made a decision which was - if considered objectively and with regard to the special circumstances of the case - justified."

While hearing the appeal, the court of appeal of Amsterdam concluded that the physician had decided to administer euthanasia because, in the view of the physician, each additional day of life

---

27. *See above* for the text of the article.

28. HR Nov. 27, 1984, NJ 1985, 106 m.nt. Th.W. Van Veen.

was a heavy burden to the patient and caused her unbearable suffering. The Supreme Court construed "his judgment" as "his professional judgment as a physician."

The court of appeal had rejected necessity, reasoning that the physician had not proven the absence of other choices convincingly enough. The requirement of no alternatives had not been met. The court of appeal indicated it had doubt as to this particularly important subject. The Supreme Court held that it was the task of the court of appeal to dispel this doubt. It should have investigated whether, on the basis of the general medical principles including standards of medical ethics, there really had been necessity, as argued by the physician. The Supreme Court did not state precisely what questions the court of appeal should have sought to resolve, since the answers depend on several factors which may differ from case to case. For the Alkmaar case, however, the Court gave the following examples:

*   whether - and if so, to what extent - a constant deterioration in the patient's condition and/or a further increase in her suffering which she already found unbearable, could be expected, based on professional medical judgement,

*   whether, in combination with the danger of further deterioration, the patient . . . . could be expected not to die with dignity,

*   whether - and to what extent - there was still any alternative way left to alleviate her suffering.

The court of appeal had also considered the fact that the physician had consulted his assistant and the son of the patient, but it found them neither sufficiently objective nor sufficiently independent. The Supreme Court did not find this reasoning sufficient since it left the possibility that euthanasia by the suspected physician was justified by the doctrine of necessity, given objective medical standards. In a later euthanasia case the, Supreme Court continued this line of thought holding that not consulting another physician did not automatically preclude the medical defense of necessity.

The Supreme Court nullified the decision of the court of

appeal. The case was reconsidered by another court of appeal which came to the conclusion that the physician had acted out of necessity.

In its second euthanasia case,[29] the Supreme Court again acknowledged justification of the act by a physician as a result of necessity. The court of appeal Leeuwarden had rejected this defense, reasoning that, by promising to administer euthanasia, the physician had put herself in a position which rendered a successful defense of justification by reason of necessity impossible (culpa in causa). The Supreme Court rejected the conclusion of the court of appeal that it

> "was beyond doubt that the physician honestly believed that she - being a physician - did not have any other option but to let the patient die. The latter's situation . . . . as well as her suffering and the pressure she had exerted on the physician to allow her to die and the other factors which played a role in this case should have been reason enough for the court of appeal to investigate . . . . whether, according to general medical standards and pursuant to contemporary standards of medical ethics, circumstances existed which should be acknowledged as an emergency."

Accordingly, in case law justification, the defense of necessity is the best option as lawful excuse for euthanasia carried out by a physician. But since justification by reason of necessity - due to its very nature - is a rather open ended type of lawful excuse, it is supplemented with elements of medical justification, with the result that the difference between necessity and medical justification has become minimal.

Although no physician has yet been condemned for euthanasia, many physicians are unsatisfied with the jurisprudence. They want a law which gives them - in their eyes - more legal security and which also prohibits the Public Prosecutor from "unnecessarily" beginning prosecution, because they feel threatened by prosecution. In the last few years, the Public Prosecutor has utilized a prosecution policy (made possible by the principle of discretionary powers) requiring that each known case of euthanasia be discussed by the five Procurator General of the court of appeals. The Public

---

29. HR Oct. 21, 1986, NJ 1987, 607, m.nt. Mulder.

Prosecutor thus derives euthanasia criteria. Although the criteria are well-known, the Public Prosecutor does not publish its criteria. It fears that in doing so it would give the impression that the Ministry of Justice, as the highest authority of the Public Prosecutor (and therefore the government approves) them. In truth, there is a split in the government about regulating euthanasia. These different views are reflected in the action of the two chambers of the parliament.

B. Euthanasia and Future Law in the Netherlands

1. Introduction

By the initiative of Mrs. Wessel-Tuinstra, a member of parliament for the democratic party, "D 66," a proposal for an act on euthanasia, was introduced in parliament on April 12, 1984.[30]

In her opinion, society was in urgent need of legislation in this field and, therefore, she was not prepared to wait for the report of the Government Commission, installed in 1982, which would report in 1985.[31]

In this report, a majority of 17 members of the Commission were in favor of a restricted legislative adoption of the existing practice, while two members dissent because they declined to liberalize euthanasia. The opinion of the majority, which will be called the commission's proposal, will be discussed below. It influenced the first draft of the government's euthanasia law which was called a "Proeve," a sort of trial proposal.[32]

First, the above mentioned proposals will be compared as to their main characteristics. Then we examine the draft act presented by the government on December 11, 1987, a draft that is inconsistent with the other proposals.

---

30. Wetsvoorstel van het lid Wessel-Tuinstra ter verandering van de artikelen 293-294 Sr, Tweede Kamer (TK) 1983-1984, 18331, nrs.1-3.

31. *Rapport van de Staatscommissie Euthanasie*, DEN HAAG 1985.

32. TK 1985-1986, 19356, nr.2.

2. The Essence of the First Three Proposals on Euthanasia

The government commission proposed a revision of Articles 293 and 294 DPC and
an addition of some new articles at the same time. The penalty up to 12 years imprisonment was reduced to four years. Both the Commission and Wessel-Tuinstra added to Article 293 a second paragraph with a special ground for immunity: "The purposeful killing of a patient upon his request is not an offense if performed by a physician in conformity with medical and ethical criteria."

Wessel-Tuinstra even proposed immunity for active euthanasia performed by a third person in close cooperation with a physician under the same conditions if the patient is in a state of emergency with no chance for improvement.

The government, however, has chosen to use a special "personal" formulation of the defense: "Physician shall not be punishable when he . . . ." It focuses on "personal" blameworthiness as determinative, but in the subsequent text of the second paragraph inserts the criteria according to which the medical administering of active euthanasia may be justifiable.

These criteria are more or less similar to the conditions in the other proposals.

As the government adopted personal grounds for defense, it also provided in Art. 293 DPC that, in the case of the immunity of an actor, accomplices should not be punished.

Both the Government Commission and the government allow only a physician to practice euthanasia. Wessel-Tuinstra does not exclude anybody else. In the next paragraphs of the proposed Article 293, three drafts enter into details about the standards of careful medical practice.

The following conditions are mentioned:

* The patient's request has been expressed deliberately and consciously, after being sufficiently informed about his situation.

* The physician must be convinced about the voluntariness and the evenness of the patient's decision.

* The physician must consult an independent doctor.

* The physician must keep a diary of developments in the patient's condition.

* If the patient is no longer competent to express his will, the physician may administer active euthanasia on the ground of a former statement in writing by the patient, if he is convinced that this instrument was made deliberately and with due deliberation.

As to the patient's prognosis, the following conditions are essential: The Government's Commission demands a state of necessity without the possibility of a change for the better, which also is the criterion used in Wessel-Tuinstra.[33]

Apart from that, both the Commission and Wessel-Tuinstra keep to the current text of Art. 294 DPC, with the exception that in Wessel-Tuinstra's proposal incitement to suicide shall be punishable by up to 12 years imprisonment. The maximum punishment in cases of aid in suicide is raised from three to four years to make possible the application of certain means of coercion such as pretrial detention.

The Commission's proposal to allow euthanasia of comatose patients without a directive if the above-mentioned conditions are met has provoked serious criticism and has not been adopted in the other proposals.

Also, the Commission has proposed that some life-shortening acts not be punishable provided that these acts are indisputably a form of medical treatment. The government has adopted this proposal unaltered in the so-called "Proeve" and the new provision reads:

"The following shall not be considered as criminal homicide or causation of death in the sense of this section:
a. Withholding or withdrawing medical treatment on the expressed and serious request of a patient.
b. Withholding or withdrawing medical treatment in cases where such treatment, according to current medical standards, does not serve a reasonable interest of the patient.

---

33. Gewijzigd wetsvoorstel van het lid Wellel-Tuinstra ter verandering van de leden 293 en 194 Sr, TK 1985-1986, nr. 18331. *See* especially: nr. 18331, nr. 11.

c.   Withholding treatment of an accidental illness of a patient who has lost consciousness irreversibly according to current medical standards.

d.   Life shortening as an accidental result of a treatment necessary for and directly applied to alleviate serious suffering of a patient."[34]

3. The Government's Proposal About Euthanasia in 1987

The proposals of Wessel-Tuinstra and the "Proeve" were due to be considered in parliament on February 17, 1986. However, at the very last moment, the government postponed the deliberations in parliament because it wanted to introduce a new draft act because of the criticism the proposals had provoked and the dissension about it in society.

Prof. Dessur, a former criminologist, had made a comparison with euthanasia practiced before World War II in Nazi-Germany, and by doing so she had excited strong feelings of dismay in certain circles of society.[35]

From the subsequent public discussion, it turned out that there were at least three different points of view.

The first group preferred the development of case law by the judiciary to a revision of the criminal code. In case law, grounds for immunity could be developed just as the medical exception and the state of necessity had been developed. Such development was reputed to be more flexible than new statutory provisions.

The second group preferred a restatement of the criminal code in conformity with the proposal of Wessel-Tuinstra.

The third group opposed any liberalization of the legislation on euthanasia and wanted strict enforcement of current law.

However, the government had promised to present a draft of a new act on euthanasia in parliament and, taking into account the opposition in society, it considered a more restricted restatement of the present law. Therefore, some questions were addressed to

---

34. TK 1985-1986, 19359, nr.2, p. 4.

35. C.I. Dessaur, *Euthanasie: de zelfmoord op zieke en oude mensen*, DELIKT EN DELINKWENT (DD) 913 t/m 917 (1985).

234

the "Raad van State" (Privy Counsel) for advice.[36] It finally issued a new proposal. The regulation of euthanasia should not be enacted into the criminal code, because of the dissenting opinions in society, but the law could list treatments which should be considered ordinary medical acts and Article 293 DPC would not be applicable.

To make possible the defense of necessity in cases of euthanasia the Raad suggested amending the criminal code to provide a special ground of justification: medical necessity.

Apart from this special ground, a doctor engaged in euthanasia could always invoke the general ground for justification provided in Art. 40 DPC, namely necessity related to a situation in which the actor had to make a choice for the lesser of two evils.

The government adopted these proposals and sent them to the national health council and the attorney-generals of the five courts of criminal appeal for advice.

Both answered with severe criticism and, at the same time,the proposals were rejected in legal literature.[37]

The main objection was that the criminal code was not the proper place for a special regulation regarding the medical profession. Further, it was argued that issues that were self-evident should not be inserted into the criminal code, let alone the enumeration of conduct that was not to be regarded as an open text rule, to be developed by the courts.

In its draft of December 11, 1987,[38] the government agreed with some of the above mentioned criticism and, therefore, proposed to maintain the current Article 293 DPC, reducing the maximum penalty from 12 to 4-1/2 years or a maximum fine of fl. 25,000. The remaining regulations concerning the definition of euthanasia were to be inserted into the act about the medical

---

36. TK 1985-1986, 18331, nr. 43C.

37. Gezondheidsraad, *Advies inzake zorgvuldigheidseisen euthanasie*, DEN HAAG 1987, en TK 1986-1987, 19359, nr.8. *See* for the literature e.g.: W.C.M. Klijn, *"Euthanasie" en het kabinet*, NJB 233 (1987) and J. Woretshofer, *Het tweede advies van de Raad van State inzake euthanasie* 840-48 DD (1987).

38. TK 1987-1988, 20383, nrs. 1-3.

practice, in which there would be an enumeration of acts that are not to be considered as euthanasia. The exempted acts were the acts already mentioned in the "Proeve" with one exception. The ground, "withholding treatment of an accidental illness of a patient who has lost consciousness irreversibly according to current medical standards" was dropped from the government's draft.

The remaining regulations about the definition of euthanasia were also to be added to the new provisions. In a further provision, the conditions were enumerated for a successful defense on the ground of necessity. These conditions don't differ essentially from those already mentioned as the "Proeve".

What to think about this new proposal?

The proposal implies a special statutory arrangement, creating a specific ground for a defense, in a special code, apart from the criminal code.

As to the conditions creating immunity for aid in dying, great differences occur as a result of the open test rule of the duty of care.

The various proposals stress the importance of the duty of care, but a legal formula will never cover all possible situations, so this provision cannot assure that a physician who has met the strict legal conditions will be found not guilty on the ground of necessity.

The draft proposal of the government did not bring about more consensus between advocates and opponents of active euthanasia, and, for this reason, it has not yet been presented to parliament.

On the January 17, 1990 a new commission was installed by the Minister of Justice and the Secretary of State for Public Health to investigate how medical practice in this field has been developed in recent years.

The commission has to report before August 1991. Prof. J. Remmelink, at present Attorney General of the Supreme Court of the Netherlands and formerly Professor of Law, presides.

Special attention will have to be given to the practice of active euthanasia and of finishing life support treatment with or without a directive of the patient. The inquiry will also have to deal with alternatives to euthanasia and the withdrawal of life support treatment.

Finally, the opinions of the legal profession about the limits of the duty of medical care, the fight to alleviate pain and suffering and the refusal to continue medical treatment, allowing the patient to die from a natural cause, have to be reported.

To demonstrate the deep dissensions about euthanasia among the Dutch people and members of the medical profession, a look at two recent cases will serve.

4. The Cases Stinissen and Baby Ross

Mrs. Stinissen

Mrs. Stinissen fell into a coma in 1974, when she was 31, as a result of a medical mistake when she was anesthetized in a hospital. When there was no improvement in her situation, she was transferred to a nursing home where she was put on artificial life support.

In 1989, her husband asked the clinic to stop the artificial feeding and hydration since his wife had been comatose for 15 years. The administration of the nursing home refused to comply with this request so Mr. Stinissen brought an action in civil court, asking that they order a lethal injection for his wife. The president of the court of first instance dismissed the claim but the court of appeal disagreed. It held that the feeding and hydrating of Mrs. Stinissen had to be regarded as a medical treatment. Because medical treatment in this case had no further purpose, and since the condition of the patient was not expected to change for the better, there was no obligation on the part of the physician to continue treatment.[39]

After this decision, the administration and doctors of the clinic agreed to the withdrawal of artificial life support. But then the Dutch Society of Patients (NPV) intervened in court asking for an order to prolong life support. Both the court of first instance and the court of appeal held that the society did not have standing to pursue its claim because it was not entitled to interfere with the

---

39. Hof Arnhem, Oct. 31, 1989, NJ 1989, 909.

interests of a patient without his or her consent.

In addition, the courts held that the responsibility of stopping a medical treatment belonged to the physician.[40]

After these court decisions, the artificial feeding and hydrating of Mrs. Stinissen was withdrawn. She died within 11 days.

Citing this case, a member of the medical profession published an article in a medical magazine in which he protested against what he called the interference of outsiders in questions he believed were the exclusive responsibility of a doctor. This opinion has been sustained, from a legal point of view, by the former professors in criminal law, Enschede, Langemeijer and Van Veen. However the opinion is only shared by a small minority of the public and has not been accepted by the judiciary so far.

On the contrary, many people think that a final decision about the life and death of a patient is part of the autonomy of the patient himself. If a patient is no longer competent to express his will, then a subrogate decision might be taken by legal representation, in close co-operation with the attending physician.

This opinion was also held by the present Minister of Justice, when he answered the questions of members of parliament in January 1990. In an article in the Dutch Lawyers Weekly Magazine (Nederlands Juristenblad) of February 9, 1990, the public health lawyer Gevers found that there was no unanimity as to the question whether artificial feeding and hydrating had to be seen as a medical treatment. In his view, they are primarily normal care but there might be some situations in which the technical-medical aspect was so predominant that one could no longer speak of nurture, as when providing food and liquid prevents the natural death of terminal patients.

In Mrs. Stinissen's case, the withdrawal of artificial supply would have caused gradual starvation and desiccation and there would not have been a natural death.

Whether withdrawal was justifiable in this case can only be answered by comparing the consequences of continuation of treatment and withdrawal against the background of the interest of the patient. But more than the interest of the patient is at stake.

---

40. Hof Arnhem Jan. 16, 1990. TvGR 1990/39. TIJDSCHRIFT VOOR GEZOND-HEIDSRECHT is a magazine for health law.

238

The interests of close relatives should be taken into consideration. One could add that even the interests of society may count.

Does this mean that "quality of life" arguments may justify the active ending of the life of a comatose patient even without any formal directive?

One would be inclined to say that human life cannot be regarded as human any longer when only vegetative functions remain. In case of terminal patients, a positive answer seems to be much easier.

The Case of Baby Ross[41]

It is extremely difficult to decide if life-support treatment should be given in the case of severely handicapped new born babies. The parents of Baby Ross were confronted with the birth of a child with Down's-syndrome and a closure of the stomach and bowels. They consulted their general practitioner and informed him that they were considering refusing a life saving operation. The physician informed the public prosecutor. Consequently, the parents were temporarily deprived of their parental authority. Control of the child was given to the Juvenile Board but the director of this board also refused to agree to an operation. After having consulted a medical-ethical commission, a surgeon made the decision not to operate and to end his treatment. The child died after a few days. The public prosecutor then charged the surgeon with malicious homicide by withholding necessary medical treatment.

The court of criminal appeal held that the surgeon had not breached his professional duty of care by deciding that medical treatment of a new born child is not required if, notwithstanding the treatment, the chance of serious suffering remains. The issue has to be decided ultimately by the physician who would perform the operation on the child. The parents' point of view might also be taken into consideration.

The Supreme Court upheld the verdict of the court of appeal. In his commentary as to the disposition of this case, Prof. Mulder ascertained that in a case of treatment or withholding of treatment

---

41. HR April 28, 1989, NJ 1990, 46 m.nt. G.E. Mulder.

related to new born children with innate mental and bodily deficiencies we must accept a certain amount of discretion in the physician and respect a decision taken after a conscientious deliberation between the doctor and the parents. On the other hand, the ruling of the court has been criticized because the bodily defect of the child could have been addressed by an operation which had a fair chance of success. The decision not to operate obviously decided that the child would die.

Some regard this case as the next step on a slippery slope. The divergency of views in society makes it almost impossible for the legislature to give a clear answer. Some people want to respect the decision of the parents while others demand that society protect the life of the helpless.

Whether there will be a law concerning euthanasia will not be known until the results of the commission Remmelink are known in 1991.

In the meantime, in February 1990, the figures of a poll by the Vara, a broadcasting company, have been published. According to this poll, about 17% of all deaths in the Netherlands result from some form of euthanasia. At the same time, in about one third of these cases, the will of the patient was not consulted. If these figures are correct, society is in urgent need of a law on euthanasia. However, the impact of such a law cannot be predicted because physicians could continue the existing practice of issuing a certificate of natural death in cases of euthanasia and this practice cannot be controlled.

DEATH BY DIRECTIVE*

*George J. Alexander***
United States

On April 16,1986 the California Court of Appeal for the Second District upheld Elizabeth Bouvia's petition to remove a feeding tube from her stomach. Approving her wishes, the court noted: "It is not a medical decision for her physician to make. Neither is it a legal question whose soundness is to be resolved by lawyers and judges. It is not a conditional right subject to approval by ethic committees or courts of law. It is a moral and philosophical decision that, being a competent adult, is hers to make alone."[1]

Bouvia v. Superior Court[2] caps a decade of development of California law with respect to control of medical life support. It falls on a background of technical development that allows the marginal postponement of death, often at great expense, for an extended time. Increasingly, someone must make a choice to allow life to end rather than to rely on natural process. This new and unwanted obligation has forced patients, their families, the medical community and the courts to face issues previously avoided.

In the tradition of individual autonomy, the choice has ostensibly been left to each individual patient but has usually, in fact, been made by doctors applying "medical standards." Physicians have assumed the responsibility, leaving patients and their surrogates to

---

* This article was published previously in 28.1 SANTA CLARA LAW REVIEW 67 (1988). © by George J. Alexander.

** Professor of law and former Dean, Santa Clara University; A.B., 1953, J.D., 1959, University of Pennsylvania; LL.M., 1963, Yale University. The author acknowledges the invaluable assistance of his research assistants, Holly Harris and Susan Meyer.

1. Bouvia v. Superior Court, 179 Cal. App. 3d 127, 1143, 225 Cal. Rptr. 297, 305 (1986).

2. *Bouvia*, 179 Cal. App. 3d 1127, 225 Cal. Rptr. 297 (1986).

go through courts to assert their right to decide. Commonly, unlike Elizabeth Bouvia, those affected were incompetent to choose by the critical time. Making decisions for them has proven perplexing both to surrogate decision-makers and to reviewing courts. California created a statutory directive through which one could make a prospective choice. Fifteen years later, such a statute has been adopted by all states and the District of Columbia.[3] It is seriously flawed and in need of revision.

I

The ability, medically, to support life despite the failure of bodily functions grew significantly in the latter half of this century. Aggressive use of ventilators was a post World War II development.[4] Dialysis machines did not become available until the sixties.[5] Intensive Care Units (ICUs), the locus of most critically ill patients, existed in about ten percent of hospitals in the sixties and are virtually universal today.[6] Heart and kidney transplantation, not to mention open heart surgery and more minor replacement of arteries and valves, have joined the repertory of medical responses.[7] Some artificial body components have been in use for

---

3. *See infra* note 136.

4. Russell, TECHNOLOGY IN HOSPITALS: MEDICAL ADVANCES AND THEIR DIFFUSION 76 (1979).

5. *Id.* at 111.

6. U.S. OFFICE OF TECHNOLOGY ASSESSMENT, INTENSIVE CARE UNITS (ICUS): CLINICAL OUTCOMES, COSTS, DECISION MAKING (1984). "From 1981 AHA survey tapes, it can be estimated that 78 percent of hospitals larger than 200 beds have a separate ICU." *Id.* at 15.

7. *See generally* U.S. HOUSE OF REPRESENTATIVES, SUBCOMMITTEE ON INVESTIGATIONS AND OVERSIGHT OF THE COMMITTEE ON SCIENCE AND TECHNOLOGY, NEW OPPORTUNITIES IN TREATING KIDNEY DISEASE (1982); PRESIDENT'S COMMISSION FOR THE STUDY OF ETHICAL PROBLEMS IN MEDICINE AND BIOMEDICAL AND BEHAVIORAL RESEARCH, DECIDING TO FOREGO LIFE-SUSTAINING TREATMENT 1 (1983) [hereinafter PRESIDENT'S COMMISSION REPORT].

some time, but artificial hearts,[8] artificial blood[9] and artificial skin[10] are now available to add to the reservoir of donated supply. Diagnostic improvements such as computed tomographic (CT) and nuclear magnetic resonance (NMR) scanners have all added greatly to the efficacy of new drugs and procedures.[11]

One can see the effect of new medications and processes in the changes in patterns of death. Contrasting the present with the turn of the century, one notes that communicable diseases have greatly declined as a cause of death while degenerative diseases have become more prominent. Heart disease, cancer and cerbovascular disease have replaced influenza, pneumonia and tuberculosis as major causes of death.[12] The dying population is older, more likely to be in a hospital and to have suffered from the cause of their death for an extended period than was previously true.[13] By 1949, half of all deaths occurred in hospitals. The percentage has increased about ten percent per decade. Modern medicine has gotten the population past life threatening diseases and to the point at which death more commonly comes from gradual bodily failure than from sudden infection. Its success has, in turn, increased life expectancy thereby increasing the elderly, more frail population.

Not surprisingly, these changes have created more disputes concerning treatment of the terminally ill, some of which have found their way to court. The litigation to date has typically

---

8. *See generally* Bernstein, *The Artificial Heart: Is it a Boon or a High-Tech Fix?* 236 NATION 71, 71-72 (1983).

9. James, *Researchers Step up Efforts to Develop Synthetic Blood*, Wall St. J., Sept. 4, 1987, at 17. *See generally In Science,* 37 CHANGING TIMES 16 (1983); *Slick Substitute Does Blood's Job*, 91 SCIENCE DIGEST 76 (1983).

10. Stipp, *Scientists Seeking to Put Life into Body Replacement Parts*, Wall St. J., Sept. 25, 1987, at 25.

11. Institute of Medicine, A CONSORTIUM FOR ASSESSING MEDICAL TECHNOLOGY 3 (1983).

12. PRESIDENT'S COMMISSION REPORT, *supra* note 7, at 5.

13. PRESIDENT'S COMMISSION REPORT, *supra* note 7, at 17-18.

concerned petitions to require patients to submit to life support or to require health care professionals to withdraw it.

The law has treated life support refusal as if it were a problem rarely to be confronted. In fact, the choice whether to continue to provide medical support is one that increasingly has to be made by someone. It has been estimated that it may be involved in at least six percent of the cases in hospital wards.[14] Statistics are difficult to gather since death is normally recorded as having resulted from an underlying disease rather than as a result of a decision to remove support.[15]

A recent empirical study of long term dialysis patients[16] provides some indication of the process. In a group of 1766 patients being treated for end-stage renal disease by dialysis, 155 died because dialysis was ended.[17] They represented nine percent of the patient group and twenty-two percent of those who died. Sixty-six of them were considered competent to make their own decision and did so, although in six cases, ending treatment was first suggested by a physician or by family. Discontinuance did not follow a set pattern although age and diabetes were the highest risk factors. Of the competent patients who discontinued treatment, about half did so at a time during which they were not experiencing medical complications.[18] Those who discontinued when a medical complication such as amputation or blindness occurred were not distinguishable for other characteristics from

---

14. Lo & Schroeder, *Frequency of Ethical Dilemmas in a Medical Inpatient Service*, 141 ARCH. INTERN. MED. 1062 (1981).

15. PRESIDENT'S COMMISSION REPORT, *supra* note 7: "[I]f an otherwise dying patient is not resuscitated in the event of cardiac arrest, or if pneumonia or kidney failure goes untreated, the underlying disease process is said to be the cause of death." *Id.* at 68-69.

16. Neu & Kjellstand, *Stopping Long-Term Dialysis*, 314 NEW ENG. J. MED. 14 (1986).

17. *Id.* at 15.

18. *Id.* at 18.

those who remained on dialysis under those circumstances.[19]

II

Studies of attitudes about death show great diversity of opinion.[20] Some hold life very precious and want to remain alive as long as possible irrespective of pain and discomfort.[21] Others want death to come quickly once they are diagnosed as incurably ill and death is probable from their disease.[22] There are many points of view between these polar extremes.

That there is substantial interest in hastening rather than prolonging death is demonstrated by the apparent interest in directives to physicians to withhold life support. An estimated five millon such directives have been executed.[23] It is also popularly reported that in the Netherlands one in six deaths were actively caused by physicians at their patient's request.[24]

Limitation of medical life support may also become a product of cost containment efforts. During the last few years, there has been increased concern about the costs of health care. In fact, the United States is the best example of the fact that expenditures on medical care vary directly with the wealth of countries[25] in the manner usually associated with luxuries and contrary to the pattern of necessities.

It is easy to illustrate the high cost of medical treatment

---

19. *Id.*

20. See PRESIDENT'S COMMISSION REPORT, *supra* note 7, at 21-22.

21. PRESIDENT'S COMMISSION REPORT, *supra* note 7, at 21.

22. PRESIDENT'S COMMISSION REPORT, *supra* note 7, at 21.

23. Nelson, *Doctors Debate Right to Stop 'Heroic' Effort to Keep Elderly Alive,* Wall St. J., Sept. 7, 1982, at 20, col. 1.

24. *60 Minutes*, The Last Right? (C.B.S. television broadcast Jan. 5, 1986). *See infra* note 176.

25. Maxwell, HEALTH AND WEALTH 41 (1981).

controlling for changes in population (i.e. by units of care). In 1950, a day's stay in a hospital cost $14. It rose to $133.00 by 1975 and was at nearly $300 in 1982.[26] The day rate at Stanford Hospital is now between $466 to $544 depending on the room type. In real dollar terms, it has more than doubled just since 1965.[27] Medical care grew from 5.3% of the gross national product in 1960 to over 10% by 1984.[28] Per capita annual expenditure has increased over ten times between 1950 and 1980.[29] It is especially important to note that critical care administered in Intensive Care Units constitutes ten to fifteen percent of that amount, about 30 billion dollars.[30]

Terminally ill patients account for a disproportionately high percentage of medical costs. In 1974, Selam Mushkin[31] estimated that over 20% of all non-psychiatric hospital and nursing home expenditures in non-governmental facilities were spend on the care of the terminally ill. Although only 5% of all Medicare enrollees died in 1967, 22% of all reimbursements were made on their

---

26. Menzel, MEDICAL COSTS, MORAL CHOICES 1 (1983).

27. Id.

28. Freedland & Schlender, National Health Expenditure Growth in the 1980's, 4 HEALTH CARE FIN. REV. 4 (1983).

29. Id.

30. The total cost of hospital care for 1984 was $157 billion. UNITED STATES ACCOUNTING OFFICE, CONSTRAINING NATIONAL HEALTH CARE EXPENDITURES: ACHIEVING QUALITY CARE AT AN AFFORDABLE COST, Sept. 30, 1985, at 10. OFFICE OF TECHNOLOGY ASSESSMENT, INTENSIVE CARE UNITS (ICUs): CLINICAL OUTCOMES, COSTS AND DECISION MAKING 22 (1984). The Office of Technology Assessment reported that the percentage of total hospital care costs attributable to ICUs is 15-20%. Combining the two figures, the total cost of ICU care for 1984 would be $23.7 to 31.5 billion. Id.

31. S. Mushkin, CONSUMER INCENTIVES FOR HEALTH CARE 183-216 (1974).

behalf.[32] The Health Care Financing Administration reported that the cost of such care ranged from nineteen to twenty-two percent of all reimbursed Medicare charges from 1974-1976.[33] Detsky found that "the data indicate that the use of resources for dying patients exceeds resources use for other high cost patients."[34]

The Massachusetts General Hospital patient classification system and the Therapeutic Intervention Scoring System provide improved data for prognosis.[35] Quite consistently, there is an inverse relationship between favorable prognosis and expenditure.[36]

The high cost of critical care both in absolute terms and in relationship to the total cost of medical care has brought considerable current focus on it in the medical community. The fact that prognosis has become as reliable as it has results in some pressure for cost containment through limitations on expenditures for what is correctly perceived to be a high-risk, high-cost, low-yield group. Reducing marginally effective therapies (those that add only slightly to the welfare of patients in general or which add to welfare of only a small group of patients) seems a likely choice.[37]

---

32. Bayer, *The Care of the Terminally Ill: Mortality and Economics*, 309 NEW ENG. J. MED. 1491 (1983).

33. *Id.*

34. Schroeder, Showstack & Roberts, *Frequency and Clinical Description of High-Cost Patients in 17 Acute-Care Hospitals*, 300 NEW ENG. J. MED. 1306 (1979).

35. Cullen, Ferrara, Briggs, Walker & Gilbert, *Survival, Hospitalization Charges and Follow-up Results in Critically Ill Patients*, 294 NEW ENG. J. MED. 982 (1976) [hereinafter Cullen]; Silverman, *The Therapeutic Intervention Scoring System: An Application to Acutely Ill Cancer Patients*, 3 CRIT. CARE MED. 222 (1975) [hereinafter Silverman].

36. Civetta, *The Inverse Relationship Between Cost and Survival*, 14 J. SURG. RES. 265 (1973).

37. Silverman, *supra* note 25, at 224-25. *But see* Scitovsky & Capron, *Medical Care at the End of Life: The Interaction of Economics and Ethics*, 7 ANN. REV. PUB. HEALTH 59, 70, 73 (1986) (asserting that the difficulty of separating

Technological advances continue. It is not possible to be certain about their future costs. It is always possible that low cost alternatives will be found for presently expensive treatment without a diminution of effectiveness and that new therapies will provide savings over those in place. But cost savings have not been the rule to date. It consequently seems prudent to estimate that new technology will add to or at least maintain present costs. The aging of the population will contribute increasingly to the demand for expensive therapy. Critical care patients are, of course, disproportionately elderly.[38] Consequently, even providing continued support at present per capita levels will amount to a reduction of available resources for patients. For example, heart transplants cannot be provided to most of those whose lives they might extend.[39] It is possible to acknowledge that fact without admitting to health care rationing because it can be blamed on the scarcity of appropriate organs to transplant. The excuse is quite temporary. Artificial hearts have been developed and used.[40] They will, no doubt, be perfected in the near future. It is estimated that some 50,000 people per year would be suitable candidates for such hearts. The cost, when the device is perfected, is likely to be at least $50,000 per patient with additional first year costs of about $100,000. The total cost would be between $2.5 and $5 billion plus follow up costs.[41] Similar expenses attend liver and other transplants.[42] A transplant is, of course, only one of many

---

dying patients from those critically ill prospectively is insuperable and that, in fact, expenditures on those who die are actually less than treatments for critically ill patients who survive).

38. PRESIDENT'S COMMISSION REPORT, *supra* note 7, at 17-18.

39. Efforts to improve the chances of locating a transplant organ for their children have led several parents recently to make public appeals on television.

40. *See* Bernstein, *supra* note 8, at 71-72.

41. H. Aaron & W. Schwartz, THE PAINFUL PRESCRIPTION: RATIONING HOSPITAL CARE 125 (1984) [hereinafter PAINFUL PRESCRIPTION].

42. *Id.*

treatments which might be beneficial. In the United States, an estimated two million patients die per year.[43] An increasing number of patients utilize intensive care;[44] the average cost for ICU treatment is $14,000 exclusive of physician fees and many other costs.[45] If everyone died in an ICU, that cost alone would be 28 billion dollars.[46]

The pressure of costs has led a number of commentators to predict that substantial reductions in resources will follow.[47] A common focus of procedures which might lead to savings is reducing the range of persons admitted to intensive care and reducing such care for those for whom it is marginally useful. Since Great Britain has a system which delivers health care at substantially lower costs, British experience is one indication of the broader range of changes that might be anticipated.

As in the United States, there is no express rationing system for health care in Great Britain.[48] Appropriate care standards accommodate the more limited resources. Some practices which would be common in the United States are rarely available but their unavailability is explained, within the system, by asserting that the

---

43. NATIONAL CENTER FOR HEALTH STATISTICS, VITAL STATISTICS OF THE UNITED STATES: MORTALITY PART B 7 (1973); U.S. GOVERNMENT PRINTING OFFICE, FACTS OF LIFE AND DEATH 31 (1978).

44. *See generally* Greenberg, *Forward Cautiously, With the Forward Plan for Health,* 293 NEW ENG. J. MED. 673 (1975). Singer, *Rationing Intensive Care: Physician Responses to a Resource Shortage,* 309 NEW ENG. J. MED. 1153 (1983).

45. Cullen, *supra* note 35.

46. Cullen, *supra* note 35, at 986.

47. *See, e.g.,* PAINFUL PRESCRIPTION, *supra* note 41, at 122; Mechanic, *Cost Containment and the Quality of Medical Care: Rationing Strategies in an Era of Constrained Resources,* 63 MILBANK MEM. FUND Q. HEALTH & SOC. 453 (1985) [hereinafter Mechanic].

48. PAINFUL PRESCRIPTION, *supra* note 41, at 123-24.

treatments are medically inappropriate.[49] The result is reflected in standards of care which have already incorporated the scarcity of supply. To a physician accustomed to practicing in the United States, the standards of care would, consequently, represent substantial diminution of optimal care.

Using the magnitude of utilization in the United States as a base, some forms of care are available in substantially reduced measure in Britain. Per capita expenditures run about one third as high as those in the United States.[50] The British perform half as many X-rays and use half as much X-ray film for each examination as in the Untied States.[51] The rate of treatment for chronic renal failure is less than half.[52] Dialysis is carried out at less than one third the United States' rate.[53] Parenteral nutrition issued one quarter as often and CT-scanning equipment is only one-sixth of that available here.[54] Coronary-artery surgery, which has become an important life sustaining procedure in the United States, is performed in Britain one tenth as often as in the United States.[55] Intensive care beds are available in numbers one fifth to one tenth as many.[56] Undoubtedly, British expenditures are quite lavish when compared to expenditures in underdeveloped countries.

There are other British treatments and procedures which are provided as readily as in the United States. These include treatment for hemophilia, radiotherapy for cancer, bone marrow transplantation, and chemotherapy for cancer of the sort highly

---

49. PAINFUL PRESCRIPTION, *supra* note 41, at 25.

50. PAINFUL PRESCRIPTION, *supra* note 41, at 84.

51. PAINFUL PRESCRIPTION, *supra* note 41, at 28.

52. PAINFUL PRESCRIPTION, *supra* note 41, at 28.

53. PAINFUL PRESCRIPTION, *supra* note 41, at 28.

54. PAINFUL PRESCRIPTION, *supra* note 41, at 28.

55. PAINFUL PRESCRIPTION, *supra* note 41, at 28.

56. PAINFUL PRESCRIPTION, *supra* note 41, at 28.

responsive to such treatment (far less for less responsive sorts.)[57] The reasons underlying the difference are not officially articulated but one can speculate about some of them. There seems to be a preference for treating those who will benefit the most. Thus, treatment for hemophilia, which strikes young patients, is applied less frequently while dialysis, mostly required for the elderly, is utilized far less.[58] Chemotherapy in the most tractable cases is on par with the Untied States and in more hopeless cases it is far more rare.[59] Relative expense probably explains the dearth of CT scan equipment.

A lack of formal rationing and medical justification of the standard of care being applied tends to obscure the relative scarcity of the extant system. Some clues help to illuminate the matter. The existence of queues, for example, indicates unmet demand. In Britain in 1979, of 566,000 patients awaiting surgery of all kinds, thirty-one percent had waited for more than one year. Seven percent of those on the waiting list were classified urgent and nearly three fourths of them had been waiting more than a month.[60] In the United States, on the other hand, there appears to be a surplus of available hospital space and surgical talent despite some local shortages.[61] With the exception of organ transplants, there appears to be no queue for medical procedures. Organ transplant procedures have escaped public wrath in part because the supply of organs is so short as to mask the rationing which takes place. When rationing criteria come to light, they can

---

57. PAINFUL PRESCRIPTION, *supra* note 41, at 28.

58. PAINFUL PRESCRIPTION, *supra note 41, at 29-31, 37-40.*

59. PAINFUL PRESCRIPTION, *supra* note 41, at 28.

60. Aaron & Schwartz, *"Special Report" Rationing Hospital Care: Lessons from Britain*, 310 NEW ENG. J. MED. 52, 54 (1984) [hereinafter Aaron & Schwartz].

61. TASK FORCE REPORT ON THE DEPARTMENT OF HEALTH AND HUMAN SERVICES, PUBLIC HEALTH SERVICE, HEALTH CARE FINANCING ADMINISTRATION, PRESIDENT'S PRIVATE SECTOR ON COST CONTROL 62 (1983); AMERICAN MEDICAL ASSOCIATION, THE AMERICAN HEALTH CARE SYSTEM 48 (1984).

evoke heated condemnation.[62]

Physicians say that they generally provide appropriate services on a first-come first-served basis if there are any temporary shortages. A study of practices during an extended nursing strike, supports this viewpoint.[63] Most notably, the death rate appeared not to have been affected by the cutbacks, suggesting that the attention to the admitted critically ill was maintained functionally static.[64] Most of those who write about the need to ration available treatments speak of the problem as though it looms in the future but does not exist today.[65]

Aaron and Schwartz,[66] who have compared the British and American systems, come to the conclusion that while the American system can absorb mild budget cuts without changing the provision of services significantly, severe cuts would lead to following the British archetype.[67] In such a future, they conclude, terminal care would be much reduced. The reduction would follow redefinitions of standard medical care. According to Lo and Jonsen, some categorical removal of patients from life support by redefinition of appropriate care standards has already taken place in the United States. Patients with end-stage lung disease are generally not financed for extended use of ventilators. Patients with intractable

---

62. In June, 1986, Loma Linda University Medical Center refused to consider an infant, Baby Jesse, for a desperately needed heart transplant because his young parents were unmarried. Loma Linda felt that they were unprepared to give Baby Jesse the extensive post-operative care which would be required. Loma Linda offered the baby's parents a compromise: if they would give up custody of Jesse to his grandparents, it would consider him for a transplant. The parents agreed, and Jesse ultimately received a heart after a well-publicized battle. Wallis, *Of Television and Transplants*, TIME, June 23, 1986, at 68, 127.

63. Singer, Carr, Mulley & Thibault, *Rationing Intensive Care - Physician Response to a Resource Shortage* 309 NEW ENG. J. MED. 1155, 1158 (1983).

64. *Id*. at 1159.

65. *See, e.g.,* Aaron & Schwartz, *supra* note 60, at 52.

66. PAINFUL PRESCRIPTION, *supra* note 41.

67. *See supra* notes 55-65 and accompanying text.

gastrointestinal hemorrhage do not receive unlimited quantities of blood. Neither practice has been formally proposed or defended.[68]

Although he has not obtained much following for his position, former Colorado governor Lamm has strongly advocated reduction of expenditures on health care for the elderly.[69] He proposed redirecting the resources to meeting the needs of groups who have not already had as an extensive a use of public benefits as the elderly.

While his position has drawn strong criticism, it raises perspectives which cannot be ignored. As previously mentioned, the increasing elderly population is causing unprecedented medical expenses.[70] Likewise, the different costs of their care are creating other financial crises. The social security system is in danger.[71] Non-medical facilities to provide food and shelter are inadequate both in numbers and in quality.[72] The lower fertility of recent generations[73] has left a smaller number of workers to provide the resources with which to provide for their elders. In many respects the deficits of the present are legacies created by the expenditures of the elderly for which payment will be extracted

---

68. Lo & Jonsen, *Clinical Decisions to Limit Treatment*, 93 ANN. INTERN. MED. 764 (1980).

69. N.Y. TIMES, March 29, 1984, at A16, col. 4: N.Y. TIMES, April 1, 1984, at A22, col 1.

70. Mechanic, *supra* note 47, at 465-66.

71. N.Y. TIMES, February 16, 1984, at A23, col. 1. (Report by Committee for Economic Development warns that if U.S. economy does not perform as well as Congress expects, Social Security could reach another crisis in the 1980s. The 1983 amendments provide very little margin of safety); N.Y. TIMES, August 14, 1985, at A1, col 8.

72. Friedland & Marotto, *The New Homeless and Community Public Policy* (paper presented at the 80th Annual Meeting of the American Sociological Association, Washington, D.C., August 26-30, 1985).

73. Scitovsky & Capron, *Medical Care at the End of Life: The Interaction of Economics and Ethics*, 7 ANN. REV. PUB. HEALTH 59, 60 (1986).

from the young. A rebellion against a future in which such burdens increase seems quite plausible. Hints of sharper future generational division are already abundant.[74]

The law respecting a right to choice has also seen a period of rapid acceleration. Before this decade of active litigation concerning life support removal, few cases had tested a patient's control of refusal of medical procedures. Some cases announced the paramount right of patients to control the limits of their treatment even if death resulted,[75] but several well known cases concerning Jehovah's Witness patients are contrary.[76] In those cases, courts ordered blood transfusions over the religious objections of members who would have died had they not received blood. In *Application of the President and Directors of Georgetown College,*[77] a young

---

74. Callahan, SETTING GOALS: MEDICAL GOALS IN AN AGING SOCIETY (1987); Longman, BORN TO PAY (1987); Longman, *Age Wars: The Coming Battle Between Young and Old*, FUTURIST, Jan-Feb 1986, at 8: King, *The War Between the Generations,* NEWSWEEK, Apr. 14, 1986, at 8.

75. *See, e.g.,* Rasmussen v. Fleming, 154 Ariz. 207, 211, 741 P.2d 674, 678 (1987) (en banc); Tune v. Walter Reed Army Medical Hospital, 602 F.Supp. 1452, 1455 (DC 1985); *Bouvia,* 179 Cal. App. 3d 1127, 225 Cal. Rptr. 297 (1986); *In re* Osborne, 294 A.2d 372 (D.C. App. 1972); Satz v. Perlmutter, 362 So. 2d 160 (Fla. Dist. Ct. App. (1978), *aff'd,* 379 So. 2d 359 (Fla. 1980); *In re* Spring, 380 Mass. 629, 405 N.E.2d 115 (1980); Superintendent of Belchertown State School v. Saikewicz, 373 Mass. 728, 370 N.E.2d 417 (1977); Lane v. Candura, 6 Mass. App. 377, 376 N.E.2d 1232 (1978); *In re* Conroy, 98 N.J. 321, 486 A.2d 1209 (1985); Downer v. Veilleux, 322 A.2d 82 (Me. 1974).

76. *See e.g.,* United States v. George, 239 F. Supp 752, (D. Conn. 1965); *Application of* President and Directors of Georgetown College, Inc., 331 F.2d 1000 (D.C. Circ.), *reh'g en banc denied,* 331 F.2d 1010 (D.C. Cir.), *cert. denied sub nom.,* Jones v. President and Directors of Georgetown College, Inc. 377 U.S. 978 (1964); John F. Kennedy Memorial Hosp. v. Heston, 58 N.J. 576, 279 A.2d 670 (1971); Powell v. Columbian Presbyterian Medical Center, 49 Misc. 2d 215, 267 N.Y.S. 2d 450 (Sup. Ct. 1965); Collins v. Davis, 44 Misc. 2d 622, 254 N.Y.S.2d 666 (Sup. Ct. 1964); *In re* Estate of Dorone, 349 Pa. Super. 59, 502 A.2d 1271 (1985), *aff'd,* 539 A.2d 452 (Pa. 1987). *But see Osborne,* 294 A.2d 372 (D.C. App. 1972); *In re* Melideo, 88 Misc. 2d 974, 390 N.Y.S. 2d 523 (Sup. Ct. 1976).

77. 331 F.2d 1000, *reh'g en banc denied,* 340 F.2d 1010 (D.C. Cir.), *cert. denied sub nom., Jones,* 377 U.S. 978 (1964).

mother of a seven month old child was admitted to Georgetown Hospital suffering from a bleeding ulcer. When she refused a blood transfusion, the hospital obtained a court order to administer it. The case has been explained as having upheld the mother's duty of care for her infant child and as lacking more general application.[78] However, subsequent cases involving Jehovah's Witnesses allow a patient to refuse medical treatment even when minor children are present.[79] Nonetheless, it has proven to be the high water mark for paternalistic intervention to require treatment.

Ten years ago, the matter of Karen Quinlan began a process of reexamination of the sparse precedents from which a consensus developed which allowed the President's Commission for the Study of Ethical Problems in Medicine and Biomedical Behavior Research (hereafter the President's Commission) to conclude that "decisions about healthcare [including the choice to forego life sustaining treatment] ultimately rest with competent patients."[80]   I   n the period since *In re Quinlan*,[81] at least seventeen states and the District of Columbia have produced decisions dealing with the termination of life support.[82] Although many allude to counter-

---

78. *See, e.g.,* Winthrop University Hospital v. Hess, 128 Misc. 2d 804, 490 N.Y.S. 2d 996 (Sup. Ct. Nassau Co. 1985) (Court ordered blood transfusion for mother of infant); Holmes v. Silver Cross Hosp., 340 F. Supp 125, 130 (N.D. Ill. 1972) (A father can be forced to undergo a transfusion if his refusal would devastate his dependents); Heston, 58 N.J. 576, 279 A.2d 670 (1971) (ordered a blood transfusion for a pregnant woman).

79. *See, e.g.,* Wons v. Public Health Trust of Dade County, 500 So. 2d 679 (Fla. Dist. Ct. App. 1987); St. Mary's Hosp. v. Ramsey, 465 So. 2d 666 (Fla. Dist. Ct. App. 1985).

80. PRESIDENT'S COMMISSION REPORT, *supra* note 7, at 2.

81. 70 N.J. 10, 355 A.2d 647, *cert. denied sub nom.,* Garger v. New Jersey, 429 U.S. 922 (1976).

82. Tune, 602 F. Supp 1452 (D.D.C. 1985); Rasmussen, 154 Ariz. 207, 741 P.2d 674 (1987) (en banc); *Bouvia,* 179 Cal. App. 3d 1127, 225 Cal. Rptr. 297 (1986); Bartling v. Superior Court, 163 Cal. App. 3d 186, 209 Cal. Rptr. 220 (1984); Barber v. Superior Court, 147 Cal. App. 3d 1006, 195 Cal. Rptr. 484 (1983); *Conservatorship of* Drabick, 200 Cal. App. 3d 185, 245 Cal. Rptr. 840

vailing state interests in supporting life, no appellate decision has found any of them decisive. Four interests have been mentioned: the interests in preserving life, preventing suicide, safeguarding the integrity of the medical profession and protecting innocent third parties.[83] Since the cases have typically concerned patients who

---

(1988), *cert. denied*, 109 S.Ct. 399 (1988); Foody v. Manchester Memorial Hosp., 40 Conn. Supp. 127, 482 A.2d 713 (Conn. Super. Ct. 1984); McConnell v. Beverly Enterprises - Connecticut, Inc., 209 Conn. 692, 553 A.2d 596 (1989); Severns v. Wilmington Medical Center, Inc. 421 A.2d (Del Super. Ct. 1980); Corbett v. D'Allessandro, 487 So. 2d 368 (Fla. App. 1986); John F. Kennedy Memorial Hosp., Inc. v. Bludworth, 452 So. 2d 921 (Fla. 1984); *Satz*, 362 So. 2d 160 (Fla. Dist. Ct. App. 1978), *aff'd*, 379 So. 2d 359 (Fla. 1980); *In re Guardianship* of Barry, 445 So. 2d 365 (Fla. Dist. Ct. App. 1984); *In re* L.H.R., 253 Ga. 439, 321 S.E. 2d 716 (1984); *In re Estate of Longeway, 133 Ill. 2d 33, 549* N.E.2d 292 (1989); Downer v. Veillux, 322 A.2d 82 (Me. 1974); *In re* Gardner, 534 A.2d 947 (Me. 1987); Brophy v. New England Sinai Hosp., Inc., 398 Mass. 417, 497 N.E.2d 626 (1986); *Spring*, 380 Mass. 629, 405 N.E.2d 115 (1980); *Saikewica*, 373 Mass. 728, 370 N.E. 2d 417 (1977); *In re* Torres, 357 N.W. 2d 332 (Minn. 1984); Cruzan v. Harmon, 760 S.W. 2d 408 (Mo. 1988) (en banc); *In re* Conroy, 98 N.J. 321, 486 A.2d 1209 (1985), *In re* Quinlan, 70 N.J. 10, 355 A.2d 647, cert. denied sub nom., Garger, 429 U.S. 922 (1976); State of New Mexico *ex rel.* Smith v. Fort, No. 14,768 (New Mexico 1983) (order granting alternative writ of prohibition); Delio v. Westchester Co. Medical Center, 129 App. Div. 2d 1, 516 N.Y.S. 2d 677 (1987); *In re* Eichner, 102 Misc. 2d 194, 423 N.Y.S. 2d 580 (1979) *modified*, 73 A.D. 2d 431, 426 N.Y.S. 2d 517 (1980), *cert. denied sub nom., Storar v. Storar, 454 U.S. 858 (1981);* In re Storar, 52 N.Y. 2d 363, 420 N.E. 2d 64, 438 N.Y.S. 2d 266 (1981), *cert. denied*, 454 U.S. 858 (1981); *In re* Westchester Co. Medical Center on behalf of O'Connor, 72 N.Y. 2d 517, 534 N.Y.S. 2d 886, 531 N.E. 2d 607 (1988); Winthrop University Hosp. v. Hess, 128 Misc. 2d 804, 490 N.Y.S. 2d 996 (1985); Leach v. Akron General Medical Center, 68 Ohio Misc. 2d 1, 426 N.E. 2d 809 (1980); *Estate of* Leach v. Shapiro, 13 Ohio. App. 3d 393, 469 N.E. 2d 1047 (1984); Gray v. Romeo, 697 F. Supp 580 (R.I. 1980); *In re Welfare of* Colyer, 99 Wash. 2d 114, 660 P.2d 738 (1983), *modified sub nom., In re Guardianship of* Hamlin, 102 Wash. 2d 810, 689 P.2d 1372 (1984).

83. *See, e.g.,* PRESIDENT'S COMMISSION REPORT, *supra* note 7, at 181-83; *Bartling*, 163 Cal. App. 3d at 195, 209 Cal. Rptr. at 225 (1984); *Satz*, 362 So. 2d 160, 162 (Fla. Dist. Ct. App. 1978), *aff'd*, 379 So. 2d 359 (Fla. 1980); *Spring*, 280 Mass. at 640, 405 N.E. 2d at 123 (1980); *Brophy*, 398 Mass. 417, 497 N.E. 2d 626 (1986); Commissioner of Correction v. Myers, 379 Mass. 255, 261, 399 N.E. 2d 452, 456 (1979); *Saikewicz*, 373 Mass. at 738, 370 N.E. 2d at 424.

were either terminally ill or in a chronic vegetative state, there was little purpose in maintaining life for the benefit of others. It has been possible to assert that neither suicide nor threats to the sanctity of life were involved. Resulting death occurred, it was said, because of the patient's underlying condition. Most of the decisions also fit within the ambit of prevailing medical practice which permits allowing patients a comfortable death when further treatment is futile.[84]

Quinlan expressly based its decision on the constitutional right of privacy and many of the later courts have agreed.[85] Massachusetts' Supreme Judicial Court indicated that the right "is an expression of the sanctity of individual free choice and self-determination as fundamental constituents of life" and that the value of life is not lessened by a decision to refuse treatment but by the failure to allow patient choice.[86] In addition to the right of privacy held to govern such cases, the Supreme Court of New Jersey in *In Re Conroy*[87] noted that there is also a common-law right to self-determination in these cases and that courts could rely on either. While it, as most other courts, emphasized that neither right was absolute and reviewed the variety of state interests that militated against such decisions, it concluded: "In cases that do not involve the protection of the actual or potential life of someone

---

84. *See* Lo & Jonsen, *Clinical Decisions to Limit Treatment*, 93 ANN. INTERN. MED. 764, 764-68 (1980).

85. *See, e.g., McConnell*, 209 Conn. 692, 553 A.2d 596 (1989); *Drabick*, 200 Cal. App. 3d 185, 245 Cal. Rptr. 840 (1988), *cert. denied*, 109 S.Ct. 399 (1988); *Bouvia*, 179 Cal. App. 3d 1127, 225 Cal. Rptr. 297 (1986); *Bartling*, 163 Cal. App. 3d 186, 209 Cal. Rptr. 220 (1984); *Barry*, 445 So. 2d 365 (Fla. Dist. Ct. App. 1984); *Brophy*, 398 Mass. 417, 497 N.E. 2d 626 (1986); *Spring*, 380 Mass. 629, 405 N.E. 2d 115 (1980); Saikewica, 373 Mass. 728, 370 N.E. 2d 417 (1977); *Quinlan*, 70 N.J. 10, 355 A.2d 647, *cert. denied sub nom., Garger*, 429 U.S. 922 (1976), *In re* Colyer, 99 Wash. 2d 810, 689 P.2d 1372 (1984).

86. *Saikewicz*, 373 Mass. at 742, 370 N.E. 2d at 426.

87. 98 N.J. 321, 486 A.2d 1209 (1985). *See also, Gray*, 697 F. Supp 580 (R.I. 1988); Gardner, 534 A.2d 947 (Me. 1987); *In re* Grant, 109 Wash. 2d 545, 747 P.2d 445 (1987); Corbett, 487 So. 2d 368 (Fla. App. 1986); *Cruzan*, 760 S.W. 2d 408 (Mo. 1988).

other than the decision-maker, the state's indirect and abstract interest in preserving the life of the competent patient generally gives way to the patient's much stronger personal interest in directing the course of his own life."[88]

Despite the fact that most of the reported cases concern patients unable to voice a choice, the courts have agreed that the rights of choice of the competent and incompetent are identical.[89] However difficult to effectuate, there seems no principled reason to deny equal rights to incompetents. Thus, recent developments in rights of choice are probably of equal importance to both groups. Two recent California cases,[90] all involving competent patients, have made recent additions to the law.

William Bartling[91] was 70 years old when admitted to the Glendale Adventist Hospital. He had emphysema, arteriosclerosis and an abdominal aneurysm as well as a lung tumor. In taking a sample of tissue from his tumor for biopsy, the needle punctured and collapsed one of his lungs. His tumor proved malignant, the puncture did not heal and his lung did not re-inflate. At that point, a tracheotomy was performed and a ventilator installed. Despite his opposition to using the machine, his doctors insisted that it remain connected as he would die otherwise; ethical concerns barred their acceding to his contrary wishes. Bartling tried several times to remove the breathing machine and finally his hands were placed in restraints to prevent further efforts. He brought an action

---

88. *Id.* at 350, 486 A.2d at 1223.

89. *See, e.g.,* Cleburne v. Cleburne Living Center, Inc., 473 U.S. 432, 439, 105 S.Ct. 3249, 3254, 87 L.Ed. 2d 313 (1985); *Bartling*, 163 Cal. App. 3d 186, 209 Cal. Rptr. 220 (1984); *Foody*, 40 Conn. Supp. 127, 482 A.2d 713 (Conn. Super. Ct. 1984); *Severns*, 421 A.2d 1334 (Del. Super. Ct. 1980); *Bludworth*, 452 So. 2d 921 (Fla. 1984); *Saikewicz*, 373 Mass. 728, 370 N.E. 2d 417 (1977); *Torres*, 357 N.W. 2d 332 (Minn. Ct. App. 1984); *Quinlan*, 70 N.J. 10, 355 A.2d 647, *cert. denied sub nom.*, *Garger*, 429 U.S. 922 (1976); *Eichner*, 102 Misc. 2d 184, 423 N.Y.S. 2d 580 (1979), *modified*, 73 A.D. 2d 431, 426 N.Y.S. 2d 517 (1980), *cert. denied sub nom.*, Storar v. Storar, 454 U.S. 858 (1981).

90. *See infra* note 97.

91. *Bartling*, 163 Cal. App. 3d 186, 209 Cal. Rptr. 220 (1984).

to require that the ventilator be removed. In a deposition, he indicated that he did not want to die, that he understood that removal of the ventilator might well cause his death and that he nonetheless wanted it removed. The trial court denied his request for an injunction on the grounds that he was neither terminally ill nor permanently comatose and that the law permitted removal of life support only under one of those circumstances. He appealed but died prior to the appellate hearing, still connected to a ventilator. The court of appeal heard the case, notwithstanding his death, because of the importance of the issues. It reversed the lower court, stating, "if the right of a patient to self-determination as to his own medical treatment is to have any meaning at all, it must be paramount to the patient's hospital and doctors. The right of a competent adult to refuse medical treatment is a constitutionally guaranteed right which must not be abridged."[92]

Bartling v. Superior Court[93] left open four important issues concerning competent patients wishing to refuse treatment. Had he stated that he wanted to die rather than to live without a ventilator, would the state interest in preventing suicide have overcome his interest in control of his treatment? Would the court have granted his injunction if his life expectancy in treatment had been longer? Testimony in the trial court had given him up to a year to live if he could be weaned from the ventilator. Would the same result apply if he were less seriously ill? Could he have chosen to end artificial feeding in place of removing his ventilator?

Bouvia answered three of those questions. Elizabeth Bouvia was a 28 year old woman whose cerebral palsy, complicated by painful arthritis, had made her quadriplegic and unable even to sit upright. She had been bedridden and in severe pain. Her ability to take nutrition by mouth was so limited that her doctors felt it necessary to feed her through a nasogastric tube to sustain her life. She objected and, unlike Mr. Bartling, claimed that she wished to die rather than to undergo further life in her helpless condition. When refused, she also brought suit. To the trial court, her wish to die was an improper motivation. Invoking the state interest in

---

92. *Id.* at 195, 209 Cal. Rptr. at 225.

93. 163 Cal. App. 3d 186, 209 Cal. Rptr. 220 (1984).

260

preventing suicide, it refused her petition. Since that refusal, she has recanted her desire to die but a second court did not believe her recantation. The court of appeal, however, held that her decision to let nature take its course was not the equivalent of a decision to commit suicide and that the trial court erred when it made her motives determinative. Testimony put her life expectancy at fifteen to twenty more years to which the court commented, "It is incongruous, if not monstrous, for medical practitioners to assert their right to preserve a life that someone else must live, or, more accurately, endure, for 15 or 20 years."[94] It also found the fact that she chose to remove a nutritional tube unexceptional.[95]

Although these two cases advance decisional law to some extent, neither is very shocking. While Bartling and Bouvia were alive when they resisted further life support, the perception of the quality of their remaining lives evokes outrage at the indignity of insisting on their submission to the insertion of unwanted tubes. Although the removal of nutritional support has been quite controversial, it has recently been accepted by the Judicial Council of the American Medical Association as an acceptable response to those permanently comatose.[96] New Jersey has even more recently resolved other procedural questions in similar circumstances.[97]

---

94. *Bouvia*, 179 Cal. App. 3d at 1143-44, 225 Cal. Rptr. at 305.

95. "[S]ubstantial and respectable authority throughout the country recognize the right which petitioner seeks to exercise. Indeed, it is neither radical nor startlingly new. It is a basic and constitutionally protected right." *Id.* at 1139, 225 Cal. Rptr. at 302.

96. Wallis, *To Feed or Not To Feed*, TIME, Mar. 31, 1986, at 60.

97. *Conroy* involved an eighty-four year old woman living in a nursing home. 90 N.J. 321, 485 A.2d 1209 (1985). She was legally incompetent, but had limited ability to interact cognitively with her environment. She had a variety of health problems which rendered her unable to swallow enough food and fluids to sustain her life. However, she was not unconscious, comatose or in a persistent vegetative state.

Ms. Conroy's nephew and guardian petitioned the court to remove the nasogastric tube which supplied life-sustaining nutrients and fluids. The Supreme Court ultimately blocked removal of the tube, but it established three tests which may be employed to remove such life-sustaining treatment.

As is often true in times of social transition, case law has created fictions to avoid affronting previously accepted norms.[98]

These tests, as the subsequent cases make clear, are limited to the factual situation at issue in *Conroy*. They apply only to incompetent, elderly, nursing home-bound patients, not in a permanent vegetative state, whose illness will result in the patient's death in a short period of time.

There are three tests described by the court. The "subjective test" allows removal of life-sustaining treatment whenever there is clear and convincing evidence that if the patient were competent, he or she would have declined the treatment. *Id.* at 360, 486 A.2d at 1229. The "limited-objective test" allows discontinuance of the treatment when there is some trustworthy evidence that the patient would have declined the treatment and the surrogate decision-maker is satisfied that the burdens of continued life outweigh the benefits. *Id.* at 368, 486 A.2d at 1232. The "purely objective test" permits removal of the treatment when the burdens of continued life clearly outweigh any benefits. *Id.*

In re Farrell involved a thirty-seven year old competent, terminally ill patient suffering from Lou Gehrig's disease. 108 N.J. 335, 529 A.2d 404 (1987). Mrs. Farrell lived at home, but died during the pendency of the action in the supreme court. She petitioned the court to allow the removal of her respirator. The court found that she had the right to the removal of the respirator; in its decision, the court announced the procedures which must be followed in the case of competent, adult patients who are living at home and request the removal of life-sustaining treatment:

> First, it must be determined that the patient is competent and properly informed about his or her prognosis, the alternative treatments available, and the risk involved in the withdrawal of the life-sustaining treatment [citation omitted]. Then it must be determined that the patient make his or her choice voluntarily and without coercion. After these assessments have been made, the patients' right to choose to disconnect the life-sustaining apparatus must be balanced against the four potentially countervailing state interests . . . . To protect the patient who is at home, we require that two non-attending physicians examine the patient to confirm that he or she is competent and is fully informed about his or her prognosis, the medical alternative available, the risk involved, and the likely outcome if medical treatment is disconnected.

Id. at 354, 529 A.2d at 413, 415.

The court also stated that judicial review is not required except in unusual situations where there is a conflict among family members or the physician involved. *Id.*

---

98. *See generally*, Campbell, *Fuller On Legal Fictions*, 2 LAW & PHIL. 339, 347 (1983).

262

In life support termination, there is a fiction of medical determinism. Patients are seen as passive victims of their illness. They do not choose to die; death overtakes them. Their physicians do nothing to help them die. Death overwhelms them, too.

Bartling, presumably on advice of counsel, testified that he did not want to die. After an unsuccessful attempt to have her way despite a candid admission that she proposed to starve herself to death, Bouvia changed her story (perhaps honestly) to indicate that she would not seek to die. That allowed the courts in both cases to adopt the now common deterministic theme that death, when it comes, comes from the underlying illness not the termination of treatment.[99]

The fiction requires that any action taken which will lead to death be described as, at worst, surrender to the futility of further treatment. Thus, the removal of Ms. Bouvia's nasogastric tube has to be distinguished from discontinuing her feeding on the grounds that inserting the tube was a medical procedure when initiated and that its removal is the termination of a treatment. Of course, there are valid medical aspects of artificial feeding. It has medical consequences on other aspects of bodily functioning and the ability to fight disease. It sometimes involves serious risks. Artificial nutrients are readily distinguishable from normal food in appearance and formulation. Eating by mouth is not. When the American Medical Association's Judicial Council approved removing artificial feeding and hydration in some instances they could discuss the matter in the same manner as other aspects of treatment.[100]

---

99. In *Bouvia*, the court stated: "[Bouvia's] decision to allow nature to take its course is not equivalent to an election to commit suicide with real parties aiding and abetting." 179 Cal. App. 3d at 1146, 225 Cal. Rptr. at 306. In *Bartling*, the court stated: "Several doctors also expressed the view that disconnecting Mr. Bartling's ventilator would have been tantamount to aiding suicide. This is not the case, however, where real parties would have brought about Mr. Bartling's death by unnatural means by disconnecting the ventilator. Rather, they would merely have hastened his inevitable death by natural causes." 163 Cal. App. 3d at 196, 209 Cal. Rptr. at 225.

100. *Barber*, 147 Cal. App. 3d at 1016, 95 Cal. Rptr. at 490. *See also, In re* Estate of Longeway, 133 Ill. 2d 33, 139 Ill. Dec. 780, 549 N.E. 2d 292 (1989).

Using medical explanations also has its utility for the courts. It removes the responsibility for decisions that seem harsh when explained in plainer language. To let a person starve herself to death is certainly less palatable than to permit the removal of a medical feeding tube. All the better if the patient will also agree that her purpose is not death but simply relief from the intrusion.

Rhetorical use of medical imagery to create the illusions that underlie legal fictions does not, of course, mean that the issues are truly medical. Blaming the underlying disease rather than the act of life-support removal is romantic but illogical. A person who removed a feeding tube from a recovering patient temporarily dependent on it would have a difficult time persuading anyone that the resulting death was caused by the underlying illness not by the removal of the tube. Although it is true that artificial feeding differs from normal eating, providing food and liquids is so psychologically bound to a level of expected non-medical care that physicians, not to mention lay people, have difficulty in equating its removal with the removal of respirators and other less commonly provided forms of help.[101] To make a case depend on whether the person wishes to die as opposed to having necessary life support removed (a distinction the Bouvia appellate court would not abide)[102] is too transparent to be useful and too insensitive to be ethical. If she were not aware of probable lethal consequences would she be competent to direct removal?

III

As choice issues are masked as medical decision, their answers are increasingly relegated to medical decision makers such as the

---

101. *See generally*, J. Quinlan, KAREN ANN: THE QUINLANS TELL THEIR STORY 282 (1977).

102. *Bouvia*, 179 Cal. App. 3d at 1145, 225 Cal. Rptr. at 306. The court stated: "[T]he trial court seriously erred by basing its decision on the 'motives' behind Elizabeth Bouvia's decision to exercise her rights. If a right exists, [which the court determines it does] it matters not what 'motivates' its exercise. We find nothing in the law to suggest the right to refuse medical treatment may be exercised only if the patient's motives meet someone else's approval." (emphasis in original).

American Medical Association Judicial Council. At the moment, for example, would other doctors with patients like Bouvia be prevented from ethically removing artificial feeding on request because it has only been officially approved for permanently comatose patients?[103]

If one can believe removal of food and water can be relatively painless,[104] it may have practical advantages. It provides a manner of allowing death for virtually any unconscious patient. Thus, it responds to one concern about an estimated 10,000 permanently comatose patients alive today. Also, unlike the removal of a ventilator which for many would cause death in minutes, death from deprivation of nutrition is likely to take place more slowly. In cases in which death is not imminent but the patient has suffered a great loss to the quality of life and wishes not to be rehabilitated to live under new circumstances, food and liquid withdrawal may provide a reflective period in which reconsideration is possible without thwarting an autonomous choice to die shortly if that persists. For the physician, the added time may provide reassurance that options have been carefully considered by the patient, the friends and family if the patient wishes to involve them and the hospital staff. Of course, the acceptance of death by deprivation of nutrition has brought renewed interest in more active lethal choices.[105]

The insistence of the courts that ethical concerns of physicians be a factor in counterbalancing the wishes of a patient for life support removal is itself a product of using medical metaphors in adjudicating the issue. As in the abortion cases in which a similar obfuscation took place, the proper role of physicians must be articulated differently. It must really be the woman, not her physician, who decides whether to carry the fetus after the

---

103. *See In re* Jobes, 108 N.J. 394, 529 A.2d 434 (1987); *In re* Peter, 108 N.J. 365, 529 A.2d 419 (1987).

104. *See, e.g.*, Jobes, 108 N.J. 394, 529 A.2d 434 (1987); Peter, 108 N.J. 365, 529 A.2d 419 (1987), but see Conroy, 98 N.J. 321, 485 A.2d 1209 (1985).

105. *See supra* note 82.

physician has provided appropriate information. The fact that some doctors dislike abortions and that the Hippocratic oath prohibited them does not give physicians the right to make the decision which is constitutionally protected for pregnant women. In removal of life support, *Bouvia*, helps to focus a definition of an appropriate physician's role which is more complicated than in the abortion cases.

Bouvia's case is clouded by the enormity of her distress as a quadriplegic with numerous additional medical problems. If weighed by medical standards, however, the result might be more questionable. A number of others live in similar conditions. She will remain sensate and her pain is presumably controllable with medication. It is certainly appropriate for her physicians to feel that she can lead a productive life, and they should be willing to contribute their skills toward that end. That the court would not accept the physician's conclusion in preference to hers seems to capture the appropriate role for both. The physician's function initially is to diagnose and to indicate the prognosis for the future. That role can be negatively determinative but should not bar a patient's unwillingness to undergo further suffering. If, for example, the physician concludes that a patient would die shortly regardless of treatment and that treatment would neither prolong life nor reduce suffering, they should have no obligation to treat irrespective of the patient's wishes. Their obligation then would merely be to provide for comfort to the extent possible. The question of what is medically feasible should belong to the experts in medicine.[106]

Having determined that Ms. Bouvia's life support is feasible, the balancing that remains weighs the quality of her life against the pain and suffering that continued life promises her. Neither the doctors nor the courts bring expertise to that narrow question. It has to do with a variety of traits that are uniquely hers.[107] Experiences of being dependent on others for almost all activities may seem to her totally unacceptable while others may find such

106. Lo & Jonsen, *Clinical Decision to Limit Treatment*, 93 ANN. INTERN. MED. 764, 8766 (1980).

107. *See generally* PRESIDENT'S COMMISSION REPORT, *supra* note 7, at 21-23.

help acceptable in a life they find productive. Her lack of personal privacy may seem intolerable for reasons which may not be universal. No adequate objective measure of life quality can substitute for a personal decision. Similarly, the fact that she refuses to consent to being nourished by tube ought not to raise medical concerns. Whether or not tubal nutrition and hydration are considered treatment does not address the question of whose decision controls whether she allows herself to be kept alive. While the approval of the American Medical Association's Judicial Council for removal of artificial feeding of permanently comatose patients[108] should ease the concerns of doctors, it should not govern the limits of such removal. The patient's consent is a necessary prerequisite to such feeding, not because it is a treatment, but because the law at least makes an unconsented touching tortious.[109]

Others may seem less sympathetic in their plight than Ms. Bouvia. Each will have to confront the quality of life that they can anticipate if they remain alive. So long as they have had the opportunity to weigh life quality as they perceive it, it is improper to reject their conclusion.

IV

Many of the competent ill will not need help from courts or hospitals if they decide to forego further life support. It is usually possible to arrange a transfer to a doctor or institution that will view one's plans more sympathetically or, that failing, to leave the institution and go home to die even if one's doctors disapprove.[110] Problems concerning competent patients are far less difficult than those of incompetent individuals. All courts that have

---

108. Wallis, *To Feed or Not to Feed,* TIME, Mar. 31, 1986, at 60.

109. Subsequent to the appellate decisions, Ms. Bouvia filed a lawsuit against her health care providers and the Glenchur Medical Center for battery. *See also,* Cruzan v. Director, Missouri Department of Health, 110 S.Ct. 2841, 2846 (1990).

110. *But see* Jobes, 108 N.J. 394, 529 A.2d 434 (1987) (asserting difficulty in finding a transfer institution).

decided the issue also have held that the right to refuse treatment was equally available to an incompetent patient but disagreed on methods of determining the choice.[111] Quinlan held that Ms.

---

111. *See, e.g.*, Saikewicz, where the court noted that the doctrine of substituted judgment should be used to determine the patient's wants and needs. 373 Mass. 728, 370 N.E. 2d 417 (1977). It stated:

> We take a dim view of any attempt to shift the ultimate decision-making responsibility away from courts of proper jurisdiction to any committee, panel or group, ad hoc, or permanent. Thus we reject the New Jersey Supreme Court in the Quinlan case of entrusting the decision whether to continue artificial life-support to the patient's guardian, family, attending doctors and hospital 'ethics committee.'

Id. at 758, 370 N.E. 2d at 434. Other courts have agreed with the New Jersey Supreme Court's handling of the *Quinlan* case. In *Severs,* the court appointed the husband as guardian of the wife's person and allowed him authority to make medical decision for her. 421 A.2d at 1347. The court stated: "The Court of Chancery, in our opinion, may recognize the right of the guardian to vicariously assert the constitutional right of a comatose ward to accept medical care or refuse it." *Id.* at 1347. However, the court required that the guardian submit to an evidentiary hearing before the court will grant him the authority to discontinue his wife's life support system.

Still other courts require a rigorous procedure be followed for terminating an incompetent patient's life-support system. In *Colyer,* the court required that the following procedure be followed to terminate an incompetent's life-support system. 99 Wash. 2d 114, 660 P.2d 738 (1983):

> 1. There must be a unanimous concurrence of the treating physician's diagnosis by a prognosis board. The prognosis board is comprised of two disinterested physicians. They must find that the patient's condition is incurable and there is no probability that the patient will return to a cognitive life. If no agreement can be reach, the court can make the findings by clear and convincing evidence.
> 2. The court must appoint a guardian ad litem for the purposes of representing the patient at the guardianship hearing.
> 3. The appointed guardian may exercise the patient's right to refuse medical treatment only if he deems it is in the best interest of the patient.
> 4. Alternatively, the court may appoint a guardian ad litem and judicially determine what is in the best interest of the incompetent patient.

Peter involved a sixty-five year old nursing home patient who was in a persistent, vegetative state with no hope of recovery. Although terminally ill, she may live for an extended period of time. 108 N.J. 365, 529 A.2d 419 (1987). Ms. Peter executed a durable power of attorney which appointed a surrogate decision maker for medical decision, but it did not specifically authorize the removal of any life-sustaining treatment. The attorney-in-fact petitioned the court to remove the nasogastric tube which sustained her life.

The New Jersey Supreme Court first re-emphasized its prior holding that incompetency does not effect a patient's right to refuse or forego life sustaining treatment. "All patients, competent or incompetent, with some limited cognitive ability or in a persistent vegetative state, terminally ill or not terminally ill, are entitled to choose whether or not they want life-sustaining treatment." *Id*. at 372, 529 A.2d at 423. The New Jersey court then held that the tests articulated in *Conroy* are limited to their facts; it specifically held that the limited-objective and pure objective tests are inapplicable because "by definition such patients . . . do not experience any of the benefits or burdens" which the tests attempt to balance, and the court must instead be guided by *Quinlan*. *Id*. at 376-77, 529 A.2d at 424.

However, in this case, Ms. Peter left clear and convincing evidence of her intention to remove life support apparatus, so the court applied the *Conroy* subjective test. "[T]he *Conroy* subject test is applicable in every surrogate-refusal-of-treatment case, regardless of the patient's medical condition or life-expectancy." *Id*. Under this test, life-sustaining treatment may be removed when there is clear and convincing evidence of the patient's intentions. If the *Conroy* subject test cannot be met because there is not clear and convincing evidence of the patient's intentions, the *Quinlan* test must be used. Once the subject test is met the following procedures must be followed:

[T]he Ombudsman . . . must be given the opportunity to investigate and prevent any possible mistreatment of elderly nursing home patients who have been declared to be in a persistent vegetative state. Therefore, before life-sustaining treatment is withdrawn or withheld from such a patient, the surrogate decision-maker should inform the office of the Ombudsman for the Institutionalized Elderly that a decision to forego treatment has been made. The Ombudsman should secure two independent medical opinions to confirm the patient's medical condition, the medical alternatives available, the risks involved, the likely outcome if medical treatment is discontinued and that there is no reasonable possibility of the patient's recovery to a cognitive, sapient state.

Id. at 383-84, 529 A.2d at 429.

If the patient has designated a surrogate decision-maker, the Ombudsman should defer to that person to make any decision once his or her investigatory role has been fulfilled. If there is no surrogate specifically chosen, the Ombudsman, with the advice of the attending physician, should ascertain whether there is a close family member who is willing to make the medical decisions. If there are no close family members, it will be necessary to have the court appoint a guardian. The court specifically states that a close friend is not a proper surrogate unless the patient has formally designated that person. *Id*.

Jobes involved a thirty-one year old nursing-home patient in a near persistent, vegetative state. 108 N.J. 394, 529 A.2d 434 (1987). Mrs. Jobes' husband petitioned the court for the removal of the j-tube which was providing the food and hydration which sustained her life. The court found that this case was very similar to *Quinlan*. The court applied *Quinlan's* substituted judgment analysis to this case and found that Mrs. Jobes' j-tube should be removed. In this case, Mrs. Jobes did not make known her preferences should she find herself in a persistent, vegetative state so there is insufficient evidence to meet the *Conroy* clear and convincing test. However, under the *Quinlan* test, the proper persons to make the substituted judgment are the patient's family, which normally would include spouse, parents, adult children and siblings. If individual's from one of these groups are not available, the court must appoint a guardian; the court also gives a health care professional the right to ask for a guardian if he or she determines that the family is not looking out for the best interest of the patient. *Id.* at 419, 529 A.2d at 338. The *Quinlan* test requires the concurrence of a hospital prognosis committee which is not required in a nursing home. However, the court held that the decision making process should be substantially similar, but it recognized that there are safeguards present in a hospital which are not present in a nursing home. *Id.*

> For non-elderly non-hospitalized patients in a persistent vegetative state who, like Mrs. Jobes, have a caring family or close friend, or a court-appointed guardian in attendance, we hold that the surrogate decision-maker who declines life-sustaining medical treatment must secure statements from at least two independent physicians knowledgeable in neurology that the patient is in a persistent vegetative state and that there is no reasonable possibility that the patient will ever recover to a cognitive, sapient state. If the patient has an attending physician, then that physician likewise must submit such a statement. These independent neurological confirmations will substitute for the concurrence of the prognosis committee for patients who are not in a hospital setting and thereby prevent inappropriate withdrawal of treatment.

Id.

Judicial review is not required for the decision to forego the life-sustaining treatment; it may be used only in special circumstances which may occur when there is a conflict among the family, the guardian, or the physician. Any interest person can petition the court in such a situation. *Id.* at 423, 529 A.2d at 449.

The New Jersey Supreme Court also held that the nursing home could not refuse to participate in the withdrawal of the j-tube from Mrs. Jobes. The trial court had found that the nursing home objected to the removal on moral grounds and that, therefore, it need not participate in the withdrawal. The supreme court found that if the nursing home were permitted to refuse to allow the withdrawal while Mrs. Jobes was a patient there, it is likely that her wishes may never be carried out due to the difficulty in finding a facility which would

Quinlan's guardian and family should render their best judgment of what she would have chosen to do in the circumstances. Later courts have opted for more rigorous inquiry standards.[112] Substituted judgment, that is judgment made by a surrogate on the basis of what the patient would have wished, has been approved by courts and the President's Commission[113] as appropriate, at least in cases in which there is clear evidence of the patient's desires.[114] Morally and legally, this means of determining individual wishes comes closest to allowing the autonomy of competent patients to make choices based on different perceptions of life quality. In those case in which there is insufficient data to allow substituted judgment, some courts have adopted a best interest test by which surrogates would decide whether to remove life support.[115] However, some courts have held that when a patient

---

take her and participate in the removal. Since this nursing home did not put the Jobes on notice that it would not participate, it may not now assert their moral right. The court does not decide whether notification would insulate a nursing home from participation in removal of the j-tube. *Id.* at 425, 529 A.2d at 450.

112. *See supra* notes 97 & 111. *See also,* Cruzan v. Director, Missouri Department of Health, 110 S.Ct. 2841 (1990).

113. *See* PRESIDENT'S COMMISSION REPORT, supra note 7, at 132-33. See also Conservatorship of Drabick, 220 Cal. App. 3d 185, 245 Cal. Rptr. 840, cert. denied, 109 S.Ct. 399 (1988); *In re* Estate of Longeway, 133 Ill. 2d 33, 139 Ill. Dec. 780, 549 N.E. 2d 292 (1989).

114. *See, e.g., McConnell,* 209 Conn. 692, 553 A.2d 596 (1989); *Gardner, 534 A.2d 947 (Me. 1987),* Jobes, 108 N.J. 394, 529 A.2d 434 (1987); *Leach,* 68 Ohio Misc. 1, 426 N.E. 2d 809 (1980); *Longeway,* 123 Ill. 2d 33, 139 Ill. Dec. 780, 549 N.E. 2d 292 (1989); Cruzan v. Harmon, 760 S.W. 2d 408 (Mo. 1988).

115. *See, e.g.,* Foody, 40 Conn. Supp. 127, 482 A.2d 713 (Conn. Sup. Ct. 1984). In *Foody,* the court stated:
If the exercise of the right is to be maintained where no expression has been made by an incompetent patient as to treatment, it must take place within the context of an analysis which seeks to implement what is in the person's best interests by reference to objective socially shared

is in a persistent vegetative state, a best interest test may not be used because there are no benefits to weigh against burdens.[116] Typically, a best interest inquiry balances the benefits and burdens of continuing treatment. Others have refused to do so[117] or have accomplished the same end by ruling that life continuation is always in the best interests of a patient who has not indicated contrary wishes.[118]

---

criteria.
Id. at 129, 482 A.2d at 721. *See also, Colyer*:

A guardian of the person has the power to 'care for and maintain the incompetent or disabled person, *assert his or her rights and best interests,* and provide timely, informed consent to necessary medical procedures.' (quoting WASH. REV. CODE 11.92.040(3)(emphasis in original). As refusal of life sustaining treatment is an individual's personal right, we conclude that under this provision the guardian has the power to assert such a right.

99 Wash. 2d at 129, 660 P.2d at 746-47. *See* also *Conroy* where the court stated:

In the absence of trustworthy evidence, or indeed any evidence at all, that the patient would have declined the treatment, life-sustaining treatment may still be withheld or withdrawn . . . if a pure-objective test is satisfied. . . . [T]he net burdens of the patient's life with the treatment should clearly and markedly outweigh the benefits that the patient derives from life.

98 N.J. at 366, 486 A.2d at 123.

116. *Jobes*, 108 N.J. 394, 529 A.2d 434, (1987). *Peter* 108 N.J. 365, 529 A.2d 419 (1987).

117. *Jobes*, 108 N.J. 394, 405 N.E. 2d 115 (1980); *Saikewicz*, 373 Mass. 728, 370 N.E. 2d 417 (1977).

118. *See, e.g., Saikewicz*, 373 Mass. 728, 370 N.E. 2d 417 (1977). The court stated: "Should the probate judge then be satisfied that the incompetent individual would . . . have chosen to forego potentially life-prolonging treatment, the judge shall issue the appropriate order. If the judge is not so persuaded, or finds that the interest of the state require it, then treatment shall be ordered." *Id.* at 757, 370 N.E. 2d at 434. *See also Conroy*:

When the evidence is insufficient to satisfy either the limited-objective test [life-sustaining treatment may be withheld when there is some trustworthy evidence that the patient would have refused treatment and the decision maker is satisfied that the burdens outweigh the benefits] or purely objective standard [the net burdens of the patient's life with

Beyond determining an appropriate standard, courts have taken quite different approaches to questions concerning oversight of the procedure. New Jersey's high court indicated that it expected family concurrence and review by a hospital ethics committee.[119] In the case of patients from nursing homes, it also wanted review by an Ombudsman already charged with oversight of the elderly in such institutions.[120] Its Massachusetts counterpart denied the right of any group to make such a decision without reference to courts.[121] The New Mexico Supreme Court believed itself powerless without legislative direction[122] but the Legislature quickly provided a procedure by which a substitute judgment made by all of the family in good faith would suffice.[123]

A major problem in ascertaining the wishes of a patient has almost always arisen from the absence of an indication of what he or she would want done. There is general agreement that if the patient's wishes were known, they would be respected.

So long as a person continues to be conscious and is treated as competent, individualized treatment corresponding to individual views is possible. Making a surrogate choice for incompetents is far more difficult.

Irrespective of how it is attempted, making decisions that duplicate what another would have decided is virtually impossible. Considering the wide range in decisions which the same people

---

the treatment clearly outweigh the benefits the patient derives from life], however, we cannot justify the termination of life-sustaining treatment as clearly furthering the best interests of a patient.
98 N.J. at 368, 486 A.2d at 1233.

119. *Conroy*, 98 N.J. at 375, 486 A.2d at 1242; *See supra* note 111.

120. *Conroy*, 98 N.J. at 375, 486 A.2d at 1242.

121. *See Saikewicz*, 373 Mass. 728, 370 N.E. 2d 417 (1977). *But see Spring*, 380 Mass. 629, 405 N.E. 2d 115 (1980).

122. State of New Mexico *ex rel.* Smith v. Forte, No. 14,768 (order granting alternative writ of prohibition).

123. In 1984, the Legislature passed the Right to Die Statute, N.M. STAT. ANN. 24-7-1 to 24-7-11 (1984).

make on different occasions, the changes of mind and the alter-
ations of attitudes, it would be impossible to foretell what decision
the patient would have made at any given point. All of the prior
decisions which serve as models necessarily reflect different
circumstances. They were made when the person was healthier
and able to communicate. How would the presence of the
disabilities presently plaguing him affect the type of decision that
was formerly made? Even the patient may not have known the
answer before he experienced the differing circumstances under
which he now lives. If one adds the personal attitudes, the biases
and, perhaps, the personal motives of surrogate, the result will
certainly be a distortion of the decision which the patient would
have made himself. Realizing the impossibility of a perfect result,
courts or the Legislature must provide for some method of
surrogate decision making and will have to settle for the best
available even if that is quite imperfect.

The surrogates of choice have invariably been members of the
family.[124] However, when they make or suggest a choice respecting treatment, they appear to courts to be those most likely
to know about the patient's habits and wishes and most likely to
effectuate them.[125] The President's Commission recommends

---

124. *See, e.g., Barber*, 147 Cal.App. 3d 1006, 195 Cal. Rptr. 484 (1983);
Foody, 40 Conn. Supp. 127, 482 A.2d 713 (Conn. Super. Ct. 1984); *Severns*,
421 A.2d 1334 (Del. Sup. Ct. 1980); *Bludworth*, 452 So. 2d 921 (Fla. 1984);
Barry, 334 So. 2d 365 (Fla. Dist. Ct. App. 1984); *L.H.R.*, 253 Ga. 439, 321 S.E.
2d 716 (1984); *Spring*, 380 Mass. 629, 405 N.E. 2d. 115 (1980); *Quinlan 70
N.J. 10, 355 A.2d 647*, cert. denied sub nom., Garger, 429 U.S. 922 (1976);
Cruzan, 760 S.W. 2d 408 (1988).

125. *See, e.g., Spring.*
The judge properly relied in part on the opinion of the ward's wife of
fifty-five years. That opinion was corroborated by that of the son, and
there was every indication that there was a close relationship within the
family group, that the wife and son had only the best interest of the
ward at heart, and that they were best informed as to his likely attitude.
380 Mass. at 640, 405 N.E. 2d at 122, *See also, Bludworth*: "[T]he means
developed by the courts to afford this right [to refuse medical treatment] to
incompetent persons is the doctrine of 'substituted judgment.' Under this
doctrine close family members substitute their judgment for what they believe the
terminally ill incompetent person, if competent, would have done under these

that when there are several equally acceptable options, the one chosen should be selected by the family. The involvement of the family is so well known that those who wish otherwise are on notice to make specific provisions.[126] Unfortunately, while the interests of family members may be consistent with a patient's wishes and while they are the only available surrogates in many cases, one must consider potential conflicting interests involved as well. In some cases, the family and patient will have differing religious or ethic views about death.[127] More antagonistic relationships may attend the fact that some may have conflicting current endeavors, may be heirs on the patient's death or may bear the financial and emotional burden of the illness.

Conservatorship disputes have certainly demonstrated the potential for adversarial approaches among family members.[128] In their acting as surrogates for heath care, one would expect no better results than those achieved in property management. Most states which legislatively authorize directives to physicians respecting removal of life support, disqualify family members as witnesses because of such concerns.[129] Whatever supervisory scheme is superimposed on the charge to family surrogates, it is quite likely that they will control the process in most cases because they will be accepted as both informed and as benevolent.[130]

---

circumstances." 452 So. 2d at 926.

126. PRESIDENT'S COMMISSION REPORT, *supra* note 7, at 193 n.55 (citing Parker v. United States, 406 A.2d 1275 (D.C. Ct. App. 1979)).

127. It is less likely that such differences will exist within a family than between the patient and another surrogate chosen from a different background, however, and the family ought not to be disqualified on that ground alone.

128. Alexander, *Premature Probate: A Different Perspective on Guardianship for the Elderly,* 31 STAN. L. REV. 1003, 1010-11 (1979) [hereinafter Alexander].

129. *See, e.g.,* CAL. HEALTH & SAFETY CODE 7188 (West 1986); IDAHO CODE 39-4505 (1985); NEV. REV. CODE 449.600 (1977).

130. Alexander & Lewin, THE AGED AND THE NEED FOR SURROGATE MANAGEMENT (1972).

V

To counterbalance reliance on such surrogates in health care matters,the author recommended the use of health care durable powers of attorney in a Stanford Law Review article,[131] suggesting that they take the name of the far more limited natural death act directives known popularly as "living wills." The name has not been adopted but the device has in all fifty states and the District of Columbia.[132] Its main feature is the appointment of a surrogate of choice to direct health care and financial concerns for those

---

131. Alexander, *supra* note 128.

132. *See generally* Alexander, WRITING A LIVING WILL: USING A DURABLE POWER OF ATTORNEY (1988); Ala. Code 26-1-2 (1986); Alaska Stat. Ann. 13.26.350 to 13.26.356 (Supp. 1989); Ariz. Rev. Stat. Ann 14-5501 (1975); Ark. Code Ann. 28-68-201 to 28-68-203 (1987); Cal. Civ. Code Ann. 2400 (West Supp. 1990); Colo. Rev. Stat. 15-14-501 et seq. (1987); Conn. Gen. Stat. 45-690 (Supp. 1989); Del. Code Ann. Tit. 12, 4901-4905 (1987); D.C. Code 21-2081 et seq. (1989); Fla. Stat. 709.08 (1989) Ga. Code Ann. 10-6-36 (1989); Haw. Rev. Stat. 551D-1 to 551D-7 (Supp. 1989); Idaho Code 15-5-501 et. seq. (Supp. 1989); Ill. Rev. Stat., ch. 110 1/2 802-6 (1987); Ind. Code 30-2-11-1 to 30-2-11-7 (1988); Iowa Code 633.705 (Supp. 1989); Kan. Stat. Ann 58-610 (1983); Ky. Rev. Stat. Ann 386-093 (Baldwin 1983); La. Civ. Code Ann. 3027 (West Supp. 1990) Me. Rev. Stat. Ann, Tit 18-A 5-501 et seq. (Supp. 1989); Md. Est & Trusts Code Ann. 13-601 to 13-602 (1974) (as interpreted by the Attorney General, *see* 73 Op.Md.Atty.Gen No. 88-046 (Oct. 17, 1988); Mass. Gen. Laws ch. 201B, 1 to 201B 7 (1988); Mich. Comp. Laws 700.495, 700.497 (1980); Miss. Code Ann. 87-3-13 (Supp. 1990); Mont. Code Ann. 72-5-501 to 72-5-502 (1989); Neb. Rev. Stat. 30-2664 to 30-2672, 30-2667 (1985); Nev. Rev. Stat. 111.460 et seq. (1986); N.H. Rev. Stat. Ann 46:2B-8 (1989); N.M. Stat. Ann. 45-5-501 et seq. (1989); N.Y. Gen. Oblig. Law 5-1602 (McKinney 1989); N.C. Gen. Stat. 32A-1- et seq. (1987); N.D. Cent. Code 30-1-30-01 to 30.1-30-05 (Supp. 1989); Ohio Rev. Code Ann. 1337.09 (Supp. 1989); Okla. Stat., Tit. 58 1071-1077 (Supp. 1989); Ore. Rev. Stat. 127.005 (1989); Pa. Con. Stat. Ann., Tit. 20 5601 et seq., 5602(a)(9) (Purdon Supp. 1989); R.I. Gen. Laws 34-22-6.1 (1984); S.C. Code 62-5-501 to 62-5-502 (1987); S.D. Codified Laws 59-7-2.1 (1978); Tenn. Code Ann. 34-6-101 et seq. (1984); Tex. Prob. Code Ann. 36A (Supp. 1990); Utah Code Ann. 75-5-501 et seq. (1978); Va. Code 11-9-1 et seq. (1989); Wash. Rev. Code 11.94.020 (1989); W.Va Code 39-4-1 et seq. (Supp. 1989); Wis. Stat. 243.07 (1987-1988) (as interpreted by the Attorney General, see Wis. Op. Atty. Gen 35-88 (1988); Wyo. Stat. 3-5-101 et seq. (1985).

276

declared to be incompetent and to avoid a court imposed guardianship or conservatorship. It seeks to retain control for the person even though he or she is declared legally incompetent.

Some states now have specific durable powers for health care as statutory provisions.[133] In other states, general durable power legislation is thought to authorize the creation of health care surrogates.[134] Part of the popularity of durable powers in life support refusal cases comes from their being unencumbered by the many limitations that have attended natural death act directives. As an expression of an incompetent patient's current wishes, the

---

133. ARK. STAT. ANN. § 20-17-202 (1989); CAL. CIVIL CODE § 2431 (DEERING 1990); DEL. CODE ANN. TIT. 16, § 2502 (1983); D.C. CODE ANN. § 21-2201 (1989); 1990 FLA. LAWS 232; GA. CODE ANN. § 31-36-1 (1990); IDAHO CODE § 39-4505 (1990); ILL. REV. STAT. CL. 110 1/2, PARA. 802-1 (1988); IND. CODE 16: 8-12-5 (1990); IOWA CODE § 144(A) 7(1)(A) (1989); 1989 KAN. SESS. LAWS 181; 1990 KY. ACTS 123; LA. REV. STAT. ANN. § 40: 1299.58.1 (WEST 1990); ME. REV. STAT. ANN. TIT 18(A), § 5-501 (1989); MO. EST. & TRUSTS CODE ANN. § 13-601 (1988); MINN. STAT. § 145(B).01 (1989); MISS. CODE ANN. § 41-41-151 (1990); NEV. REV. STAT. ANN. § 449.810 (MICHIE 1989), 1990 N.Y. LAWS 752; OHIO REV. CODE ANN. § 1337.11 (BALDWIN 1990); OR. REV. STAT. § 127.510 (1989); R.I. GEN. LAWS § 23-410-1 (1989); S.D. CODIFIED LAWS ANN. § 59-7-2.5 (1990); TENN. CODE ANN. § 34-6-201 (1990); TEX. REV. CIV. STAT. ANN. ART. 4590L-1 (VERNON 1990); UTAH CODE ANN. § 75-2-1105, 1106 (1989); VT. STAT. ANN. TIT. 14, § 3453 (1989); VA. CODE ANN. § 54.1-2986 (2) (1988); WASH. REV. CODE § 11.94.046 (1989); W. VA. CODE § 16-30(A)-3 (1990); 1989 WIS. LAWS 200; WYO. STAT. § 35-22-102 (1988).

134. Society for the Right to Die, HANDBOOK OF LIVING WILL LAWS 1981-1984 (1984). Thirteen states have living will statutes authorizing the appointment of healthcare proxies. See ARK. CODE ANN. 20-17-202 (Supp. 1989); DEL. CODE ANN., Title 16 2502 (1983); FLA. STAT. 765.05(2) (1989); IDAHO CODE 39-4504 (Supp. 1989); IND. CODE 16-8-11-14(g)(2) (1988); IOWA CODE 144A.7(1)(a) (1989); LA. R.S. ANN., 40:1299.58.1 40:122 = 99.58.3(C) (West Supp. 1990); MINN. STAT. 145B.01 et seq. (Supp. 1989); TEXAS HEALTH & SAFETY CODE ANN. 672.003(d) (Supp. 1990); UTAH CODE ANN. 75-2-1105, 75-2-1105, 75-2-1106 (Supp. 1989); VA. CODE 54.1-2986(2) (1988); 1987 WASH. LAWS, ch. 162 1, sec. (1)(b); WYO. STAT. 35-22-102 (1988).

prior competent statement appears to many courts[135] and to the President's Commission the most preferable choice.[136] Given the changes of the last decade, there is a need to alter legislation dealing with both natural death act directives to physicians and the appointment of health care surrogates.

Natural death acts have been passed in all states and the District of Columbia.[137] They typically provide that if the maker is unable to give instructions, is terminally ill and death is imminent the process of dying should not be extended through extraordinary means.[138] California had further limited the ability to use a directive by requiring a period of deliberation after the diagnosis of terminal illness,[139] but that provision was dropped in 1992. Some states make directives ineffective during the pregnancy of the patient,[140] and prohibit their application to withholding food

---

135. *See, e.g.*, Bludworth 452 So. 2d 921 (Fla. 1984); *Spring*, 380 Mass. 629, 405 N.E. 2d 115 (1988); *Saikewicz*, 373 Mass. 728, 370 N.E. 2d 417 (1977); *Torres*, 357 N.W. 3d 332 (Minn. 1984); *Conroy*, 98 N.J. 321, 486 A.2d 1209 (1985); *Quinlan*, 70 N.J. 10, 355 A.2d 647, *cert. denied sub nom.*, Garger, 429 U.S. 922 (1976); *Eichner*, 102 Misc. 2d 184, 423 N.Y. 2d 550 (1979), *modified*, 73 A.2d 431, 426 N.Y.S.2d 517 (1980), *cert. denied sub nom.*, Storar v. Storar, 454 U.S. 858 (1981).

136. PRESIDENT'S COMMISSION REPORT, *supra* note 7, at 3.

137. See *supra*, note 132.

138. California Health & Safety Code section 7118 provides for a directive which states:
If at any time I should have an incurable injury, disease, or illness certified to be terminal . . . and where the application of life-sustaining procedures would serve only to artificially prolonging the moment of my death and . . . my death is imminent . . . I direct that such procedures be withheld or withdrawn.
CAL. HEALTH & SAFETY CODE § 7188 (West Supp. 1987).

139. *Id.* §§ 7188, 7191.

140. *Id.* § 7188 (West Supp. 1987); WASH. REV. CODE 70.122.030 (Supp. 1987); ALA. CODE 22-8A-4 (1984).

and fluids.[141] As mentioned, they also expressed distrust of persons with conflicting interest such as members of the family, heirs, physicians and others by prohibiting them from providing the necessary witnessing of the documents.[142]

The strictness and vagueness of provisions has proved trouble-some. Commentators noticed that about half of the California patients who were diagnosed as having a "terminal condition" did not remain conscious for the two additional weeks before they could become legally entitled to make a binding directive.[143] A terminal condition is defined in the California law as one in which death is imminent regardless of the life sustaining procedures used.[144] As the President's Commission noted, survival to complete a directive "would require a miraculous cure, a misdiagnosis, or a very loose definition of the word 'imminent.'"[145] In fact, those who could properly execute a directive had little incentive to do so because the act merely allowed the termination of treatment that could not prevent their imminent death. Although the statute was drafted with Karen Quinlan's case in mind, Ms. Quinlan would not have benefited from the Act since her death was not imminent.

Although the acts typically reserve common law rights irrespective of the utilization of a statutory directive,[146] the common law has been sparse. Had case law been better developed, there would

---

141. COLO. REV. STAT. 15-18-104 (Supp. 1986); IND. CODE 16-8-11-12 (1985).

142. CAL. HEALTH & SAFETY CODE § 7188 (West Supp. 1987); WASH. REV. CODE 70.122.030 (Supp. 1987); IDAHO CODE 39-4504 (Supp. 1987).

143. Redleaf, *The California Natural Death Act: An Empirical Study of Physicians' Practices*, 31 STAN. L. REV. 913, 928 (1979) [hereinafter Redleaf].

144. CAL. HEALTH & SAFETY CODE § 7187 (West Supp. 1987).

145. PRESIDENT'S COMMISSION REPORT, *supra note 7, at 142.*

146. California Health and Safety Code § 7193 states: "[N]othing in this chapter shall impair or supersede any legal right or legal responsibility which any person may have to effect the withholding or withdrawal of life-sustaining procedures in any lawful manner." CAL. HEALTH & SAFETY CODE § 7193 (West Supp. 1987).

have been no original need for natural death acts or their very recent adoption by many states.

The Acts cannot be viewed as an effective response to the problems of life support termination. Data on their effect on medical practice is contradictory, but demonstrates at least that they have not become a central manner of resolving life support termination decisions.[147] There is some indication that the presence of the statute has led many doctors to regard the absence of a directive as rejecting termination of life support despite the fact that their patient may have had contrary expectations.[148]

Despite its inadequacies, all states have now adopted a natural death act. Many of the Acts avoid some of the problems of the California prototype but, in the main, they copy it. Since the formalities of execution differ from state to state, there remains the additional problem that a directive executed in one state which has a natural death act will not qualify in another which has a differing one.

In 1985, the Commissioners on Uniform State Laws adopted an act entitled the Uniform Rights of the Terminally Ill Act.[149] While its adoption would eliminate inconsistencies and assure the effectiveness of directives in other states, it carries forward most of the problems of its progenitor. Only "qualified patients" are entitled to the benefits of the Act.[150] A condition to being "qualified" is a prior diagnosis of terminal illness.[151] Fortunately, the Act does not also carry forward the California limitation on making directives.[152] Any person who is at least 18 and of

147. Redleaf, *supra* note 143, at 945.

148. PRESIDENT'S COMMISSION REPORT, *supra* note 7, at 144.

149. UNIF. RIGHTS OF TERMINALLY ILL ACT, 9B U.L.A. 609 (1985).

150. *Id.* at 2.

151. *Id.* at 1.

152. *Id.* at 2(a).

280

sound mind may do so at any time.[153] Since revocation remains possible indefinitely, and can be exercised irrespective of "competency,"[154] that change brings the benefits of rumination and deliberation without limiting the effects of later perspectives.[155]

When the patient is "no longer able to make decisions regarding administration of life-sustaining treatment"[156] attending physicians shall either act in accordance with the declaration or transfer the patient.[157] The directive may request the termination of treatment which, "when administered to a patient, will only serve to prolong the dying process."[158] It is difficult to imagine a treatment that could ethically be administered only to prolong dying even without a directive. Karen Quinlan would certainly again not qualify. Further, the Uniform Act nullifies a declaration to end life support for a pregnant woman whose fetus could "develop to the point of life birth with the continued application of life-sustaining treatment" unless the directive otherwise provides[159] (the model

---

153. *Id.*

154. *Id.* at 4(a). The individual may revoke the directive at any time and in any manner regardless of the individual's mental or physical condition as long as the revocation is communicated to the physician. The intention of the Commission on Uniform State Laws is to allow an individual freedom to revoke the directive at any time without the encumbrance of complicated procedural requirements.

155. The intended result might be better achieved by a provision making the directive ineffective while the maker objects to its effectuation. Revocation normally denies the maker future use of the directive since the maker will likely be found incompetent to execute it anew.

156. *Id.* at 3(ii).

157. *Id. But see Jobes,* 108 N.J. 394, 529 A.2d 434 (1987) (transfer not permitted even on moral grounds).

158. UNIF. RIGHTS OF TERMINALLY ILL ACT, 9B U.L.A. 609 2(b) (1985).

159. *Id.* at 6(c).

declaration in the statute makes no mention of the issue).[160] It also expressly rejects mercy-killing or euthanasia negatively using three different verbs (it does not condone, authorize or approve) for emphasis.[161]

The presumption against life support termination for a pregnant woman in her first trimester, at least, seems clearly unconstitutional on privacy grounds.[162] The state's interest in the woman's life which provides balance for her interest in limiting her consent to unwanted medical treatment (especially that which merely prolongs the dying process) is quite weak. The state's interest in preventing what is essentially an abortion of the fetus if she dies before it can be saved must be even more subordinated to the woman's choice.[163] It cannot be required that she must remain alive though dying when in the normal case she is not required to consent to the use of her healthy body at least in the early months of pregnancy.[164] The denunciation of euthanasia is equally unfortunate in its lumping of active and passive euthanasia. While these terms are also quite imprecise, they connote the distinction between actively causing death as by administering a lethal agent for the sole purpose of killing and more passive acts such as decisions to forego resuscitation or removal of life support. The

---

160. *Id.* at 2(b). The declaration, which requires two witnesses states: If I should have an incurable or irreversible condition that will cause my death within a relatively short time, and I am no longer able to make decisions regarding my medical treatment, I direct my attending physician, pursuant to the Uniform Rights of the Terminally Ill Act of this State, to withhold or withdraw treatment that only prolongs the process of dying and is not necessary to my comfort or to alleviate pain.
Id.

161. *Id. at 10(g).*

162. Roe v. Wade, 410 U.S. 113 (1973).

163. *In re* A.C., 533 A.2d 611 (App. D.C. 1987).

164. *Id.*

282

former is still generally anathema in the medical community[165] and is only recently becoming accepted by the general public.[166] The latter has growing support from both groups.[167] While the attitude of the medical community ought not to be determinative of such issues,[168] it is of political importance.

In a subtler fashion, the Uniform Act shifts control further in the direction of the medical community. Several acts are criminalized by the proposed statute. Failure to record a declaration provided by the patient, altering, concealing or coercing the making of a declaration or its revocation are typical.[169] Also criminalized is the failure of a doctor who does not wish to comply with the directive to "as promptly as practicable take all reasonable steps" to see to the patient's transfer.[170] The refusal to comply is expressly not proscribed and, indeed, physicians are expressly immunized from civil and criminal responsibility as well as professional discipline for actions under the Act which "are in accord with reasonable medical standards."[171] The qualified transfer provision begs the most difficult question: what if after reasonable steps the doctor is unable to transfer the patient? Does the patient's wish or the doctor's govern? That, after all, is the central subject of the legislation.

One provision of the Uniform Act is particularly worthy of future adoption, however. It provides that the declaration may be revoked by the patient at any time and in any manner without

---

165. PRESIDENT'S COMMISSION ON THE STUDY OF ETHICAL PROBLEMS IN MEDICINE AND BIOMEDICAL AND BEHAVIORAL RESEARCH, 2 MAKING HEALTH CARE DECISIONS 234-35 (1982).

166. *Id. See also infra* note 176.

167. *See infra* note 176.

168. *See cases cited supra* note 82.

169. UNIF. RIGHTS OF TERMINALLY ILL ACT, 9B U.L.A. 609 (1985).

170. *Id.* at 7.

171. *Id.* at 8(b).

regard to mental or physical condition.[172] While such a provision leaves open a great potential for manipulation, it wisely recognized the ultimate preference for life when in doubt as to the patient's wishes. There should be a counterpart provision that a reinstatement of a declaration is acceptable on similar terms so that the underlying document is not lost because of a recanted expression of changed intentions. This purpose might be accomplished, for example, by providing that life support not be removed from patients whose last expressed wish was to have it maintained, but that the validity of the directive would not be affected unless it was validly formally revoked.

VI

While both the model act and the extant statutes fix earlier and more naive notions, case law has made many advances in dealing with specific cases. New legislation is required to consolidate the benefits of both the individual directive and the appointment of a medical surrogate for that purpose. For some persons, appointing trusted friends who understand one's point of view will be a good solution given the complexity of circumstances in which the need for a surrogate decision may be required. In other cases, there may be no one sufficiently trusted or available. A directive with necessarily more general provisions may be best in such instances. Combining both would be even more prudent. A document encompassing both would better deserve the name "living will."[173]

There are several changes which should be captured by such a new law. It should state the competent patient's right to refuse any type of treatment as well as any other form of care which is objectionable without qualifying the circumstances for such a decision. A patient should have the opportunity to prepare a directive to that effect but it should be suspended during a period in which he repudiates its direction whether competent or not. No one's life should be ended over his protest even if competency

---

172. *Id.* at 4(a).

173. Alexander, *supra* note 132.

determinations were uncontroversial. A surrogate, named in the directive, should be authorized to interpret the patient's wishes in specific circumstances. Physicians should be obligated to follow the directions provided or to transfer the patient. In cases in which transfer is medically inappropriate, doctors should comply with the directive. Failure to do so should be grounds for professional punishment and legal liability.

Public opinion is increasingly accepting the right to choose death as an alternative to treatment.[174] Case law is slowly promoting it[175] and medical opinion has come to accept both more patient control and a greater range of choice in life support removal.[176] One must still question the extent to which patient

---

174. *See, e.g., Aid-in-Dying Act Well Received*, 23 HEMLOCK Q. 1 (1986); Society for the Right to Die, HANDBOOK OF LIVING WILL LAWS 1981-1984 7-8 (1984).

175. *See cases cited supra* note 82.

176. *See, e.g.,* Society for the Right to Die, HANDBOOK OF LIVING WILL LAWS 1981-1984. 3-6 (1984). "Recent opinion polls in the Netherlands show that the majority of the Dutch population (56%) do not object to interventions taken to shorten the lives of terminally ill patients. Only about 23% of the population take a definite stand against euthanasia. The number of opponents to euthanasia decreased from about 48% in 1972 to about 43% in 1976 and to 23% in 1979." Hilhorst, RELIGION AND EUTHANASIA IN THE NETHERLANDS: ON THE CLARIFICATION OF TWO OPPOSITE FACTORS 9 (1982). "According to the most recent poll in 1985, 67% have no objection against active euthanasia and 84% are not against passive euthanasia." Admiral, *Active Voluntary Euthanasia*, VOLUNTARY EUTHANASIA 186 (1986).

In 1985, "[o]ne-sixth of all the people who died in Holland, some 20,000 people, were killed by doctors on purpose, and not one of those doctors went to jail, even though it is illegal to practice euthanasia." *60 Minutes: The Last Right?* (CBS television broadcast Jan. 5, 1986). The Euthanasia Society in the Netherlands has been working to make active euthanasia legal. However, active euthanasia is "classed in the criminal code as a form of murder punishable by up to 12 years in prison. But so long as doctors meet medical and ethical criteria developed in a series of judicial decisions since 1973 they are seldom prosecuted." WALL ST. J., Aug. 21, 1987, at 11, col. 4. These standards have also been incorporated into guidelines promulgated by the Dutch Medical Association. The doctor may not actively euthanize a patient unless the request comes from the patient, himself/herself; the patient must be competent and fully conscious; and the patient must ask repeatedly for the procedure. In addition, the patient must

autonomy ideals are actually incorporated into medical practice.

Even expressed agreements which seems to prevail cannot be trusted to have changed procedures well entrenched in a prior time when the patient's participation in decision making was less valued. One must sill inquire to what extent competent patients are consulted about their wishes, especially life and death decision.[177] A study completed by the President's Commission

---

have physical or mental suffering which is deemed to be unbearable, and there must be no chance for improvement. *Id.*

"Efforts to get clarifying legislation on euthanasia through the Dutch Parliament have thus far failed; the issue splits the two parties in the governing coalition. The Christian Democrats prefer keeping euthanasia a crime, with very limited exceptions; the small Liberal Party would like to move toward legalization. The government still hopes to have a proposal ready for debate this fall but is having a hard time working one out." *Id.* at 11, col. 4.

Doctors are usually not prosecuted for engaging in active euthanasia if the judicially created guidelines are followed. However, because the prosecution decision is left in the hands of the 2090 local prosecutors, doctors are uncertain as to whether they will be prosecuted. *Id.* For example, a doctor in Amsterdam was charged with administering active euthanasia in the case of a thirty-two year old multiple sclerosis victim. He was tried at The Hague, and he admitted that he had given the patient a fatal injection. Because the patient was in a great deal of pain and facing a terminal illness, the judge found that the doctor was faced with a conflict: his duty to the patient and his duty to obey the law. The judge found him not guilty. *60 Minutes: The Last Right?* (CBS television broadcast Jan. 5, 1986). On the other hand, in the sixty-five cases of active euthanasia reported to the Ministry of Justice, nine resulted in prosecution. Wall. St. J., Aug. 21, 1987, at 11, col. 4.

Therefore, it seems that the reality in the Netherlands is that people are allowed to plan their deaths due to the availability of euthanasia. However, the government has not sanctioned the practice. Courts are forced to indulge in a legal fiction that adherence to guidelines means that no crime has been committed although it is clear the letter of the law is broken.

In California there was an initiative proposed for the November 1988 ballot which would have allowed physician assisted euthanasia. It did not qualify for the ballot.

177. A perspective may be obtained by looking at the procedures of Stanford University Hospital with respect to "do not resuscitate" orders. OFFICE MEMORANDUM FROM STANFORD UNIV. MEDICAL CENTER COMMITTEE ON MEDICAL ETHICS TO STANFORD UNIV. MEDICAL CENTER, MEDICAL NURSING AND PATIENT SUPPORT STAFF (Jan. 1985) (Draft Ethics Committee Mailing #2). It begins with a recognition of the importance of patient participation.

found that 41 % of physicians would either provide the patient with a straight forward, statistically based prognosis for the disease or tell the patient that it is likely that he will die within a year. However, only 41% of physicians surveyed said they would provide the patient with a hard estimate.[178] The survey under-

---

We would like to feel confident that DNR orders at the Stanford University Hospital are consistently executed with knowledge by and the informed consent from patients or their legal guardians. We are aware of many instances of competent patients who have clearly and consistently requested not to be resuscitated and who still end up undergoing CPR. At the end of the spectrum, the potential for problems in communication at a major teaching hospital regarding this issue . . . [is shown by a study which concluded that] of 157 physicians responsible for care of patients who underwent CPR at Beth Israel (Boston) Hospital in 1981, 151 professed to believe that families of patients should be involved in DNR decisions. However, of the 154 patients who were resuscitated, only 19% actually discussed this with their doctors, and only 33% of the families were consulted. Further interviews with 24 mentally competent patients who survived resuscitation revealed only weak correlation between patient and physician perception of any communication that did take place.

Id.

To insure that patients be afforded better opportunities for participation, Stanford distributes a Patient's Rights and Responsibilities statement which includes an invitation to discuss "issues of withdrawing or withholding of life support in the setting of terminal illness" with their physician and to obtain further information at the Patient Relations Office. The policy statement itself, however, is less encompassing. A "No Code" order should be considered when the patient has an irreversible, incurable medical condition and death is expected to occur as a result of the patient's underlying medical problems. Once these criteria are satisfied, then the attending physician must exercise his or her best judgment to determine whether a no code order is appropriate.

The hospital distributes copies of both directives to physicians and durable power for health care forms for those who choose to contact the Patient Relations Office and presumably acts consistently with their requirements when they are made known. The exclusion of both the patient and the family from those who must exercise judgment about no codes probably is simply inartful.

178. President's Commission for the Study of Ethical Problems in Medicine and Biomedical and Behavioral Research, MAKING HEALTH CARE DECISIONS v.2 223 (1982).

taken by the Stanford Law Review[179] shortly after the passage of the California Natural Death Act[180] found a gap between physician views that patients had a right to make informed decisions about life support after they are diagnosed to be terminally ill and assuring that they were informed. Some assumed that other doctors had informed them. Others were euphemistic in their description (for example suggesting that the patient put his affairs in order). Some informed the family but not the patient. A small percentage (7%) indicated that they sometimes did not tell patients even if neither they nor their family knew independently.[181] All answers were self assessments. It seems likely that the answers overstated the information that was actually passed.

The active public discussion of death issues will probably increase the amount of information that patients have. Many more persons will have heard of the issues concerning life support and will know to ask about them. Members of the family and friends will likewise probe more. Each experience of a close friend dying in a hospital will also increase the sophistication of those who participate in making late life choices or hear about their being made. Doctors will likely improve in their communication and consultation as their audience learns to expect participation. Thus, it may now be possible to use a device as new as a living will on a larger scale.

If living wills are to be effective for more than a small group of the well-informed, there will have to be a commitment to providing publicity about the options available. The general public will have to be urged to consider life-end issues earlier in their lives and model living wills will have to be made easily available. The fact that as many as five million have already chosen to draft directives under the present unfavorable circumstances[182] indicates that there is potential for involving a far larger number.

---

179. Redleaf, *supra* note 143.

180. CAL. HEALTH & SAFETY CODE §§ 7185-7195 (West Supp. 1987).

181. Redleaf, *supra* note 143, at 929.

182. *See* Nelson, *supra* note 23.

There is insufficient data to determine the costs of providing only as much life support as patients want. It seems quite probable that the costs are less then the amount spent at the moment. Prior systems of health reimbursement which compensated health providers for service provided with little control of the extent of treatment, medical predilections for life over death (a normally excellent perspective) and a growing concern for potential legal liability have no doubt kept many patients in treatment when they would have preferred an earlier death. Reimbursement reform combined with relief from concern about exposure to law suits should make a noticeable difference. Given the reluctance to cut health care resources that has existed to date, the government and private employers may be wiling to support the amount of medical life support that is desired. In any event, the adjustments should diminish the reductions that are made if further cost cutting measures are instituted. There is reason to believe that many patients with incurable and ultimately terminal diseases seek to be spared the full course of possible treatment to keep them alive.[183]

If no changes in present practices are made, on the other hand, the threat of reductions by changes in medical standards of care seems quite likely. In an egalitarian manner, all would be denied some of the less promising forms of life support. Given the higher percentage of older patients who chose to end dialysis support,[184] one could conclude that dialysis might properly be age restricted in the British manner. Certainly, dialysis was less effective for older and diabetic patients than for the general population. On the other hand, it should be noted that a majority of patients continued treatment at least during the minimum year they were studied. For them, unavailability would have meant death.

Generally, egalitarian reductions would result in denying persons who feel strongly about continuing to "fight" death irrespective of odds the resources to do so as well as likely keeping many alive after they pass their own point of decision to die.

---

183. PRESIDENT'S COMMISSION REPORT, *supra* note 7, at 95-100.

184. *See supra* note 16.

Denying the former group its preference would be even more acceptable at a time of resource depletion in which funds for such people could only be obtained by increasing the risks to the remainder of those requiring health care.

INDEX

294

CURRENT ISSUES
IN INTERNATIONAL AND COMPARATIVE LAW

KLUWER ACADEMIC PUBLISHERS – DORDRECHT / BOSTON / LONDON